MARVIN

Also by Donald Zec

MARVIN
THE STORY OF LEE MARVIN

DONALD ZEC

St. Martin's Press
New York

Zee, Donald.
  Marvin.

    1. Marvin, Lee. 2. Moving-picture actors and
actresses—United States—Biography.
PN2287.M523Z4   1980   791.43′028′0924   [B]   80-51817
ISBN 0-312-51780-7

To Paul

Acknowledgments

I would like to thank the many people who talked to me about Lee Marvin. As a long-standing victim of the alphabetical order, I recognise its limitations in determining the value of each contribution, since all were equally generous with their time and reminiscences; particularly, Richard Brooks, Tristram Coffin Colket the Third, MD, William A. Fraker, Kenneth Hyman, Millard Kaufman, Stanley Kramer, Joshua Logan, Stuart Rosenberg, Don Siegel, Elliot Silverstein, Don Weiss, Keenan Wynn, Terence Young, and of course Michelle Triola-Marvin. St Leo College, Dade City, Florida were helpful and genial hosts and Mr Jack Betz of Sarasota was most forthcoming about his celebrated ex-classmate. My interviews with the former Betty Marvin, now a serene and happy Mrs Gerald Mollner, were invaluable, leading to the added bonus of their friendship. I am indebted to my friend, author Anthony Fowles, for his valued comments and, as with previous work, to my wife Frances, for her unflagging assistance in the preparation of the manuscript.

Finally I am glad to acknowledge the customary goodwill and co-operation of Mirror Group Newspapers Ltd.

Donald Zec, London, 1979.

Chapter One

'I'm not his psychiatrist. I don't know whether he has one or needs one. I'm only saying that to understand him, one needs some help.'

Stanley Kramer

The man was wearing a hairnet, a red, black and yellow bathrobe, and carrying a revolver. By the time the police finally overhauled him he'd shot up a couple of mail boxes, but spilt no blood, not even his own. Recognition was swift. No mistaking that slack, punchy grin. Clouded eyes expressing guilt and cheerful remorse from a familiar face whose bleached bony architecture seemed to revert to its Neanderthal beginnings. Shaking their heads in the manner of old campaigners, the officers delivered the ritual rebuke conceding that as misdemeanours went this fell short of Lee Marvin's record as one of Hollywood's champion disturbers of the peace. The trigger-happy ex-Marine who, in his juicier moments, reprised his not unspectacular war in Iwo Jima by enfilading the glasses along his bar on Malibu with a favourite .45. Or, when day was done, shooting out the undefended street lights on some film location when tequila chased by boilermakers had brought out the marksman in him, 'watch this, baby – KAVOOM!'

Hell-raising on a superstar level goes back to pre-Errol Flynn. Like the punk marauders of today it is narcissistic, anarchic on a strictly self-serving level, with a part of the mind constantly zeroed in on the gossip columns of tomorrow. But the good-

7

natured terrorism which passes for the life and times of Lee
Marvin raises him high above that level. Given that you do not
win a Purple Heart for malingering, or an Oscar for a dud
performance, Marvin paid his dues as a gutsy Marine in World
War II and as Kid Shelleen in *Cat Ballou*. The sub-plots surrounding both these events, recounted with the gallows humour
which even that arch needler Humphrey Bogart might have
envied, are, as they say in the trade, alone worth the price of
admission. And if impact is the test of superstars, then Marvin's
seismographic reading is always wavering on Red Alert.

Josh Logan, who directed Marvin in that dire $18 million
splurge *Paint Your Wagon*, observed after the dust had settled,
'Not since Atilla the Hun swept across Europe leaving five
hundred years of total blackness has there been a man like Lee
Marvin.' Since Atilla was a dab hand at fratricide and genocide,
with an active sideline in extortion, Marvin (or the Hun) may
have a case for the courts. Either way the unexpurgated version
of the Marvin-Logan confrontation was a joy to unravel. Yet
for all the genial backstabbing and tight-lipped enmities between
the main contenders ('We're in a fucking mess up here, and
nobody's talking to anybody!') *Paint Your Wagon* comes out as
one of Lee Marvin's milder enterprises.

At the wrap-up party on the Peckinpah production of *The
Losers* which Marvin wrecked with a touch of real class, onlookers were in shock, the security guards in awe. Anyone who
doubts Lee's liquored-up prowess for shattering people, places
and parties, then lurching away from the carnage with a smile
on his lips and love in his heart, should note this fragment from
his recollection of the affair:

> Wham goes the table, and thirty feet of hors d'oeuvres are
> kissing the floor and I have Sam (Peckinpah) up against the
> wall with his feet off the ground . . . I was told they sent for a
> nurse and she came at me with a needle so I grabbed her by
> the breast and threw her on the deck. Then they got some
> muscle to hold me down and finally cleared me and the rest
> of the debris off the premises.

To regard this boozy jape merely as a piece of self-indulgent
social vandalism is to misread Lee Marvin by a mile. He has
more style, and class than that. Behind the frontal assault, the
verbal bullying and hardcore descriptives, there is an honesty

just as brutal. Equipped with the device which Hemingway earlier dubbed as the 'built-in shit detector' Marvin is swift to spot the true from the bogus. The honest broker from the ten-cent hustler.

Descended from some distinguished Marvins, honour, courage, and his own special brand of decency are the basic, but well-camouflaged, elements in his spiky persona.

To get to the core of Lee Marvin – his ominous capacity for violence no less than the soft-centred gentleness he disclaims with the obscenity of the day – you need his version of his life and turbulent loves. I talked to him of course. But as other explorers on that rocky safari have discovered, Marvin at full spate, the liquor and the sass in him, is a mind-shredding on-slaught of a man. What commences as a courteous exercise in character revelation convulses into black comedy. Normal language is suspended while our hero launches into Marvin vernacular – a crude patois of barrack-room dirt and Holly-wood smart talk. With it you get all the stage business, the finger stuck out like a revolver, thumb cocked; the *zap* and the *Kavoom*, and his definitive put-down of people and perform-ances, a derisory gesture towards his crotch. Words, sentences are telescoped like a malevolent ticker-tape machine. No obscenity emerges from that sagging mouth without each syl-lable being savoured. His two favourite four-letter words, describing sex and excrement, are given the lingeringly expres-sive vibrato. It is all part of the macho act of course. The con-versational test-run in which Marvin lays down ground rules; lets it be known that anybody who wants earnest declarations, nudging anecdotes or pre-digested quotes might do better with a Heston or a Newman.

But even with Marvin's own vivid, and, as it turned out, highly articulate contributions it seemed prudent to seek further evid-ence elsewhere. Producers, directors, writers and others who've worked with him had vastly different tales to tell, anecdotes to relish. But uncannily there was an instant identical reaction from all of them the moment his name, and the project, was mentioned. Surprise first, signalled by a sudden upward flick of the eyebrows. Then a slow, thoughtful nodding of the head, acknowledging the logic of the scheme. Finally the rueful smile of pained experience as from one just informed in a whisper that the major surgery was a success.

I recall seeing it on the bluff features of a retired monk, Father Marion formerly of St Leo College, Dade City, Florida. And on the face of a brilliant surgeon, dedicated tippler, and sometime songwriter, Tristram Coffin Colket the Third, MD. He, like Keenan Wynn, served their long 90-proof apprenticeship with Marvin bar-hopping at Hollywood's surf-side playground on Malibu. Blood flowed, bones were broken, glasses smashed, and police placated. Hell on the Pacific may be a fair description of those Marvin years.

Though the catalogue of Marvin incidents may be long, crass, and not infrequently crotch-oriented, those nearest to the heat and falling masonry speak more in admiration than in sorrow. With Marvin, they figure, you have to take the rough with the rough.

Even Michele Triola the 'scorned woman' who obtained the historic legal rights of a mistress (and sent Hollywood's clandestine lovers into panic stations) told me with curious logic: 'Lee is probably the most pure man I have ever known in my entire life. That's why I have to sue him.' Her case, 'Marvin v Marvin' came to court in January 1979. The lurid disclosures, no less than the legal implications, were to reverberate across America.

Betty Marvin, the tall, cultured artist who divorced him after fourteen years of traumas laced with tender loving kindness, was similarly magnanimous. They both still carry the scars she says, but declares that despite all the fights, the hurting. and the spate of trial separations, 'no couple stay together for close to sixteen years unless the good moments outweigh the bad.'

The armoury of guns in the house, and his almost clinical affinity with violence in cold blood, life with Lee Marvin had as sharp an edge to it as the Hudson Bay axe he kept behind their bed. Though, she says, 'I really think Lee worked very hard at the marriage, loving me as much as he was capable of loving any woman,' the former Mrs Marvin recognised the power and unpredictability of Lee's sudden lusty impulses. So there were times when he would end up in the company of other women. 'There is a certain type which makes herself available for these kind of men,' though she added, smiling delicately, 'I have never found that alcohol and sex are such great partners.' Nevertheless while she could predict how a formal dinner party at a friend's home might begin, its finale largely hinged on Lee's capricious urges of the moment with 'Oh, God, he's going to piss in the prize plant' an average apprehension. But while this may bespeak a poor sense of time and place, and maybe of direction too, he frequently compensated with a stirring show of chivalry.

Only a man of Marvin's blue-blooded lineage could, when confronted by a beauty at a party whose right breast had waywardly dropped out of its bra-cup, gently reseat it on its plinth, then bow out like Raleigh from the first Elizabeth. He was no less gallant at an exclusive gathering in London's fashionable Eaton Square, telling an English lady in her seventies, 'I bet you got the prettiest pink little clittie in the room!' Challenge Lee Marvin on the dubious taste of this unsolicited testimonial and you get the surprised 'who, me?' routine, the hurt smile, the despairing sigh that so kindly a gesture could be misconstrued. It is a game of social brinkmanship that requires style and an unerring judgement. Humphrey Bogart drew the blue-print. Sinatra added some zingy material of his own. Marvin has sharpened the script with some gamey contributions from the US Marines.

Complex, intimidating, with an unnerving self-assurance, Lee Marvin possesses the essential personality bait that hooks an audience. Of thousands. Or of one. The power generates from a lean, taut, physical presence. From the hard, high battlement of his forehead, the basilisk grin, down to his combat boots, he is in control. He creates tension, and feeds on it. He transmits danger. On or off the screen. The face, rutted like a bad cart track, is perfect territory for the cold sneering smile or rasping insult. We learn, the hard way, that this surface malevolence is a disguise for the more praiseworthy qualities he'd stomp you for discovering. But it is as vital to his screen image as that boyish blue-eyed smile is to Paul Newman's.

For more than twenty years Lee Marvin has been the definitive bully of the screen. Terrorising widows, taunting cripples, shooting, knifing, maiming and raping – the Marvin technique is the slow burn, the neatly-layered sadism. He is the consummate psychopath, the more terrifying when sparingly demonstrated, the more credible when masked by that slow laconic smile. Vital to the Marvin menace is the feeling of battened-down rage; of a dangerous anger beneath the surface calm. The title sequence in *The Dirty Dozen*, where Marvin, the campaign-hardened officer, reviews the hand-picked killers selected for a crucial mission, perfectly illustrates the point. Stiff as a flagpole he takes with apparent composure the bad-mouthing from one of the men. Only the faint twitching of a muscle on the side of his face gives a clue to the slow-erupting anger within him. Suddenly he springs round, chops and clumps the man into a broken heap on the ground. He straightens his well-cut uniform, then smiles. For the first time. The demolition is savage, and final. The overture performed, the theme of violence stated, Marvin is supremely revealed in control of the character, and of the movie.

Marvin's track record as the mean, sardonic bad man owes plenty to films like *Bad Day at Black Rock, The Professionals, Point Blank,* and *The Killers.* But it was Fritz Lang's gangster classic *The Big Heat* (1953) that staked Marvin's claim as the all-time champion of the breed. Even way back in those supporting actor days Marvin's mastery of this kind of role was clearly demonstrated. He could hit marks, handle props, do business with the flair and competence of the seasoned star. He belongs to that small band of actors able to convey intelligence, and just as deftly, the lack of it. He can run up and down the IQ scale, here a sharp cynical wit, there a dangerous maniac with a just-smashed bottle in his hand. As a killer he offers no redeeming qualities. He asks for no sympathy, and gets none. He is downright mean. The mind is rivetted to the assignment, and the pay-off. The perfect hit-man. He is dead on target ten years later with the Don Siegel remake of *The Killers.* He is again the cold-blooded, calculating sonofabitch hoodlum. But this time the terror has an edge to it, induced by a scary touch of malice in the role.

The period between *The Big Heat* (1953) and *The Killers* (1964) proves that though some of Marvin's movies like *The Man Who Shot Liberty Vallance* (1962) can miss heavily, he is always interesting, never a carbon copy. The battalion of directors who pulled no punches recalling some of the more shuddering moments working with him, unanimously respect him however for his rare talent in bringing original ideas to every role he plays. Don Siegel said it. Elliot Silverstein said it. Stanley Kramer said it. And likewise Josh Logan, Don Weiss. Stuart Rosenberg, Richard Brooks, Terence Young and William A. Fraker. With their hands on their hearts they could not fault the actor. On Lee Marvin, the man, however, there was not the same glowing unanimity. Some winced, others, remembering some gruesomely funny incident, yelped like moon-struck coyotes.

What stands out is that whatever reactions Lee Marvin induces in his friends and the rest of the walking wounded, indifference isn't one of them. Marvin offers – and demands – commitment, not just eye to eye, but gut to gut. It makes waves, creates uneasiness. In the environment of, for the most part, shallow relationships, no one wants to go in that deep. Unlike the glossier, hard-laminated male superstars who seem to be impervious to shock, bruising or other human hazards, Marvin strides into harm's way convinced something good will emerge from the debris. This sense of an intrinsic, uncompromising integrity in Marvin is central to almost all the evidence offered – whether for or against. Some of the reminiscences still hang in the mind, long after the interviews took place. For instance there was this off-the-cuff memoire from that incisive, veteran scriptwriter Millard Kaufman (*Bad Day at Black Rock, Raintree County,* etc.). He delivered it against a fortuitous background of thunderous rock-blasting near his mountain-top eyrie overlooking California's San Fernando Valley.

The last time I worked with Lee was on *The Klansman* which bombed out for a number of reasons which do not concern us immediately. A year later I met him again in Arizona and asked him if he'd ever been back to Oroville where the film was made. He said yes he had. He'd been passing through and stopped long enough to call on just one person out there who interested him. He took the guy and his wife out to dinner. It was his driver on the location. Now in a way this was typical of Lee. He's not interested in pomp, rank, or circumstance. I knew this driver and he was a very supportive shit-kicker from the backwoods. But there was a sort of stubborn integrity to the man which Lee saw, and admired. So in that one night he had in the area, this was the one man he wanted to spend it with.

Kaufman's first picture with Lee Marvin was *Bad Day at Black Rock*. There was the instant rapport you would expect from two men who had served in the Marine Corps in World War II. Says Kaufman:

He escaped death by inches at least twice to my certain knowledge. I was hit a couple of times myself but nothing like the way Lee was. I understand his almost mystical love for the Marines. I enjoyed it too, if you can say that getting shot at in anger can be an enjoyable experience. But Lee had a real feeling for those men. With them he found what he seemed to be searching for, some lost arena of satisfaction and fulfilment that he found nowhere else – not even in his success as an actor. Some people say so many things about people they don't give a damn about. Well I give a damn about Lee. He has values. He is sensitive, and enormously bright.

He is also a phenomenally physical actor. He has great powers. You can feel his impresses. Nobody can direct anyone to handle a gun the way Marvin does it. It's fantastic. He can take a handgun or a rifle and throw those damned things around like they were educated toothpicks. One of the reasons Lee is so good is he has this marvellous ability to not 'don't just stand there, *do* something' but to stand there and *not* do something. As Gable said, 'I don't care how much dialogue you give to anybody else in the picture, I want the one last word, and I want to exit, and I want them to look at me go.' Reaction. Nobody's better at it than Marvin. When his cerebral machinery is cranking in there, you can *feel* it. Of course he can't play the weak stuff, can't resist the macho pose. He was pissed pretty good on *The Klansman* but he never did anything except act well, both on and off the screen. Correction. A couple of times off the set he was a pain in the ass. But he showed up for work, and did the work regardless. One day Marvin and Burton wanted me to go to lunch with them. I said, 'I've got work to do,' which was a lie, but I didn't want to get caught up because I'm not the strongest person in the world. But actor O. J. Simpson went with them. When he came back he said to me, 'Holy Moses! Do you know what those guys had for lunch?' I said, 'Yeah,' he said, 'Do you know how much?' I said, 'No.' And he said, 'Seventeen martinis apiece!' And then they went back to work. But the director Terence Young called off the rest of the day. I've seen these fakirs who can do anything, total control of their bodies right down to their extremities. They can do impossible things with say, their little toe or their penises. Lee Marvin can do the same. This physical power maybe makes it difficult for him ever to play a weak man. To some extent he is imprisoned in that dominant physique. But within that configuration, I think Lee Marvin could do just about anything.

Less forthcoming was director Michael Ritchie (*The Candidate, Prime Cut, Downhill Racer, The Bad News Bears*, etc.). He firmly declined to take any part in the proceedings. With good-natured inflexibility he said, 'I am prepared to talk about, say, Robert Redford, Walter Matthau or any other pleasurable subjects, but not about Lee Marvin. He said some wicked things about me to *Rolling Stone* and I am not disposed to reply in kind. Nor on the other hand am I disposed to say anything favourable either.' Cut and print.

Well nothing is that terminal in movies. Rashly calling Michael Ritchie a sonofabitch in December 1972 may not preclude Lee Marvin from recanting by 1980. One fine talent needs another – and will cross a field of horse manure if necessary to get to it. Maybe it is the price that has to be paid for a true original. That originality has surfaced like a blazing sunrise through several Marvin movies. There was a fine example of it in *Raintree County* (1957) with Marvin playing nothing more vicious than a small-town braggart-cum-dandy. His death soliloquy (applauded by the grips and crewmen at the close) is given added poignancy by a deep, moving, vocal colouring. His voice is probably the one tangible asset he possesses which could be described as being beautiful. Resonant, low-pitched, it is also flexible, able to snap out the hood's freezing monosyllable or flare off alarmingly into a Widmarkian cackle. How much of that deeper timbre is due to training, Marine Corps yammering or the gravel-smoothing decades of tequila, is a matter for expert judgement. Certainly the women who, for better or worse, have shared his bed and buffoonery, nominate the Marvin voice as being crucial to his brusquely tender sex appeal. He needed it. When the drink was in him, like the potion in Dr Jekyll, the result was a grimacing metamorphosis from gent to ape. An articulate ape to be sure. But drink doesn't fool him. 'Get juiced enough and you'll roll around with a buffalo and think she's beautiful.' A statement from the buffalo could clinch it.

The bizarre effects of liquor on his private and professional life cannot be overlooked in any authentic profile of Lee Marvin. But if there was social carnage at times, there were also some hilarious moments too. The ritual, during those well-soused years on Malibu, fell into a pattern. The wife, or whoever was back home minding the store, would have the car on the forecourt and the black coffee on the hob. Then, on occasions, the phone would ring as a frantic bartender pleaded, 'Kindly come and collect Mister Marvin before war breaks out!' At which point the guardian angel with whatever beefy assistance was on hand, would do an emergency pick-up with Marvin crooning a soaring aria of repentance. Tutored by summer stock and the late John Ford, Lee Marvin can be the Larry Olivier of eloquent self-reproach. Police, hospital attendants, shocked hostesses, stunned passers-by had to admit that even pie-eyed on a stretcher or prone on the sidewalk, Marvin never gave a bad performance. He makes outrage legitimate. This enabled him to say things to the late Vivien Leigh for example, which from any other actor would have earned her Ladyship's well-known Siberian put-down. But Lee's amiable obscenities (aristocratic disdain brings out the worst in him) actually increased the subtle vibrations that hummed between them. Likewise Jeanne Moreau, Vivien's Gallic equivalent, who after working with him on *Monte Walsh* declared him to be one of the most exciting men she had ever known. The contrast between the corrugated Marvin and the slender, elegant Parisienne was akin to cow-pat and caviare. But Jeanne Moreau wasn't deceived by the wrapping on the package – and what passed between them after the day's love scenes was perhaps no break in continuity.

But while the two women he married, and the third he spectacularly didn't, concede the sensitivity and plain decency of the man, they do not ignore his darker side. The strange fascination for guns. The irresistible attraction towards risky one-to-one confrontations. The palate for violence. Any child who can bodily throw a room-mate out of a second-floor window is clearly no Doctor Spock prize exhibit. Any actor who can wrap a banjo around the skull of a foolishly persistent saloon-bar jerk is not first choice on Gregory Peck's party list. True the picture brightens over the later years. But the progress is slow. And here I may as well declare an interest. I found Marvin's direct, down-the-line style a refreshing change from the uptight wariness of your average male superstar. The unreasonable violence, the social raffishness all happened, of course. But with it all there were always strict codes of honesty and concern. Behind the garrulity and the terror game there was, and is, the genuine liking of people who, he would admit, he needs more than they need him. But when the drink and the demons are cavorting around inside him, then Lee Marvin, as much in conflict with himself as anybody else, can be the boor of the week.

Well we shall come to that. Understanding it better against the lurid backdrop of Marvin's war. Knowing something more about the strange atmosphere in the Marvin home at Woodstock, New York. A scene which the first Mrs Lee Marvin described to me as 'straight out of Eugene O'Neil'. But she says it with a smile and some tenderness, implying that it was a fair bargain for the love of Lee. So we get the sour incidents and the belly laughs, star wars, and the close encounters of the worst kind. Lee Marvin, who now lives in Tucson, Arizona, spent several years at a beach house on Malibu. It was far enough from the smog and smart talk of Hollywood to make Lee feel at ease. Close enough to the ocean rollers and the clean Pacific breezes to make him feel happy. The interior signalled the tastes and style of its celebrated owner. Some fine books, hunting trophies, fish lures, a Spanish guitar and pictures of his yacht, the 56ft *Blue Hawaii* dancing at its moorings in the Phillipines. Fishing the giant marlin, the snap of the suddenly taut line like the crack of a .22 is music to his soul.

Strapped in a seat on heaving deck, the battle between him and the big fish joined, Lee Marvin is on a direct line to ecstasy. He had been sounding off that morning about guns, and death, whorehouses and bad people of which he had had first-hand experience. It was a lot of sludge to shovel at one sitting. He decided he needed air. Fresh stuff. Hauling his six feet three inches out of a chair, he went out on to the verandah. He took a deep lungful of the salty, unpolluted Pacific breeze and invited me to have a swig of it too. He screwed his eyes down to a long thin line of birds floating beyond the surf then panned along the beach. 'That bird,' he said, 'is, unless I am mistaken, the lesser marbled godwit. Not to be confused with the Hudsonian godwit, or the Siberian black-tailed godwit.' This was a lot of godwit by any standards. But Lee, soaringly at one with Nature, was now turning his attention to the sea. 'There's a big ocean out there,' he said, 'and man, you're only seeing the top of it!'

The same may be said of movie stars.

Prepare to submerge.

Chapter Two

'He was a wild, crazy kid. If he thought he'd
done nothing wrong and somebody said "Take
your punishment or else," Lee would say, "Okay,
else." '

Father Marion Bowman,
Abbot of St Leo College

On 26 April 1969, the Honorary Degree of Doctor of Fine Arts
was conferred on Lee Marvin at the St Leo College, near Dade
City, Florida. He was in distinguished, if controversial company.
Alongside him on the dais, the 589th Air Force Band unleashing
Elgar's *Pomp and Circumstance* was the Honourable Melvin R.
Laird then United States Secretary of Defence. A soft breeze
rustling their gowns and tassles they received their citations
with the self-conscious smiles of infants at prizegivings. It was,
according to a sardonic observer at the time, 'just a good old-
fashioned American God and Country Baccalaureate and Commencement . . . for the members of the class of 1969, safely
carried out in the true traditions of the United States of
America.' For as everybody, including the celebrated gentry on
the rostrum, knew, less than a mile away road blocks and
Florida Highway Patrolmen in riot gear were keeping 250 anti-
Laird protestors at bay, with spotter helicopters sweeping overhead. Nothing was going to stop the happy audience of 3,500
graduates, parents, guests and dignitaries from enjoying their
day on the sunlit campus of St Leo. And nothing was going to
stop Lee Marvin doing likewise. As he stood there, the silver-

white sideburns frothing out beneath the black mortarboard, he could scarcely suppress the horse-laugh erupting inside him.

But was it so bizarre, the notion of Lee Marvin, PhD (Hon.)? The bloodline, whatever it may have been laced with later, had a gallant and distinguished beginning. Matthew Marvin, a Scots Stewart related to Charles I sailed to America in 1634. He became the first Chief Justice for the State of Connecticut. A General Seth Marvin fought with the North in the Civil War. A brilliant young professor, Ross G. Marvin, served with the legendary Arctic explorer Admiral Robert Edwin Peary (1865–1920) on two Polar expeditions as his assistant and secretary. He died on the second in 1909. He was twenty-seven. Boasting a judge, a general, an explorer, enlivened by a touch of Charles I – the Marvin lineage looked set to produce some formidable sons. And one of these, a prime example of the breed, was Lamont W. Marvin, Lee's father. He was born in Manhattan. His ancestors had moved there after the Revolutionary War. Lamont Marvin was raised in the austere, high-principled shadow of his famous forbears. The home was macho-dominated with antique pistols and swords upstaging the Dresden china in the glass cabinets. Decency, honour, duty were the components of Marvin Senior's patriotism. He preached it as fervently as he sang *Rock of Ages* at Sunday chapel. And he practised it in World War I, enlisting as a private, rising to Captain. Serving with the American Expeditionary Force in France he returned to the US with a hero's medal, a sackful of souvenir weapons, and an urge to extend the Marvin line. He was 6ft 3in tall, ruggedly handsome, and, with a voracious appetite for reading, had all the words required for skilful wooing.

He needed them to land the slim, elegant beauty whom he married after World War I. Lamont's wife Courtenay, soon demonstrated she was no 'plucky little woman' dutifully baking, bedmaking and breeding while the husband took care of life's weightier preoccupations. A career woman, writing on fashion and beauty for Helena Rubinstein and others, she was an emancipated female long before Germaine Greer and Erica Jong chained themselves to the railings of Womens Lib. Lamont himself was involved with the media, though on a more prosaic level than the fragrant cloud on which Courtenay floated. He worked as an advertising executive, plugging first American apples, then the citrus fruits of the South. Though dirt shook off his products and sequins glittered on hers, they could speak the same language at nights – of layouts, design, catch-phrases and campaigns. 'All the white-collar Madison Avenue bullshit, you know,' was how Lee Marvin was to describe it years later, tactfully holding off until neither was alive to hear the jibe.

But Madison Avenue, for all its twenties chic, was good to the Marvins. They lived comfortably with Lamont's aesthetic inclinations and Courtenay's flair producing a home of some style. Their first son, Robert, was born in 1921. Lee arrived three years later, on 19 February 1924. Lamont Marvin, the slaughter and harsh disciplines of the war still gnawing at his mind, had firm ideas on how his two sons would be raised. Parading a variety of virility symbols – guns, muscle and back-bone – he set the pattern for the infant Marvins' development. But while the solemn young Robert reflected his mother, Courtenay's, conventional obedience to authority – Lamont's, the sassier Lee kicked against it from the start. Any expert embarking on a definitive thesis on The Problem Child could find useful source material in the early life of Lee Marvin.

When he was launched, initially, on the public-school system in New York, the authorities concerned were soon enquiring what they had done to deserve it. Him. Lee Marvin. Toe-to-toe confrontations between teacher and this mutinous half-pint resulted invariably in a defeat for scholarship. At four going on twenty, he would fix his instructor with a chilling stare and faintly contemptuous smile anticipating The Killers by thirty-six years. The number of occasions Lee Marvin ducked school, pleading urgent business elsewhere, do not figure in any records. Nor the total of flunked tests. Headteachers are reluctant to catalogue their most spectacular failures. Lee Marvin is equally hazy about the number of schools in New York that expelled him on a 'we-can't-take-any-more-of-it' ticket. He was enrolled at P.S.165 and then returned to Mr and Mrs Marvin some months later with every good wish for the monster's future. Some place else. The picture at the Mahumit School, New York, was the same. Bad. Marvin Junior was rebellious, unreceptive to authority and an unsettling influence on his classmates, so the official litany insisted. (The said accusers, viewing Marvin years later in *Bad Day at Black Rock*, *The Big Heat* and other hoodlum epics, must have subconsciously sniffed 'type-casting'.) Lee Marvin remembers he was a problem from the beginning.

There was the kindergarten on Long Island where the rot started. Things were going pretty good there for about three or four weeks. Then there must have been a Parent-Teacher-Association meeting or something. Anyway my mother went to the school and the teacher said, 'How did your son enjoy the business trip to Chicago?' My mother said, 'I beg your pardon?' And the teacher, a woman, said, 'Well, Lee told us he had to go to Chicago on a business trip with you. He hasn't been in school for four days.' On the way home my mother said, 'What kind of nonsense is all that about a business trip to Chicago?' I told her they were putting some buildings up along the street and I just hung around watching them every day. Much more fascinating than algebra which I didn't give a rat's ass for anyway. Maybe there was a Tom Sawyer or a Huck Finn calling me at some distance. I don't know. I had twice run away from schools to go fishing and the State Troopers brought me back. I loved the sea even then, I was only around five or six. It grabbed me so deeply it was enough for me to stand for hours and just watch it. Everything else bored me. I was a daydreamer. I really didn't give a damn for the formal stuff they fed me with.

With ancestors who led armies or scaled polar ice-caps on legendary expeditions, Lee Marvin's inability to stay put at a school desk or bring an apple for teacher, was understandable. His father compounded the confusion. At home most nights – they had now moved to Woodstock – he'd have both sons, Lee and Robert galvanised by his tales of World War I. While Courtenay sat writing about the latest fashions and French perfumes, Lamont expounded on the slaughter, the freezing trenches, but mostly of individual heroism on the battlefield, though omitting to mention his own. The medals would come out. And then the guns. Both boys were peering through the sight-aperture of a rifle, flinching at the crack of a .45 before they could multiply double figures.

Guns were to become more than an obsession with Lee Marvin. They became his virility badge whenever he figured his manhood was on the line. 'I don't know why it gives me pleasure to hit something in the distance with a weapon,' he said once. 'And I don't want to know. When I spent my spare time hunting I'd squeeze a trigger sending the striker forward to hit the percussion cap . . . the kinetic charge of gunpowder ignites and sends the missile out of the bore, twisting with absolute accuracy. When you discover that feeling within yourself sexually then you don't need a rifle anymore.' As he told *Playboy*, 'I know where my cock is at last so I don't need to prove my masculinity.'

But did Lamont Marvin need to prove his? When both sons enlisted to fight in World War II, Lamont instantly joined up as well. Patriotism or Freudian paternal ego-flexing? (The point is nicely probed when the first Mrs Lee Marvin has her say.) So Lee was raised on gun talk, in the sweet-smelling atmosphere of Courtenay Marvin's world of Helena Rubenstein. It was no substitute for a formal education. Bounced out of four public schools – he was caught smoking with three females in one of them – Lee Marvin was tried out as a boarder in private establishments. No discernible improvement resulted. It just took a little longer for the bad news to reach home. The crunch came following a bizarre event at Oakwood, a Quaker school at Poughkeepsie, NY. Lee Marvin's recollections of the affair (he tossed a room-mate out of a window) were amiably imprecise, admittedly after the fifth vodka-martini of the morning.

There were four of us to a room in this place. It was a nice long building, typical two-storey dormitory with shiny wooden floors which we had to take turns sweeping and cleaning. Well we were a little late for class and it was my turn to sweep up. Well there's this room-mate who's the second guy to throw garbage on the floor. He was holding the dust-pan and I swept the stuff into it. He dumped it all out of the window. I said, 'What did you do that for? Now we'll have to go out and clean it up.' He said, 'You something something sonofabitch!' I said, 'Hey, you call me that again and you're going out the window.' And he said it again so I was trapped by my own statement. I threw him out the window. I must admit he was smaller than me which made it kind of easier. It was an 18ft drop. Trouble was the building faced the athletic field where everybody was being called to attention just before the bell. So the whole school saw this guy sailing out and landing butt-first on the lawn. I could pull in a big audience even then.

22

But even Quakers have a cut-off point for tolerance. The ritual recriminations followed. Lee Marvin was rebuked for taking the law, and room mates, into his own hands. His expulsion was a formality. 'Okay so I didn't dig the school bit,' he says testily. 'But there was a whole lot of life going on around it. I liked being out in the woods, watching creatures eat, fly, and fornicate. I liked to throw a line into the water and wait for a big fish to figure out whether I was worth taking on. All that's learning too.'

Lamont and Courtenay Marvin surveyed their maverick son, wondering despondently where to go from there. They had their problems too. Courtenay's work, writing fashion and beauty articles, meeting the top brass of advertising agencies and publishing houses, kept her firmly tied to the Madison Avenue scene. Lamont had now become advertising manager for the Florida Citrus Commission based on Lakeland, a soporific no-place two hundred miles north-west of Miami. He commuted between there and New York where Courtenay remained. The question, what to do about Lee, scarcely arose. He had failed in New York. It was Florida's turn to defend itself against Lamont Marvin's second son. (Somewhere between departure and arrival Marvin had a short, doomed stint at a naval Academy. The notion envisaged was that the starched disciplines of the navy would shake the hell out of the young rebel. Good thinking. Bad news. The punk cadet swore at an admiral and summarily received the nautical heave-ho.)

And so they took the route to the South where they teach good manners, call their fathers and their betters 'Sir' and nobody takes lip from half-assed youngsters. This had to be right for Lee. Thus reasoned the upright Mr Marvin as, with gloomy Dickensian overtones, he took his incorrigible son on the train out of New York. In Marvin's vernacular of the later years, 'it was shit or bust time'. If he didn't make it in Florida which was too frigging dull for delinquency he was going to make it no place. With a sheaf of school dismissal notices passing for Lee's curriculum vitae, Lamont Marvin had to be pessimistic. But his stubborn son had the spunky confidence of the born mercenary. He was thirteen years old. Tall, tough, with all the plusses that make for champion athletes except one – he was no team man. None of this 'all for one and one for all' bullshit moonshine. Lee Marvin had been genetically structured for the one-man feat. The solo effort. His fantasies didn't run to triumphant ball game combinations or rowing to victory with a Harvard eight. He was the lone round-the-world yachtsman. The old man and the sea. And all-time favourite, Ross G. Marvin, of the North Pole.

But the visions faded fast at his first view of his new environment. Lakeland, bisected diagonally in a line drawn from Daytona Beach to the north-east and St Petersburg to the south-west, was deep in the redneck territory of the '30s. The centre for America's citrus industry it was a small sun-baked bastion of stiff-collared respectability. With flourishing Southern courtesies and genteel bigotry they talked religion, money, and black servant irritations. As the Marvins' train curved through the orange plantations Lee noted the large white-stuccoed mansions of the rich, and, strategically elbowed into the outskirts, the corrugated-iron shacks of the negroes. All the race-talk of the cocktail set he'd been raised on in New York – and been mystified by – was now given substance. Black farm-workers straightened up in the sun, and waved at the train. Lee wondered what the hell they had to wave at. When he grew up to discover that 'other races, creeds and colours weren't really any worse than mine' it was a revelation for him.

Lamont Marvin and son checked into the Terrace Hotel, a sombre, turn-of-the-century edifice which dominated the town's mainstreet intersection. Lee was enrolled at Lakeland High School. His records, unaccountably, were lost as, history repeating itself, he was chucked out for bad-mouthing a teacher. But though two other schools in the area ditched him too the main protagonists allowed that there was more good in young Marvin than bruised the eye. Cecile Gober, Lamont Marvin's secretary for the five years he was based on Lakeland, speaks of the rangy teenager she knew as though the flawless image of Robert Redford had become lodged on her inner retina. A formidable local figure now living at Polk City near Lakeland, she remembered Lee as 'a swell youngster, a fine human being who just didn't happen to like school very much. He was lonely and never had many friends. Sure he was mischievous – and don't ask me, Sir, what he did because I just wouldn't tell y'all a single thing without Mr Marvin's express permission. All I know is he just thought his father hung out the sun. They were great together here. But when it came to school, well all I can say is Lee was in a mighty hurry to get out and fight in the war'. As much in a hurry as Lakeland High wanted to be rid of him.

By now Lamont Marvin reckoned he'd played all his aces with Lee. At a rough guess – Lee Marvin's own statistics are whimsically vague – he'd kissed off eight schools. He could now be officially designated as a Problem Child. 'I . . . mean . . . a . . . pain . . . in . . . the . . . ass!' declares the latter day PhD with well-spaced emphasis. Lamont Marvin hunted around for the one establishment that could hawser Lee Marvin to his desk. Some place where they didn't exactly break a mutinous spirit. They merely hammered it into shape. St Leo Preparatory School, St Leo, near Dade City, Florida, seemed to have been founded with that, and Lee Marvin, in mind. A Benedictine monastery and preparatory school for a hundred pupils, it was billed as an establishment 'dedicated to the education of young men in a healthful, wholesome Christian atmosphere'. No doubt about that. No doubt either that it was also the grim, end-of-the-line persuader for the bright but anti-social dropouts from the public school system. Sons from wealthy, broken homes of the East; the unruly offspring of cigar millionaires of Havana; high IQ'd misfits short on love and parental understanding.

Or for just plain difficult customers, like the pale, correctly-dressed young Marvin who shook hands with his father one sad morning then walked quickly towards a smiling, black-clad monk waiting at the door. Lee was taken to his small, white-washed room, then shown the monastery, the classrooms, the long dormitory that looked out on to the athletics field, and the monks' cemetery beyond. A huddle of old limestone buildings, the campus is in good saint country. The signposts on the small tracks through the orange groves, alongside the lakes, south to the Withlacoochee River or west to Thirteen Mile Pond, pointed to San Antonio, St Joseph, St Catherine, St Petersburg, or just plain honest-to-goodness Providence. Devoutly, but not exclusively, Catholic, St Leo College, like the sleepy suburb it curls up in, takes its name from the first of the thirteen Popes of St Leo who led the Benedictines from the year 440 to 1903. (Josh Logan who likened his 'wanderin' star' to Attila the Hun may care to know that it was this Leo who turned Attila back from the gates of Rome.)

25

Official records of the battle, Lee Marvin versus St Leo, seemed to have been sunk without trace. Like other significant data of Lee's abortive schooldays, information became scarcer as his reputation grew larger. Maybe when you start handing out honours degrees in Fine Arts to one of your famous sons it is no time to disclose how, say, he once baited an Abbot or occasionally glared the saintly fathers to a reverential standstill. They've kept the good stuff though. Mr Allan J. Powers, who tub-thumps for St Leo under the imposing title Vice-President Development and Public Relations, will happily paint rosy tints around Marvin's chequered reputation. He produced evidence, on worn-to-withering programmes, of Lee Marvin's first faltering steps as an actor. With him in this 3,000 miles-off-Broadway production, were such characters as Freckles, Fat Dutchy, Dum Dum, The Gimp, Brother Nasturtium, Brother Geranium, and Brother Hollyhock. Lee Marvin was Brother Orchid though he hardly looked like it. Allen Powers was also able to offer proof of Brother Orchid's prowess on the athletic field. One report of the time reads: 'St Leo's classy track team ran rough-shod over all opposition to capture the Catholic State track crown for the fourteenth time in the fifteen years of the meet's history. Lee Marvin copped the low and high hurdles and the javelin throw . . . ' But on the subject of Lee Marvin, the slack-grinned scourge of the Benedictines, Mr Powers is cheerfully mute.

Many of the monks who engaged in soul-to-soul combat with Lee in the slightly less than two years he was at St Leo are now enjoying a bit of peace in the college cemetery. Today, if they were around to tell the tale, they would speak of an abrasive, odd-man-out of a student who made his own rules, preferred his own company. His formative years having been spent in the South he was an expert on the high falutin' rituals of Southern courtesy. But behind it was a steely obstinacy and the short-fused violence which was to persist long after the exasperated Fathers of St Leo showed him the door. The two old campaigners, on opposite sides of the barricades, remember Lee Marvin with the standard reaction of the rueful amusement cross-battened with respect. One is Father Marion Bowman, Abbot of St Leo, Lee's teacher and track coach. The other, Jack Betz, his former room-mate. One speaks for saints, the other for sinners. Jack Betz, like Lee Marvin, had been thrown

26

out of several schools before he too was delivered unto St Leo for salvation. He was thrown out of there too. For seven years he was Mayor of Sarasota, a small town on Florida's west coast, a couple of backward somersaults from the famous John Ringling Circus and Museum to the east. Dressed with the sober elegance of an English barrister – and, despite the southern cadences, sounding that way too – Jack Betz leaned back behind the heli-pad of an executive desk and rooted both for Marvin and St Leo.

The place was really strict and if they couldn't handle you they just threw you out. It was a preparatory school then which prepared you for college. It was very oriented to the church. You went to mass whether you were Catholic or not. And we had some pretty tough people there. I mean really tough – the sort that played football without knee pads just to prove it. Lee? Well he was something special. As I remember it we all called him 'Horseface'. I was there for four months before I knew his real name. He had an exceptional physique, took on the javelin, the heavy shot-putt and boxing. He was quick and strong. But I look back now and see he could never take the discipline of the team. He was always alone. He would just have to have made a good marine. He was the individual you could always count on. He could shoot his mouth off when it was needed, but he never had a mean streak in him. He was one of those guys you looked at, and who looked at you, and you weren't going to try to prove yourself with him, because he's going to hurt you back. Even the seniors never fooled around with him. He never actually seemed the aggressive type. You just sensed it was there. You just felt you'd better not screw around with this guy because maybe this guy wouldn't know when to stop. I knew if I got into a fight with Lee and he hit me, he wouldn't step back to see how bad he'd hurt me. I don't think he was the kind that hit you once. He'd swarm you.

So Jack Betz's old room-mate threw the Javelin further, jumped hurdles faster, shot the putt longer than anybody else but didn't stick around to take any bows.

But I remember this about Lee; in that kind of school system there are always minority groups being picked on. The guys who are the butt of jokes, the ones who are going to be pushed around first. Well Lee never stuck his nose in anybody's busi-

27

ness – he had enough problems of his own – anyway he never wanted to be the leader, stand up front and give the orders. But once there were these tough kids who were picking on a typical fall guy. He was in the centre of the group and they were having some real merciless fun. The kid was scared but he had no place to go. It riled Lee. Finally he sauntered up, stood there, and very quietly he said, 'Okay that's enough, you've had your fun, now break it up.' Just that, no overt show of strength. But all the young toughs got the message. It was over. I saw Lee do that sort of thing time and time again. But it was the strict disciplines of the place, what he reckoned to be the unreasonable rules, that he found hard to take. Lee wasn't girl-shy, and at that age – 'Horseface' was probably sixteen or seventeen – we liked to slip out at night to get with the girls of Dade City. Well obviously that wasn't exactly encouraged at St Leo's Benedictine establishment. In fact I really believe they loaded us up with saltpetre as a kind of deterrent.

Jack Betz laughed. But the antidote failed to suppress Marvin's exploding urges. He split frequently after lights out. Hauled up before a monk he took his punishment without a word. It was usually worth it, saltpetre or not.

Father Marion Bowman was one of the few monks at St Leo who was clued in to Lee Marvin's aberrant psyche. A hefty Friar Tuck-ish character he was quick with the jokes. An Abbot in search of Costello. Father Marion played a fair role in the development of the muscle and the mind of Lee Marvin. He differed from Jack Betz on a detail. As he remembered it, Lee Marvin was called 'Dog-face' not 'Horse-face'. He studied a college portrait. 'Clearly dog-face don't you think?' The point wasn't pressed. What mattered to the good Abbot of St Leo was that:

Lee Marvin had all the capacities of a good human being. But when he was here he was just a wild crazy kid. I don't remember too much about him academically. I used to teach track, and that's what he excelled at. Javelin especially.

There's some wild country right over across the lake. Used to be a lot of wild pigs roaming around there. Well Lee Marvin would take a long bamboo pole, fix a knife blade on the end of it, and he'd go over there and hunt pigs. He could run like the wind. He'd try and spear them. I suppose it was just a carry-over from throwing the javelin or maybe throw-

ing the javelin was a carry-over from the hunting. It was just
the crazy kind of thing he'd get involved in.

This vision of Marvin galloping after the squealing hogs with
a custom-made spear raised and ready, seems funny nearly
forty years on. But the cool savagery of it is revealing. This was
Marvin the hunter. In a fair imitation of a Masai warrior, his
manhood rested on the kill. If pigs' blood spattered the soft
greenery beneath the palms and orange trees, Marvin's sensi-
tivities were scarcely affected. The act of violence as in the
killing of a game animal, the bludgeoning of a giant marlin
hauled on to a crowded boat, has a kind of rough justice to it,
seen through Lee's eyes. 'Sure I've beat a big fish to death with
a club,' he has said. 'He was wrecking the boat so I lit into him
and didn't stop until he was dead. Once you start responding to
a stimulus like that you have no control over your emotions.'
As he told Richard Warren Lewis:

It's the same sensation of getting into a riot; when you really
start going and the adrenaline is pumping, the next thing you
know you're swinging the club or throwing the bricks . . .
you just go with it till the fish peter out, or till there's no
more windows to break or no more cops to hit. You
go into a big school of fish and you kill them and
there's blood flying all over and the guys are laughing
and killing. It's a real blood bath. There's a sense of being
cleansed when it's all over. That night you really sleep,
because you've gone your cycle.

And so while others pitched ball or made mild sport with
the Benedictine monks of St Leo, Lee Marvin stuck pigs.

It was no wonder then that Lee moved in circles far beyond
those in which the other boys moved. As a result they wrote
him down as a loner which was the way he wanted it. This
squared with his tendency to get up to all kinds of outlandish
acts in order to prove to himself he was a man. But then
maybe you have to go a little overboard if you are doubtful
of your own acceptance, to convince people you're there.

Whatever else St Leo may have been flawed on, Father Bowman's comments demonstrated they were not short on insight.
He went on:

29

But Lee must have had his problems because of course he was finally dismissed. He could be very stubborn. We had Father Raphael and Father Edward here who could get very cross easily. I don't know exactly why he was expelled. But it was probable he refused to take some punishment because he didn't feel he'd done anything wrong. Some crazy thing somebody pinned on him and he wasn't going to take the rap. He was that kind of guy. If he didn't feel guilty and somebody said, 'Take your punishment or else,' Lee would say, 'Okay, else.'

Father Marion clearly has a lot of respect for his one-time track star. But apart from the degree ceremony in 1969, has had no contact with him. 'I believe I wrote to him once since he was here, care of his agent or his lawyer – you know you can never find out where to write – but I didn't get an answer.'

News that his son Lee had been turfed out of St Leo was delivered to Lamont Marvin at the Terrace Hotel, Lakeland. The official pronouncement had a gloomy predictability to it. Lee Marvin's pathological aversion to discipline and formal teaching had received the same comeuppance it had collected in New York. He was seventeen. The year was 1941. Whatever last-ditch solutions Lamont Marvin may have hit on to bring Lee into line, young Marvin had already made up his mind. He'd had a bellyfull of bureaucratic ass-kicking. He loathed the trapped, walled-in feeling of institutionalised teaching. Florida, with its self-righteous white and segregated blacks grilling in the brassy sunshine added an edge to his discontent. He told Lamont Marvin that now that America was in the war he might just as well add his ten cents sooner rather than later. Lamont, the veteran of World War I, gave him no argument. If the services couldn't hone the rough edges off Lee Marvin, then Jesus, how are we going to win the war! 'I think you've made the right decision, son,' he said, hopeful perhaps that the generals might succeed where head teachers had failed. Lee Marvin did not wait to be drafted. He applied, and was accepted for the Marines. Interesting choice for a character with a built-in disgust for the ritual whip-cracking hog-wash of iron-hard discipline. So why the Marines? 'Simple,' Lee Marvin explained.

I knew I was going to be killed. I just wanted to die in the very best outfit. I mean I'd seen all the films. The guys going over the top with a blazing machine gun in their hands. All that stuff. But this was the real kavoom. I mean they were killing each other out there. So I figured only the best was for Lee Marvin. There are ordinary corpses. And Marine corpses. I figured on the first-class kind and joined up.

Volunteering for the Marines – they did not start drafting until eighteen months later – attracted Marvin for another reason. 'I liked the no-nonsense agreement between the Corps and the volunteer. When things got rough – and brother they got rough – they just said, "Well you asked for it, you got it."'

The monks of St Leo, led by Father Marion, assembled at the college gates to speed 'Horseface' on his way. One prayed that God would go with him. The others, and Lee, murmured 'Amen'. He took a train north to Jacksonville, changed to the mainliner to New York. 'That's where they had the biggest concentration of Marines,' Marvin said.

It goes by population with New York and Pennsylvania having the largest. My mother was living in New York, my father's work for the citrus commission pinned him down in Florida. So I enlisted and waited. But it wasn't until August 1942 that they finally said 'come'.

Eighteen years old and perkily confident down to his bootnails, Private Lee Marvin checked in to the marine base at Parris Island, South Carolina. Lean, hard and ready for inspection, he seemed to fit the marine prototype as though born with a silver bullet in his mouth. While others fumbled with their guns, Private Marvin manipulated his with a commando's skill. On the firing ranges, his cheek resting almost sensuously on the polished butt, he hit the targets with deadly precision. Discipline apart, he had the sharp eye, the muscle and the fast co-ordination that makes for warriors or West Point. But discipline wasn't apart. Not long after his arrival at Parris Island, Private Marvin went to war. Against the US Marines.

Chapter Three

'There are two prominent parts of your body in view to the enemy when you flatten out – your head and your ass. If you present one, you get killed. If you raise the other, you get shot in the ass.'

Lee Marvin.

Twenty-five years after a Japanese shell in the spine abruptly ended his war, actor Lee Marvin went back to Saipan. Debris, human and mechanical, still lay around the beaches, uncollected trophies bleaching or rusting under the burnishing sun. Clapped out tanks up-ended in the sand. Crabs scuttling in and out of blackened shell-cases. A propeller from a Zero, one end in the earth, the other pointing accusingly at the sky. And bones. Anonymous now. A skull, a jaw bone, bizarre relics of one of the most savage battles of America's war in the Pacific. The battle for Saipan began on 15 May 1944 against a Japanese garrison of 30,000 sardined into an area of seventy square miles. When they were finally crushed, the island taken, they had lost 25,000 men. American casualties were no less shattering – 16,500 killed or missing.

That night on Saipan, twenty-five years later, Lee Marvin got royally drunk. His lone recce along the deserted beaches had brought back all the stabbing pain and memories. 'Shit I can still hear the bastards!' was Marvin's thought. So he drank with an efficiency born of a quarter of a century of spectacular tippling. But the liquor, far from blunting the nightmares, gave them an edge. The sight of a couple of admirals at the other end of the bar clinched it. With the familiar illogicality of the barroom tough, Lee lurched over to them, grabbed a salt cellar and poured salt over their service hats. He mumbled that he wanted to eat the scrambled eggs on their visors and that he never ate scrambled eggs without salt. They didn't share the joke. But recognising him, aware of his reputation for crass but harmless confrontations in hostelries around the world, the admirals quietly sailed out to safer waters.

It was the uniforms that bugged Marvin. Not the men. He regarded them as the trappings of authority which stripped men of their individuality. So why, if he hated uniforms so much, did he join the Marines? The paradox didn't mystify Marvin. 'I went for the uniformity of comradeship, not clothing.' It was the mentality he objected to. It intimidated him just as it had done when, as Private Marvin L., he collected his rifle and gear at the US Marines boot camp at Parris Island, South Carolina. The Marine sergeants soon got the measure of Marvin's blank stare, the dumb insolence gift-wrapped in contempt. They threw the book at him but he stood his ground, sometimes smiling up at a bird, and naming it, while blood vessels ballooned on coarse red necks. All the published records have Marvin the marine, spending considerable time in the stockade for indiscipline or for giving such amiable advice as 'Why don't you fuck off, Sergeant!' I wrote to the Headquarters of the United States Marine Corps in Washington to get the details. The official reply, while confirming Marvin's excellent combat service, his Purple Heart and the fine battle record of his Division contained this note:

'While I am precluded from providing details on Mr Marvin's disciplinary record, I can attest to the fact that Mr Marvin was never confined in any military correctional institution. Sincerely, A. P. Brill, Lieutenant-Colonel, US Marine Corps.'

Marvin has never bothered to correct the story, presumably in accordance with every PRO's dictum: 'Never knock a good myth.' But Lee still gave his sergeant's a rough ride. They'd tried the familiar haranguing – unremitting abuse delivered an inch from the victim's ear – but Marvin grinned slowly. and just asked the guy to speak up. Reflecting the stoicism of St Leo's monks, Marvin had trained himself to 'take the shit and button the lip'. This was partly because maturity was catching up on him. But also because he had enlisted to fight the enemy, not the Marines. He may have been uncertain about his motivations, but there was no doubting his craving to get into battle. He'd flunked out of too many schools. Failed to graduate. Had booted authority in the crotch. The prognosis looked bad. At least going into action, even getting killed, had a certainty to it. You can't flunk out of a grave.

Admiral Nimitz, oblivious to Private Marvin's urge to get into action, was sure doing his best to satisfy it. Having neutralised the Japanese on the Gilbert Islands, his massive naval and air forces were preparing to do a pendulum-swing up to the heavily defended Marshall Islands. The Japanese soldiers were programmed to fight to the last man. The US Marines were required to do no less. And they were ready to go. Marvin was posted to I Company, 24th Marines, Fourth Division. He received notification of his overseas posting back home, on leave, in New York. Robert was there too, planning to join the services. Lamont Marvin had also arrived, from Florida. There was no way he was going to stay back home while his two sons went to war. He had taken the Japanese attack on Pearl Harbor as a deep personal affront. Fooling around plugging the virtues of Florida oranges was not the role this World War I veteran had cast for himself in World War II. He decided to enlist again, told Courtenay of his decision. She considered the prospect of the three men going into battle, accepting it with a sigh. There was no stopping a Marvin when his dander and his blood were up. An expert in gunnery, Lamont had quietly sounded out the local military and learned that Britain's beleaguered anti-aircraft detachments needed reinforcements. Too old to run or jump, Lamont could still read gun sightings, understand radar, and command men. He applied for a posting and was grabbed fast. General Seth Marvin, the Civil War hero, would have had a lot of time for these twentieth century Marvins, noting with satisfaction that all three were volunteers.

The night before Lee left for Camp Pendleton, the Marine base in California, Lamont went to his gun cupboard and took out a favourite, still lethal, automatic. Never had so deadly an heirloom been gifted with such tenderness. The next day, 12 August 1942, Lee went to Camp Pendleton the hard way. He hitch-hiked. Prepared for a final, paternal back-slap, he saw Lamont standing there, kit-bag in hand, and realised that the old warrior was hitching the ride south with him. Jesus Christ, he was learning more about his father every day! Lamont's motivations to get into uniform, leap into the war, would have intrigued analysts. He was brave, no question. Fiercely patriotic – that was self-evident too. But there was also the subconscious determination not to be white-feathered by his sons. That rivalry was to hit fever pitch with punches thrown when the three returned home to Woodstock.

But now, as they jolted south, father and son were jettisoning the difficult years behind them. Both now understood. The measure of Lee Marvin, overcast by the marathon expulsions, would now be really tested. The man-game. The rest was applesauce. No speeches were made. Each wished the other luck. If either were to die, well, both Marvins knew the game and accepted the ground rules. At that moment, on a short, brusque farewell handshake, Lee and Lamont Marvin were at their closest. There were battles to come, for sure. But there was no doubting the affection between the two truculent fighting-cocks. Shortly before he died in 1972, Lamont Marvin said of Lee, 'He was a wild, harmless, innocent, crazy kid. Between us though, there never was a period of misunderstanding.'

It seemed an odd setting for Lee Marvin's account of his war. Outside on the Pacific Coast Highway, the weekend limos from Beverly Hills, Bel Air and the Hollywood Hills were slotting methodically into ocean driveways like racehorses into stalls. Inside Marvin's home, his second wife, Pam, was fixing Bloody Marys, the ritual morning refreshment of the beach set. Lift the cedar shingle roofs anywhere along that Croesus-rich coastline and for certain the talk would be of percentages, screwed deals, maybe of Dyan Cannon's Primal Therapy cell on Malibu, or the favourite lament of the time, 'the fucking accountants are taking over the studios.' Inside 21404 Pacific Coast Highway the names dropped were Eniwetok . . . Kwajalein . . . Garrapan . . . Challantanoa . . . and a bitch of a mountain on Saipan called Tapotchau: Lee Marvin, white hair, blue jeans, heavy brown service boots, had in fact been talking about boats and birds. He is an expert on both.

Leaning over the rail above the sand he had indicated the Lesser Marbled Godwit, latched on to the common Sandpiper, digressed momentarily to praise 'the best piece of ass of the day!' and then gone in to show on a map where he would soon be fishing the giant marlin. With hands the size of pork joints he spread the map out on a polished ship's desk, and his finger strayed westward to the Marshall Islands. 'Je-sus Christ! Look there. I managed to get to twenty-one of those rotten little islands before they hit me.' He remembered, he said, 'every shit-scared second of it.' And no other Marine involved in what the land-based experts called 'island-hopping' would ever forget it. The American Fleet of carriers and landing craft swung the sledgehammer on to the Marshall Islands in January 1944, destroying Japanese strongholds and capturing airfields. By 4 February they had overrun Kwajalein, Eniwetok and were sweeping up to the Marianas and Saipan. Marvin, to his surprise, came out of the Marshall Islands in one piece.

In that particular shindig I was in a divisional reconnaisance company which was a derivation of the old raiders. We had to go in the night before the dawn assault and try to reconnoitre a route. It was impossible really. We'd be put down by an APD, Assault Personnel Destroyer. There were maybe 110 of us and half of us would be lost at sea in those rubber boats, you could bet. So you'd land with maybe twelve guys and you'd wander around and not see a thing because you didn't want to see anything. All you wanted to do was get off. If you were fired on you were supposed to throw a poncho over your head, whip out a blue flashlight and draw an X on the map where the fire was coming from. Well, I don't think anybody actually threw a poncho over their head, and nobody fired back either. Because once you fired you . . . were . . . dead! Of course we'd all got miserably lost and screwed up. The next morning – if you got that far – the sun would come up and there would be the whole United States Navy out there because it's D Day and they would be shelling you because if they saw you they figured you were Japs and nobody told them otherwise. So, God, it was absolute confusion. You're being hit by friend and foe. So you eventually swim out to a reef and pray; and hope Goddamit, that somebody's listening. But I didn't get hit in the Marshalls. I got my meal ticket in Saipan in the Marianas 18 June 1944.

He remembers it all in vivid detail. The bright moonlight throwing the great spread of floating juggernauts in dark extended silhouette 1,500 yards off the beaches. Then as the second-hands on blue-lit watches hit their mark the paralysing bombardment made a multi-coloured abstract of the sky and 20,000 Marines, including Lee Marvin, aged twenty, slipped into rubber boats wondering if they'd see another dawn. And this is how he told it:

We went in on Yellow Beach Two. It was morning. The first day. On a beach south of a place called Challantanoa. We clawed forward and hit the basic scrub of the beach. Beyond it were those big open fields, thousands of sticks with saki bottles on top. My assumptions then were they were used as insulators for wires that had been knocked down. But I was wrong. The Japs were using them as artillery markers. They had us nicely pinpointed on a checker-board. They didn't miss. They just knew all these points we were on and started cranking in there. The artillery got very bad, and all the bombing was coming down real heavy. We finally got to a very large trench, about, I'd say, eight hundred yards inland. There was really a tremendous downpour of this stuff so we all bailed into the trench, and we were sitting there, you know, thanking God for this kind of cover when I noticed the parapets of the trenches forward of us had firing slits and it dawned on me they belonged to them not us. I happened to say this when they started opening up at us all along the trench. We bailed out and went forward, thinking it would be better forward than backwards and they just cleaned out that trench and it must have been three thousand yards long.

So then the night came and we were very thinned out. There were about thirty yards between them and us. They could have walked across and traded yukisaki. We lost quite a few that night. But the next day we pushed towards Aslito airfield (renamed Isely Field after its capture). We got pinned down there and lost some more guys going through those cane fields. We were pulled out and on the fourth morning we were heading up into what was later called 'Death Valley' and it looked it. We had to push up this mountain Tapotchau. (An extinct volcano, rough limestone most of the way up to its summit at 1,554ft.) Well the mountain looked okay. I mean if you lived that long you could probably get to the top. Looked simple really. But nobody could get up far enough to lick the bastard. They sent one company in and they lost a pile of men real rapidly. The residue were pulled back and they sent our company in. I was the point man of the assault company so I went out with this guy Mike Harrison. We went one way, the second and third platoons went another way, and the fourth platoon someplace else. We all climbed and suddenly Mike got nailed right under the heart, or through the lung. Most likely the lung because it was pink blood, you know. He went down and I didn't know for sure what to do but anyway I stuck my finger in the hole to try to stop whatever it was that was coming out. But he was dead. We both had Browning automatics. I started firing at whatever was coming at us which was difficult when you've got one finger stuck in a guy's chest. The Nips were hitting us with machine gun fire at point-blank range. And they were laying a cross-fire behind us. It was about a fifteen-minute fire-fight and I don't think we hit one of them.

So then the Captain shouted to fall in but I couldn't get in myself. We'd just got into one knot, caught dead in an ambush, and Jesus Christ it was just decimation. We had started out with 247 men and fifteen minutes later there were six of us. 'I' Company. Third Battalion, 24th Marines. Six fellers. So anyway it was my turn to get nailed. There are two prominent parts of your body in view to the enemy when you flatten out – your head and your ass. If you present one, you get killed. If you raise the other, you get shot in the ass. I got shot in the ass.

When I got hit I recall – it's kind of interesting – the guy was on me, whoever it was shooting at me, and he was so close I could feel the muzzle blast. But being dark I couldn't see him. He got the rubber heel of my left shoe first. You know on Marine boots that's kinda heavy, with a lot of resistance, and the stuff he was firing at me was pretty good too. Anyway my leg flung out and I wasn't sure whether I was hit there or not. So I looked up and, bang, he hit right in front of my face and knocked all the stuff in my eyes so I couldn't see and I said, 'Oh Jesus!' and I just came out of rhythm, and then he knocked me in the ass, or spine, or whatever it was. I didn't know that then. All I knew was I bounced off the ground and said, 'Jesus Christ I'm hit.' And somebody shouted, 'Shut up, we're all hit!' 'But *I'm* hit don't you understand!' [Marvin creased up as he recalled the fine distinction he was drawing.] Then the confusion really started. There was our counter-attack and all that kind of stuff. The ammunition dumps are blowin' and we're getting out. I'm with a guy by the name of Pettigrew and another guy by the name of Shyte. I wasn't sure I could move at all. You know how these things work. You don't know the state you're in. It doesn't hurt that much at first. You're stunned from the neck down. You don't know the region it's in. It could be your heart, it could be anything. I just started slowly, you get used to it after a while. You start on your big toe first, you can feel that, you know, so you work up to your ankle, then your can, and then Shyte screams, 'Hey, Captain Marvel's hit in the ass.' The guys gave me the nickname 'Captain Marvel'. Well 'Marvel's hit in the ass' sounds comedic but I figured it was a little more serious than that. I mean to me, it's very serious. The machine gun fire was very heavy.

The next day they found twenty-seven gun emplacements surrounding our position. So they dumped some salt on my ass and the MO's big bandages. Well he was going to put the bandages over it so he said, 'Raise up so I can tie it' and I said, 'With all that shit flying around I'm not getting a sixteenth of an inch higher than I need to be.' So then I started crawling out, passing all these guys I knew, all lying in strange positions.

We got to a clearing, must have been about twenty feet across – say from maybe here to the end of the kitchen – and it was a fire path and . . . you . . . knew . . . it. I mean there was just no way I could crawl across because I couldn't use my legs. I said, 'I'll tell you what, if you can get me up and give me a shove towards that brush . . . ' and they said 'Okay' and they did and by God, I made it across, just fell the last five feet and slid into the scrub. I got behind this great big tree and figured, boy, that's something at least. And there was a guy sitting behind it by the name of Rose. He used to dye his underwear pink, you know, and he was just sitting there like there was no war on at all. He said, 'Where're you hit?' I said, 'I guess in the ass.' He said, 'Would you like some water?' I said, 'Jesus, yes.' So he leaned out to get his canteen up, he gave me a gulp and as he leaned out to put it back in again he got hit. He just went, 'Oh' and fell right on top of me. I couldn't get him off. He was dead but he kept looking at me. And the old panic is starting to build up right?

So then, Jesus, they start bringing the other guys out and we had a guy called Calello who had been hit in the back of the skull. A glancing blow of some nature we found out later, which had blinded him. So he was kinda screaming you know and they were trying to get him out of there, hollering for stretcher-bearers. But there weren't any and finally one did come so they got Calello on. While they were putting him on, one of the bearers got killed with a one-shot, another one got knocked right through the back killing him too, and Calello got a bullet in the hip. Calello got hit three times while he was being put on the stretcher. He was a screaming mess, you can understand that. And one guy ran by me and stepped right on my ass. I mean right on the thing. It was a big hole which I found out later was nine-by-three-by-three just lying open but I was alive and still had my .45 automatic which gave me some blast if I needed it.

Then they finally got me on a stretcher. I said, 'Do you have to use that?' because machine gun fire is about stretcher height, you know knee-high stuff, and I was stretched out, all six feet two inches of me conveniently like that. But they said, 'Let's go' – four of them – and they started running real fast which was awful, and one of them said, 'Please, please . . . ' because it was too fast and sure enough one of them went down, though he'd only tripped. He pulled himself up and we got over this small ridge, maybe only six feet high which gave us some cover, safety to some degree at last, Jesus. And when we get there here's a whole battalion sitting back smoking, just like nothing's happened.

One of the stretcher bearers announces 'Captain Marvel's been hit in the ass,' so they took me back to battalion aid and the doc was standing there with a couple of Jap pistols stuck in his belt, no shirt on, and he said, 'Do you need any blood?' I said, 'How the fuck would I know, doc?' So he said, 'Put him over there.' Now they had two groups of men; the dead men over there and the savables over here. These guys were sitting around smoking cigarettes but you just knew they were going to die. So they put me behind a stack of mortar shells and there were other dumps lying around and you could hear the stuff slamming into them. It was just frigging endless. One of our sergeants had been hit and he had an 'M' stuck on his head but he was walking – morphine, you know they used to mark you when they gave you a morphine shot – they had given me morphine by then and it helps. And the sergeant said, 'Would you like some water?' He had it in a plasma can. I said, 'Love some, sergeant' and I took a mouthful, then he took a gulp and then the whole world went WOOM! About a hundred and fifty yards in front of us one of the Japanese dumps we'd captured had been hit and you looked up and you could see those marines flying through the air, slowly, yeah, slowly . . .

It really shook the world and I'm knocked right off the stretcher on my ass, it was so . . . then the scream went up, 'COUNTER ATTACK . . . COUNTER ATTACK.' By that time I had given Shyte my pistol. He needed it. Now I was unarmed and I really got scared. They took everybody out of there, getting them back to the beach. I was about the last guy, the last of four. They put two of us in a jeep with the two ambulatories, one of them with a pistol. And we took off, really flying, except we were heading the wrong way. Going right through Japanese territory. One of the guys screamed at the driver, stopping the jeep. He jumped out but the driver fired a couple of shots and said, 'Get back in.' Then he swung the jeep round and we finally got to the beach. This was about five or six o'clock now in the evening. I'm on this tent on the beach which is the worst place to be because that's where all the supplies are loaded and BOOM . . . WHEEE . . . BRROOM . . . the stuff is really slamming in, and I'm asking 'Can't I get off this fucking island?' The answer is 'Not to-night' from the guy who's writing out the tags. By then the bleeding had pretty well stopped. I really coagulate fast.

So then an LCM (Landing Craft Medium) is going by and the guy hollers, 'Anyone going out?' So they ran me out to it and I'm on it all alone. They pull the thing out, the diesel engines start roaring, and it's a real hum, and you've got the morphine going, and you're face down on the stretcher. I remember passing ships. The LCM is looking for the nearest hospital ship. They found one. Called *Solace*. Does the name grab you? The next thing I was aware of was a pair of shiny black shoes, right there in front of my face. Shiny. It was so incongruous. So they lifted me up and they shoved me into a place that was lit up which surprised me what with the shells flying and all. Yellow walls with bright lights. And the doctor said, or somebody said, 'Where are you hit?' I told them. I was getting to know it by now. They got me to the urinary or some ward and they put me down on a real bed, you know a rack bed but with a mattress. He said, 'You can get up on that.' I said, 'But it's got sheets on it,' thinking of my shot-up ass, but they said, 'That's okay' and put me on it, dirty as I was.

Then a guy comes along, a corpsman or somebody and asks me, 'Would you like some ice cream?' I'm lying there with a nine-inch hole in my ass, souped up on morphine, and he's offering me a dish of ice cream, and would you believe it 'Moonlight Serenade' is playing somewhere on the piano. I said, 'Could you turn the lights out,' because I could still hear all the firing, but the guy understood and he said, 'No, it's okay.' Now I finally recognised some of the guys around me and they eventually did dim the lights. But you could still hear all the sounds on shore which was only about a thousand yards away. The gunfire on the beaches.

So then it all came in on me and I started to cry. Yep, I was weeping because I felt like a coward, a deserter I guess. I know a lot of other men did but it bugged me. I felt just like I'd thrown down my rifle and run. Like I'd fucked off and left them to it. That wasn't the way it was, but the morphine and the 'Moonlight Serenade' . . . anyway, I wept. Then I fell asleep. And that was about it.

But not quite. There were the thirteen months in different hospitals involving treatment for the severed sciatic nerve. He had plenty of time to think during those thirteen months on his back. He emerged from it with the unshakable credo, 'Life is every man for himself. You can't ever let your guard down, and the most useless word in the world is "HELP".'

In one of the hospitals, on Guadacanal, he was given the Purple Heart. 'It's nothing to shout about,' Lee Marvin said drily.

It's like getting a VD test. I was in this hospital ward and some guy came in and said, 'What's your name? Marvin?' He threw the salad across the bed and that was it. They should have put those Purple Hearts in the 'C' ration cans because almost everyone who didn't turn and run, qualified.

The throwaway attitude was no pose. In his book he'd done no more than survive. Physically, apart from his butt end, he was in good shape. For this he would have a permanent scar and forty dollars a week pension for life. The psychological read-out was not so neat. Emotionally, Marvin had been churned over and shredded like ploughed earth. Death at close range, seeing the bomb-blasted somersaulting bodies of the marines, the dead weight of a mortally-shot buddy pinning him to the ground, were images not easily obliterated from Marvin's inner eye. 'The memories hit me sometimes like an exploding neutron in my mind . . . ' he said, shifting his long legs, looking out to the ocean. Anything can trigger it off. A glance at a souvenir . . . the gold tooth he had off a Japanese soldier he'd killed . . . the face of his Marine sergeant, to him, the archetypal soldier hero. Then his thoughts jerk back to the Pacific and feelings of guilt, for having been hauled out of the battle, and pride for having been in it, run riot in his mind. Then, if he seeks solace in the bottle, it's wise to take to the hills. So peace made no difference to his ferocious loyalty, the word love says it better, for the US Marines. After that experience, it was big and clean, 'showbiz' would inevitably become a target for his derision and custom-made obscenities. No doubt he had been scared rigid in the Pacific. One of the last hospitals he was shipped to before his eventual discharge was on Hawaii. Almost every night before he fell asleep he had recurring nightmares. There would be these Japanese soldiers moving swiftly from tree to tree. They would come towards him but he was paralysed, unable to move. He'd raise his rifle aiming at the faces coming towards him. The light click told him there was no ammunition in the magazine. Sometimes he'd hear the shriek of shells, then the 'Moonlight Serenade' floating over the boom of the guns. He would wake up sweating. On one such session he heard an air-raid siren. He continued to hear it as he awakened, terror rising within him. Then he discovered it was a dummy run on the island for some visiting dignitary.

Lee Marvin was finally discharged from the Naval hospital in Chelsea, Massachusetts. They told him he'd been lucky. He'd been a millimetre off permanent paralysis. For all that, the morning he was handed his discharge papers at the Marine Barracks in Philadelphia, Lee was depressed to hell. 'I actually missed the Marines. Not the war and all that stuff, but, oh well, the camaraderie. Remember I'd been through plenty with these guys. You sit around with them . . . it was an emotional thing I guess. I really missed it.'

If Lee Marvin felt disoriented, exposed out of uniform, his father, discharged four days later, had his problems too. Lamont Marvin came home from England with a Military Medal, a rare achievement for an American enlisted man. Stationed first at Folkestone, then at Antwerp, he had set up the anti-aircraft gun emplacements knocking out 600 German V2 rockets. A captain in World War I he returned to America this time with the rank of First Sergeant, content with that and his medal. But like Lee he suffered from post-battle depression. He had no stomach for selling oranges in the lingering euphoria of battle-action. The two uneasy veterans met, compared miseries. Courtenay Marvin had taken a job with the Sunday supplement of the *American Weekly* which required the family to move to Chicago. Three months later Lamont Marvin suffered a shattering nervous breakdown. They moved to Woodstock, New York, Courtenay immediately giving up her career. Lee Marvin had trouble starting his. Outside of the Marines, he could latch on to nothing. It amazes him now to recall that of all things to pick on after service with the Marines in World War II he chose a course in shorthand and typing. But squiggling in notebooks, touch-typing to a Souza march, made him feel as though his manhood was fading fast. One hot Chicago afternoon he ducked out of class, went across town, and marched into a Marine Depot. 'I'd like to re-enlist,' he pleaded. The officer was sympathetic. He was familiar with the 'can't adjust' syndrome. But he reminded Lee gently of his disability, thanked him for past services, turned him round and pointed him towards home. Woodstock put out no flags for Marvin. Returned GIs were thick on the ground. He mowed lawns, swept snow off driveways, picked up a buck here and there, got his first bitter taste of the American Dream, class of 1945. The best a neighbour could offer him was a job as a plumber's apprentice. When you've handled an armoury of guns, spanners and wrenches come easy to the hand. But after the tenth sagging drain stack or spuming pipe, he began to yearn for that old friendly, foulmouthed machismo of the US Marines. Then he was called upon to clear a blocked john in the local theatre. The theatre manager was impressed.

So Marvin was not so much swept, as flushed – from effluence, to affluence.

Chapter Four

'I bought a Burberry trench coat, a snap-brim
Fedora and there was nothing I couldn't do from
"Give it to him in the gut, Ricco", to "Okay wise
guy, you're under arrest".'

Lee Marvin

So Marvin is standing back from this unclogged john in the
Woodstock Little Theatre and is so high on his performance
he'd gladly oblige with an encore. He has switched off the
suction pump and, hearing now the voices of the actors on the
stage, feels a tremor of excitement. As though he's part of
the action. Only an S-bend away from the Drama. He gives the
john a final flush, nods approvingly as the pan clears its throat,
and moves out into the semi-darkness of the auditorium. It is a
rehearsal and the director is laying it on the actors: scenes are
being shifted, script pages rustled, there's a young red-haired
beauty standing with one hand on a slender hip at stage left –
the atmosphere is as taut as grapple wire. And thrilling. Inside
Marvin's just-out-of-adolescence brain two messages flash, 'I
have to talk to that redhead!' and 'What you gonna tell her –
you shift shit for a living?' But it's all great. His kind of scene.
So he drifts over to a group milling around the director and he's
nodding and smiling like it's a Stanislavsky manual he's left outside instead of a spare ball-cock and a pump. So then this guy
examines him closely and says . . .

*

45

Lee Marvin's quick leap from local handyman to stage actor – the debut called for no more than a loud mouth and muscle – owes much to the locality in which the family lived. Woodstock, fringe town to New York, was a small, culture-conscious community to which the wealthy of Manhattan came to dodge the long hot summers. The colony attracted writers, painters, bearded oddballs and the odd shrink. Courtenay Marvin's connection with high-level publishing had opened Lee's mind to that chic literati of the *New Yorker*, Dorothy Parker, Robert Benchley, James Thurber, S. J. Perelman and Alexander Woolcott and the rest of the round table at the Algonquin. Woodstock could produce a fair show of talent of its own, much of it centred on its Little Theatre. Mowing the lawns, digging septic tanks, fixing the pipes of the town's culture-bugs gave Marvin a free ride on this bandwagon of wit and wisdom. 'I'd be hanging around there fixing something, we'd get talking away, and then they'd say, "Why don't you come over for dinner?" These were real zappy people," he said. 'You were dealing with aces.'

But they were taking him on their terms. Marvin rapidly discovered that being a war veteran with a Purple Heart and an I-was-there tale of the landings on Iwo Jima, were no automatic entry to a prime job or a soft touch. He couldn't parlay his war wound into anything useful either. There was, he discovered, a distinct disadvantage to having been shot in the rump. Not visible. A sabre slash on the cheek, a black eye-patch, these were negotiable currency in bars. 'I mean it would have been great,' Marvin grinned, 'to stand there with, say, one empty sleeve tucked in your pocket and have the character next to you go all misty-eyed and order the bartender to pour doubles. If I could have thrown open my shirt and have the guy recoil and whisper, "Oh, God . . . no!" – that would have been something! But there was no way I was going to score points by dropping my pants, bending over and saying "Get a load of what they did to me in Saipan!" '

He was having his problems with girls too. Shy as hell, with a face suggesting a bad case of faulty assembly, Marvin developed a King-sized complex inducing the familiar syndrome of aggression camouflaging reserve. He considered his ears too large; mouth large enough to take a medium shovel, and the rest of the head fine for butting and brawling. He was being overly self-critical. Famous beauties, let alone wives, will testify that the

46

alleged bad facial assemblage turned them on more devastatingly than would, say, an eager Robert Redford or persistent Mastroianni. But fresh out of the Marines, still clinging to barrack-room male chauvinism, the young Marvin was finding it hard to score. 'At that age I never really got my share. I figured something was wrong so I went to see a friend, an analyst. The session apparently produced spectacular results. 'After that,' Marvin declared, 'I was kind of up there on a dais taking this salute from thousands of women marching past me...'

But before that metamorphosis his urge to meet that redhead standing there in Woodstock's Little Theatre, carried no illusions of potential success. He would have to become part of the action first. It was a local doctor, Marvin recalls, who set it all up.

I used to do his lawns every Saturday, and he kind of took me under his wing. He'd graduated from medical school then went into mathematics. During the war he'd developed a system where you could sight off any star, not just the North Star. He became head of the American Artillery Association. He was quite an elderly man but we talked a lot and he'd have these geniuses over and occasionally we'd go out fishing which I loved. Always have. That's how I met the famous Ballantine family. Stella Ballantine was a protégé of Emma Goldman's and had a Shakespearian touring company in America. E. J. Ballantine was a fellow actor to Jack and Lionel Barrymore. He also ran Woodstock's theatre. That day when I'd fixed the john, the director told E.J. that one of the actors was sick. They needed a tall loudmouth to play a Texan and E.J. looked at me and figured I was made for the part. The actor took much longer to recover than was anticipated. By the time he staggered back, I was in business. It opened up horizons for me not only on the intellectual level but on life too. I liked the comradeship of summer stock companies. It was the closest thing to the brothers-in-arms credo of the Marines. Hard work and no bullshit.

A laudable philosophy, and as it turned out, a successful one too. It took Marvin to the American Theatre Wing in New York, under the GI Bill guaranteeing places to veterans, and he played in everything that was going. By then he'd moved to Greenwich Village – leaving only one stirred if not broken heart behind him, the shy dark-haired Pamela Feeley. She was fifteen when they met. Lee, twenty-one. Given the Commando-like bravura of his later skirmishes with women, Lee Marvin would normally have stormed right up and established a beach-head. But in those awkward years, all kinds of inhibitions swarming around inside his formidable skull, Marvin played it cautiously. As he recollected it:

I'd seen her outside her school in Woodstock and was mad to know who she was. I was having a drink with some of the guys in a bar one evening and asked them who she was and how I could get to her. One of them said, 'Stick around' and then went out. He came back and said, 'She's down at Skelly's Bridge,' which was across this little creek. So I walked down and there she was. Just standing looking at the water. I said, 'Hello.' She said, 'Hello,' and that was that. [*He looked over to the said childhood sweetheart, now his wife, and asked,* I didn't kiss you at that time, did I? *'I certainly don't think so,' she said firmly.* Oh, *Lee said,* thank you.] Well we met occasionally after that. But stopped seeing each other when I moved to New York to go to theatre school there.

Twenty years, one wife and one celebrated mistress later they were to pick up the threads. But that comes later.

Before moving to New York Marvin had toured in summer stock playing scores of easily-forgettable roles.

The first thing I did was *Roadside* by Emlyn Riggs, then *Home of the Brave, Thunder Rock,* things of that nature. The whole experience scratched either my adventurous spirit or my imagination, I don't know which. But it took me off to the GI Theatre in New York. I fell in with some really marvellous people. The war had just ended and a lot of them had been professionals before. So they were kinda warming up again. Everything was sprouting. I fell under a man by the name of Andrea Jalinski who had come from the Moscow Arts Theatre. Well I don't know, but I can say he didn't tell me one thing. I was absolutely mesmerised by the certain knowledge that I had to do everything myself. Anyway that's what Jalinski kept telling us. He'd been an actor in Russia and he could never get over his accent. So his wife did the acting while he did the coaching.

A year and a half with Jalinski gave Lee Marvin a working

knowledge of Russian oaths and a taste for hot borscht. His acting skills were mostly his own work. He began flexing his
muscles, found that producers were starting to notice him.
Three years in summer stock, good supporting roles on the stage
and in TV, had given him polish and style. There was evidently
a lot of intellectual activity behind those shiny frontal lobes.
But generally his roles were of the heavy, the threat, the heel,
the guy who never gets the girl.

I bought a Burberry trench coat, a snap-brim Fedora, and
there was nothing I couldn't do from "Give it to him in the
gut, Ricco', to 'Okay, wise guy, you're under arrest!' I was
playing either a cop, or a dope or a pickpocket or whatever.
They were these playhouse things, mainly suspense stuff. I
did a couple of hundred of them. A long endless line of mean
sonofabitches.

But they paid well. He was in there with the top guys. And
drinking. And since liquor was to become as vital an element
in the creation of Lee Marvin as that secret varnish was to
Stradivari, it might be helpful to trace it back to its source. New
York, circa 1949–50.

I was living pretty well, remember. So I could buy the drinks
and as much of it as I wanted. Or needed. But I don't know
whether I was into it real heavy at the beginning. I imagine
I was, but I was young and at that age you could throw it.
Why does one do it? Well when you're not Number One or
even Number Two you're always keyed up. You want to do
anything and everything. You get that kind of real fear drive
so . . . yeah . . . I used to drink. Particularly at night when
the pressure was off. I'd rather have been out on a boat fishing. Go down to some beach, throw a line in and then there's
nobody else in the world but you and the fish. And you both
know it. And it's the last bit of mutual respect left on earth.
But when you're working on stage or on TV those aren't the
emotions you get. So you drink. Early on it would be beer
because I couldn't drink anything else unless someone else
was buying. Otherwise it would be Martinis. We'd save up
and go over to Sardi's. [Broadway's after-theatre restaurant
where stars and producers go to celebrate or bury their dead.]
They used to have a little outside bar with maybe six or
eight stools. After about the third glass, this other guy and
myself, I guess we got not boisterous . . . well aggressive. If

49

another actor walked in we'd say, 'What an asshole!' and the bartender would say, 'You – out!' and we'd know that Sardi's would have to come off our list. There were really two groups who used to come in that place in those days, the working actors and the unemployed. And never the twain shall meet! Boy, the line from table to table was just zap zap and kerdoom. I mean it didn't matter if he was the greatest actor in the world. In the unemployed group you'd get the loud 'Why, that sonofabitch, what's he got? Do you see him? He's just a piece of shee . . . it!' Very competitive, the American system.

The exact number of occasions Lee and his tipsy cronies were asked to leave the premises, all kinds of premises, has not been listed. But Marvin reckons most estimates fall short of the true statistic. But boorish or not, it was all gestating into the crude, threatening persona of which movie hoodlums are made. Some actors play the tippling hell-raiser in public as a forlorn gimmick to hit as a 'character'. Marvin never pulled that trick. Whatever view may be taken about his spectacular encounters with the bottle, nobody could accuse him of playing to the gallery. He has said, 'Maybe these sprees are totally juvenile but they work. The aftermath is tremendous hangovers and guilt – and the pledge. Then three days later, when my joints start to creak again, I have to look around for oil.' He admits to having been drunk on occasions on film sets. But his rationale as stated to writer Richard Warren Lewis goes, 'So what? Pope Paul can't take a day off and go out and get smashed at the local gin mill, but that's one of the prerogatives I *can* enjoy.'

Whether others were to share Lee Marvin's enjoyment of his prerogatives will be seen . . . but in New York before Hollywood and the deluge, he was juicing with a passion.

It was Lee Marvin's good fortune that the director Henry Hathaway, scouting extras in New York for a Gary Cooper comedy, found Marvin's after-hours carousels easy to take. Formerly a child actor, turning to directing in 1932, Hathaway had proved he could handle the big adventure subject – and belligerent actors. He was later to make John Wayne a star, and some of the best Westerns ever. The movie for which he had earmarked Marvin as an extra was *You're in the Navy Now* a pleasant, jokey piece of fun about an experimental US patrol craft and what happens when steam turbines are installed in it. Originally titled *USS Teakettle* it starred Gary Cooper and the then lesser known players like Eddie Albert and Jack Webb. But they were class players compared with Lee Marvin, Hathaway's hired extra. The scheduled three days work spread into three weeks. Hathaway was sufficiently impressed by Marvin to put him into some additional scenes with six lines of dialogue. When the location work was completed Hathaway said to Lee, 'Come back with me to the coast, kid.' Marvin said, 'What for?' He was beginning to talk up in those days. Hathaway said, 'Oh don't be a pain in the ass . . . ' Marvin responded 'Bullshit' and on that felicitous exchange the director took his extra to Hollywood.

It was only a hit-and-run interlude. When the film wrapped, Marvin returned to New York and was immediately hired by the American National Theatre (ANTA), an experimental group on Broadway, for two shows one of which was *Billy Budd*. Not a big part. But it was Broadway. The effect on Marvin, taking bows in a hit show, Lamont and Courtenay down there, proud and misty-eyed in the stalls, was cloud-nine time. 'My entire part in the show was seven different ways of saying "Yes sir", "No sir" but I really felt I belonged in the theatre.' That euphoria, given regular booster shots in the bars on the 44th, 45th, 46th, streets and Broadway, was almost inflammable. His face was becoming as familiar to bartenders as it was to TV audiences. For actors, unless they were in the Alfred Lunt class, success on Broadway logically signposted next stop, Hollywood. Lee Marvin was not in the Alfred Lunt class. He was good on stage but he knew his limitations. His short stint for *You're in the Navy Now* had given him a chance to watch a movie star, Gary Cooper in action. Master of the slow move, the deep think, the sudden twitch of the nose which passed for a dozen lines of different dialogue, 'Coop' was a revelation to Marvin. So too was John Wayne. And Humphrey Bogart. Especially Bogey. When *Billy Budd* closed, Lee had one tour to finish. This was with the national companies of *The Hasty Heart* and *A Streetcar Named Desire*. Reminiscing on it Marvin told an interviewer with the familiar whistle-and-phwtt sound effects:

Let me tell you pal, touring was frigging tough. Introducing the Great Drama to rural areas – holy shit, 33,000 miles of one-night stands, all in the wintertime, and you got seventy-five dollars a week and had to sustain all your own expenses

51

with the exception of travel. We'd stay in places like the Pioneer Hotel in Pampas, Texas – two bucks a night, right? And about three in the morning the duck hunters would storm out on that frozen linoleum and . . . aaaghhh!

But he was getting his face seen, his name known. Especially to one of Hollywood's astutest agents, Meyer Mishkin. It was Mishkin, determined to take Marvin from thick-eared heavy to the superstar class, who insisted that Lee move permanently to Hollywood. Lee had sampled the movie town's languid blandishments even before going there to make *You're in the Navy Now* for Hathaway. He had been there seven years earlier, as a marine before sailing overseas. He, and the other liberty-ticket marines checked in at Oceanside, California, then took the bus-ride up to Hollywood and Beverly Hills. They hit the bars, did the famous footprint routine, and searched for blonde, busty sexpots on every corner. But that action was available to moguls, not marines. Going back there as an actor, late 1950 was something else. He checked into a cheap hotel in downtown Los Angeles, bought a cup of coffee and studied the trade papers. The sheer scale of the wealth, the power and the politics of the major studios and their world-famous stars, must have made Marvin feel more than surplus to establishment. Metro-Goldwyn-Mayer, with its monolithic empire at Culver City dominated by magical names like Gable, Robert Taylor and Spencer Tracy were hardly in the market for this unlovely New York actor who came on like a rogue elephant. In fact, with Mishkin's shrewd help, Marvin was at work within three days.

I wasn't exactly living it up though, [Marvin laughed, stirring an ice cube in his drink with a gnarled finger.] It was kinda Murphy's bed routine at the hotel apartment: I'd be warming it for the next guy to slot into it. In the morning I'd get up go down to Hollywood, buy the papers, get some dry cereal, put a quart of milk in the ice box and that's how it went. I know once I went to that studio I was strictly in the bottom league. They weren't in any mood for non-barrel-shirt-type guys as leading men. And those were the kind of leading men whose films I was in. It was the age of the beautiful hero. I saw it right in front of my eyes. I was just standing there rocking from foot to foot, waiting. I knew there was no place I could go except up. What was interesting then was that a guy like me, aged around twenty-seven and mid-

Western looking may have had nothing to gain, but he had nothing to lose either. If you were a Cooper or a Gable, wow, they had plenty to lose. If they blew it in a movie the whole industry shook. They didn't of course. But they always had to be in there fighting.

So Lee Marvin was no threat to Gary Cooper, Humphrey Bogart, Spencer Tracy or the other giants who called the shots in the major studios. His initial impact entering the world of the Beautiful People was strictly lightweight. His name never appeared in the gossip columns of the two reigning hell-cats of the time, Hedda Hopper and Louella Parsons. He was tippling some, but against the sensational exploits of a Flynn or a Mitchum, it didn't rate a back-page brief. He was to redeem the situation with real panache a decade or two later. Though he mostly shared the company of the grips, assistant directors, and the stuntmen, Marvin kept an observant eye on the style and stratagems of the superstars. He'd have gladly taken a chamois leather to the chromium bollards on Bogart's yacht *The Santana* just to be around the tangy charisma of its skipper. They had a love of the sea in common. Nothing else. In those days, as now, like moved with like. Bogey, for all his abrasive comments on the studio top brass, was an establishment man, part of the élite, of the blood royal. That meant him, Gregory Peck, Greer Garson, Alfred Hitchcock, William Wyler, Mr and Mrs Sam Goldwyn, and definitely not Mr Lee Marvin. Entry to that royal enclosure required substantial screen credits or the God-like endorsement of those omnipotent moguls like Louis B. Mayer, Darryl Zanuck, Harry Cohn, or Sam Goldwyn. Marvin was unlikely to achieve either with his early rag-bag of bit parts. He hardly remembers them.

Which is not surprising. Hardly anyone else does either; *Duel at Silver Creek* (an Audie Murphy Western), *Diplomatic Courier, Down Among the Sheltering Pines,* and *We're Not Married.* Riffling through the scanty records on these programmes offers no sign of gestating genius. But it was sufficient for Meyer Mishkin to convince Columbia, dominated by that front office terrorist Harry Cohn, to put Lee on a picture-to-picture contract. Cohn, for all his crude belligerence and flair for tormenting those actresses he couldn't score with, knew how to attract top talent. While other moguls pussyfooted around with 'safe' subjects or 'bankable' faces, Cohn played his hunches, and took all the stick if they failed to come off. The gambles that did come off – Sinatra's superb achievement in *From Here To Eternity* is the prime example – must also include the early work of Lee Marvin.

It was Stanley Kramer, Cohn's young whizz-kid director (a major Hollywood talent by any standards) who chose Marvin to play a World War II sergeant in *Eight Iron Men*, an adaptation of Harry Brown's play of soldiers under stress *A Sound of Hunting*. Cohn summoned the tall, thin streak of granite to his office and agreed with Kramer that there was probably more to Marvin than strained the eye. Accustomed to his contract stars quailing before him ('Don't just stand there – cringe!' goes the old Cohnism) the studio chief found Marvin no shrinking violet. Part of the paintwork above the handle on Cohn's office door peeled away from the effect of the long succession of sweaty palms that timorously pushed their way in. Told of it – by Glenn Ford – Cohn was secretly impressed and ordered that this badge of torment must never be painted over. But Marvin, having sweated at Guadalcanal, was not about to perspire in the presence of Mr Harry Cohn.

Marvin made eight pictures for Columbia. They were to establish the pattern of all Lee's screen villains of the future. And of other actors' screen villains too. True in a couple of early ones, you had to be quick to spot his name when the credits rolled. But with Meyer Mishkin adroitly calling the shots, Marvin was lucky to hit pay-dirt early on in his career. He could now go to Beverly Hills for his suits, shirts, and custom-made shoes. He drove a smart car, could afford to sit on a bar stool in the pricey gloom of the Polo Lounge at the Beverly Hills Hotel and not feel upstaged by any of the famous along the counter. His contract with Columbia had got him on to the party lists. Admittedly not the 'A' group which he probably would have ducked anyway, but the lesser echelon of writers, artists, musicians . . . and a tall music graduate from the UCLA named Betty Ebeling.

It was a typical Hollywood party, the only serious side of it being the drinking. Guests were loosely paired, their partners on departure not necessarily being the same as on arrival. Lee Marvin had come alone, reserving his options. His reputation as a benign party-wrecker still in the drawing-board stage, he made tracks for the liquor while keeping a sharp, reconnoitring eye out for possible action. He hadn't seen Betty Ebeling arrive. Had he done so he would have been stopped in mid-sips, like the other guests, by the striking entrance she made. Tall, slim, with long auburn hair, she had the sort of elegance that made the male guests guard their language, leap forward to pull back a chair, light her cigarettes. Only a year out of UCLA with honours in music, she was into composition arranging and had produced some creditable work for several theatrical productions. She had been brought to the party by the agent Robert Walker, who, as she recalled the event, met a nubile starlet there and promptly fell madly in love with her.

'He just abandoned me there and took her off somewhere for a nightcap. You know how it is,' observed the mature and magnanimous Betty Ebeling. It was not so much his sudden flight to another's nest that angered her. As she herself declared, 'I was no professional virgin at the time,' It was the fact that it left her stranded at the party, a friend's house on the Sunset Strip, without a car. 'So I was standing there in the middle of this party without an escort and no transport home. I was really furious. I went to get my coat, thinking "this is ridiculous, I don't even have money for a cab".' At which point Lee Marvin emerged from the kitchen. What followed was a formula plot for two decidedly un-formula people.

'Hi.'

'Hi.'

'I'm Betty Ebeling.'

'Lee Marvin.'

'Look, I'm in this embarrassing situation. The man who brought me here has taken an interest in someone else. Do you by any chance have a car?'

'I have a car.'

'Well I live over at Beverly Hills on Wilshire. Do you think you could do me a great favour and take five minutes out to drive me home?'

'I'll help you with your coat.'

They left together, pulled into Betty Ebeling's home for a nightcap and talked for hours. The music major of UCLA and the popular mobster of Columbia Inc. Each found with evident delight that surface impressions were highly misleading. Betty Ebeling quickly discovered that Marvin with his needling and abrasive one-liners was more kindly and soft-centred than his press agents dared admit. While Marvin was pleased to note that Betty Ebeling's gown-and-mortarboard reserve couldn't suppress the vibrant, responsive and humorous soul beneath. 'We saw each other constantly,' Betty Ebeling remembered not without tenderness.

I guess there must have been great mutual attraction. I always thought him to be a most attractive man. But Lee obviously didn't. When he was young he always thought his ears were too big for his head, his nose too short, his eyes too small. He never really liked his face. I loved it. And with it he had incredible charm and a marvellous voice. A wonderful way of moving too.

The whole masculine assemblage, plus an irresistible love potion compounded of craggy brusqueness and tender loving care. After three months of candlelit dinners, long walks on the beaches, fishing and fondling, it was apparent that the couple were grateful that Betty Ebeling had been left stranded at that party. Marvin, it seemed, eschewed the familiar kind of compliments. 'The nearest he got to telling me how beautiful I was,' Betty Ebeling laughed, 'was to say, "The one thing I like about you Betty, is you don't give a damn about how you look." '

His proposal was delivered with similar Marvin-style finesse. He had rented an apartment in Hollywood, a fifteen-minute drive from Betty Ebeling's home in Beverly Hills. Her background, strictly Victorian, baulked at the notion of living with a man she wasn't married to. Today's sexuality is a vastly different scene. 'If Lee and I had met now we might have had a chance. But in those days we both had a certain amount of guilt about sexuality.'

So each evening tryst, at her pad or his, was concluded with a 'thankyou and goodnight', when he, or she, would dutifully leave for home. But it offended Lee Marvin's concept of a mature relationship. Back in New York he wouldn't have minded the hike to and from his loved one. But no one walked in Los Angeles, particularly between Hollywood and Beverly Hills at night. The solution was obvious to him if not to Betty.

'How about coming to live with me?' he said finally.

'Oh no no no, I couldn't do that!' responded Miss Virtue, feigning shock but manifestly excited.

'Well look,' Lee grunted, 'I just can't continue to make these long drives. I'm pissed off commuting, so I guess we'll have to get married. If that's okay with you?'

There was a brief silence while both digested Lee Marvin's thorny notion of the marriage proposal. Simultaneously they exploded with laughter. If it was short on honeysuckle, the proposal was clearly strong on sincerity.

'I would hate for you to go on commuting,' Betty Ebeling said, meaning 'yes' in the language of romance. 'It was really that casual,' she recalled. 'There was no desperate love thing on his part, at least in a way that Lee Marvin could express.'

And so there was a wedding. Well, sort of. It was the kind of amiable shambles that might well have carried the familiar disclaimer, 'any resemblance to marriage ceremonies past or present is entirely coincidental.' Movie comedies have survived on lesser plots. Countdown to the affair began in the first week of February 1951. Lee was filming *Eight Iron Men* for Stanley Kramer, a wartime potboiler directed by Edward Dmytryk, at Columbia. Lee asked for a couple of days off to get married, and in keeping with Harry Cohn's steely budgeting at the time, was given Saturday and Sunday. He worked through Friday – on which day he'd rented a new apartment – and told Betty to be ready to leave for Las Vegas the following morning. He wore an open-necked shirt, jeans and sneakers, with a tie and a spare shirt in a bag. Betty Ebeling insisted on buying a dress.

Halfway along the nine-hour drive to Vegas they pulled into a filling station. Marvin went to the men's room, came out with the fresh tie and shirt on. 'Okay, here comes the bridegroom!' he warbled. It was around ten o'clock and dark when the prospective bridal pair drove into the garishly-lit mainstreet of the gambling town. The Strip. Marvin, setting the pattern for all future arrangements, had omitted to book a preacher, a hotel-room, witnesses and other trivial details. They stopped eventually outside the Wee Kirk O' The Heather, that nuptial phenomenon of Nevada. On offer – the fastest wedlock in the west. It is to this quick-service matrimonial counter that numberless movie stars have come over the years to legalise the euphoria of the preceding hours, days, or even weeks. Those hasty unions are just as hastily ended. (Some years later when Marvin was making a film in Las Vegas he found himself in a car with four other guys driving outside the Wee Kirk O' The Heather. They discovered all had been married there. They calculated how long each had been married and totalled up the score. One of the men, Lee's stand-in said, 'There's a century of horror, if you like!'

In the best tradition of those old Universal comedies, they hammered on the door of the Kirk which was opened by the sleepy-eyed incumbent in a nightshirt. You would just know that his name was the Reverend Loveable.

'We want to get married,' Marvin said.

'So I figured,' yawned the Rev. Loveable. 'You got witnesses?'

Lee looked blankly at Betty as though it was her fault. She did the packing.

'Okay no witnesses,' the reverend said wearily, 'I'll have to get the wife.'

Mrs Loveable was asleep. 'Wake up honey,' the Rev. Loveable announced close to her ear, 'we got a wedding.'

'A wedding,' Mrs Loveable intoned as she rolled out of bed. She threw a mu-mu over her head but refused flatly to be seen. 'I'll witness it from behind the screen.'

The ceremony began, Lee and Betty standing in front of the Rev. Loveable, a pair of aged, pallid insteps inside slippers being all that was visible of the witness. It was late. The Rev. Loveable, now in advancing years, was not only tired. He was getting pretty short on coherence. As Betty Ebeling recalled it:

> It was very hard to be serious. He sounded rather senile and kept forgetting part of the ceremony. He began to mumble, 'Do you Lee Marvin take this . . . er . . . you know . . . and do you Betty Ebeling take this man and all that stuff.' I mean that's what he actually said! Then he blanked out completely. Lee kissed me. He looked at me and said, 'Well I don't think I could have done better,' which was the most one could expect of Lee Marvin in saying 'I love you'. We paid up. The feet behind the screen witnessed the document and the honeymoon began.

That is they stepped outside the Kirk. 'Now where do we go?' the bride enquired. 'Aren't we supposed to go to bed together?'

Lee agreed by winking, aiming a finger at her, clicking the thumb, and going 'plutt'. But they still needed a bed. They dragged themselves from hotel to hotel on the Strip. All full.

'This is great,' Betty Marvin said. 'It's something isn't it when a bride and groom can't find a bed to slide into after their wedding!' Lee Marvin patted her as though she'd been a puppy who'd leaked on schedule.

'Let's go get a drink,' he said. They ordered a bottle of champagne at one of the casino hotels. Lee saw a soldier lose all his chips at the roulette table. He lurched over to him, put a protective arm around him, gave him a swig of the champagne and replenished the chips. Betty Marvin observed the gesture, noting Marvin's tender spot for the military. Another bottle of champagne, and Lee announced loudly, 'This is ridiculous. I've just been married and I need some sleep. Let's go home baby.'

It was exactly 1.00am when they pointed the car west along the highway to Los Angeles. Whether Lee was too tired to drive or not, Betty Marvin was too tired to care. Just outside the town their headlights picked up the figure of a soldier standing on the road. And not too steadily. He was drunk. Lee slammed on the brakes.

'Now what?' from the first Mrs Marvin.

'Wanna ride with us?' enquired ex-PFC Marvin of the US Marines.

The soldier grinned. He was three parts gone and coherent words were hard to come by. 'Get closer,' Lee Marvin said to Betty. She rested her head on Lee's shoulder and fell asleep. The drunken soldier rested his head on Betty's shoulder and also fell asleep. Lee Marvin, sleep-starved and emphatically juiced, craned forward eyes on stalks. He needed to get that reeling if not fallen warrior back to his regiment. He also needed to get his new bride into bed. Probably in that order. A hundred and fifty miles of desert driving brought them to Barstow. To an all-night pull-in for truck drivers, patrolmen, and Mr and Mrs Lee Marvin's wedding breakfast.

'Two cups of coffee,' Lee Marvin said at the counter.

'Three,' Betty Marvin said with the soldier's head still on her shoulder. 'Aren't you forgetting me?'

The soldier woke up. 'Jeeze I gotta terrible hangover,' he said, 'where am I and who are you?'

'You're at Barstow, it's 3.15am and we, believe it or not, are a bride and bridegroom just starting our honeymoon,' Betty Marvin murmured.

It was dawn when they arrived back at their new apartment.

They had jettisoned Lee's comrade at a bus station. The two men embraced, slapping each other's backs as a sliver of sun glinted over the distant hills. It was World War II again for Lee Marvin.

Betty was too tired to mock Lee with, 'Why don't you kiss him?'

Lee Marvin was too pooped to carry her over the threshold.

'I was getting a most fascinating debut,' she said, 'as Mr Marvin's ever-loving wife.'

Chapter Five

'I went over and kicked the cigarette out of the way and Brando said, "Why you sonofabitch." I said, "Well up yours too pal," then WHAM! he was giving me all of it . . . '

Lee Marvin

Curiously, Lee Marvin did not immediately take his new bride home to meet the folks. True he was still locked in filming *Eight Iron Men* in Hollywood. But as the then Mrs Betty Marvin recalled, it was four, five, or maybe six months before Lee could bring himself to tell Lamont and Courtenay Marvin that he was married. If Betty Marvin wondered about such strange reticence from this far from shrinking violet, her first visit to the Marvin home at Woodstock, New York, explained it all. Thinking back on it – the tensions, the hair-triggered violence, the verbal affrays between the father and his two sons, all beneath surface courtesies – Betty Marvin says, 'Frankly Lee's relationship with his whole family was, to me, something straight out of Eugene O'Neil. With all due respect to them, I sometimes wonder how Lee survived it at all.'

Her first visit to the Marvin home in Woodstock, as Lee's literally blushing bride, began sweetly enough. Lamont's fine breeding and Courtenay's 'Southern Lady' refinement ensured that Lee's wife would be wafted graciously across the porch. The tall, silver-haired Marvin senior, took Betty's hands in his, and after a short affectionate scrutiny told her, 'You're the daughter I always wanted.' Once inside, however, Lamont

Marvin's tender declaration was not, Betty Marvin was quick to observe, noticeably endorsed by his wife. Lee had never brought a girl friend home, let alone a bride. No other female in the house apart from the dominant, assertive, and highly-motivated Courtenay Marvin. Not, in itself, suitable plot material for Eugene O'Neil with his probes into human beings caught up in the swirling cross-currents of life. But as the months passed, and Lee's work pattern brought him more and more to New York, Betty Marvin saw beneath the Marvin patina. And there Eugene O'Neil had a play. First the props: Lamont's vast collection of guns, all in good murderous order, nurtured by their owner with a passion. The lethal extension of the man. Like the Prussian sabre and the cavalry spurs, they were Lamont Marvin's badge of honour. The main characters, we know. The outline is best left to the principal witness, the daughter Lamont Marvin 'always wanted', Betty Marvin.

> It is hard for me now as a liberated woman to understand the things that went on in that house, but they were almost beyond belief. Along with the love, and there was plenty of that, there was the fierce competition between the father and his two sons, with the mother reigning coolly supreme over them all. Lamont was very loving to me and very caring. On the other hand I knew I was not terribly welcomed by Courtenay. The guns, of course, were part of Lamont's whole machismo number. The fact that when his two sons went to war he had this need to enlist as a private – he'd been an officer in the First World War – was almost Freudian. He was not going to be bettered by his offspring. Everything in that house was so extreme. Intelligent conversation between the men would extend into heated argument, growing into actual fist fights. The father competing against two strong-willed sons. And there was also the brooding sense of a volcano. And hysteria. It was incredible for me, as a minor participant, to witness it all. And when Lee started keeping guns around the house I could see the whole pattern being repeated.

Yet despite the tensions and the outbursts Betty Marvin was the pride and joy at Woodstock. Even Courtenay Marvin came to recognise that being Lee's wife, and a pretty loyal and forgiving one at that, called for a resourcefulness over and above the line of duty. As far as Lee was concerned, Betty Marvin in the 'unliberated' role of wife, attractive hostess, and later proud mother, fulfilled his male animal concept of the perfect marital partner. When, in 1952, their first child was born, a son, Christopher, the sun shone bright over Woodstock. The arrival of the infant coincided with a sudden upswing in Lee's career. With Meyer Mishkin, his agent, charting a safe course through the minefield of lucrative but dead-end roles, Lee Marvin was carving quite a niche in Hollywood as a screen hoodlum. After throwaway roles in *Seminole, The Glory Brigade, The Stranger Wore a Gun* and *Gun Fury* Lee was ready to take on big league stuff. Two films, *The Big Heat* and *The Wild One* launched Marvin as a malevolent villain of real class and introduced an entirely new threshold of screen violence. But it took someone with a fine sense of the macabre to recognise Lee's potential.

Fritz Lang, who cut his cinema teeth in Germany making Gothic horrors peopled by dwarfs, fiends, sadists, and monocled lesbians – with the odd phallic symbol rising here and there – gravitated towards Marvin the way one vampire sucks up to another. Lang had been called into Columbia to direct *The Big Heat* (1953), a vicious gangster classic starring Glenn Ford and Gloria Grahame, with Lee Marvin as the chief hood's hired bully and hit-man. (The story: The wife of a detective is killed by a bomb meant for the cop who goes under cover to hunt the killers.) It was an important movie scripted by Sidney Boehm from William P. McGivern's novel. And nobody, but Fritz Lang, wanted Marvin in the key hoodlum role.

On the first day of shooting Marvin drove to the Columbia lot on Gower Street, Hollywood, truly scared behind that lazy grin. He had two strikes against him. He was hired, under protest, from the top brass led by Harry Cohn. And Fritz Lang's reputation as a tyrant made that other testy film-maker from old Vienna, Otto Preminger, seem almost frolicsome. When Marvin walked on to the set he approached Lang who, he noticed, had a magnum of champagne on his desk. The gold foil was off but the wire still twisted. Alongside was a bucket of ice and some glasses.

'Vould you care for a drink, sir?' enquired Lang with the exquisite courtesy of a Gestapo torturer.

'No thank you, Mr Lang,' Marvin said figuring that fancy liquor was a hazard he could afford to miss. 'But if there is anything you want to tell me about the role before we start . . . ?'

LEE MARVIN

Lang sharply brushed the query aside.
'Vot you are is vot I vant. I don't vorry about guys like you.
You are great.' Then he pointed across the stage and said,
'There are the people I vorry about.'
He was pointing at Glenn Ford and Gloria Grahame. The
stars. So Marvin said to himself, 'He loves me. I'm accepted.
Great!'
Two months later Marvin was standing at some distance from
the director when some other actor came in. Fritz Lang had
another bottle of champagne. And he was pointing at Marvin.
'Oh oh oh,' thought Marvin, 'Now Lang is "vorrying" about
me!'
Marvin was fortunate not only in being nabbed for a film that
was to become a cult classic surfacing regularly on television
and in art cinemas around the world. The star of the film, Glenn
Ford, was at his best, and Gloria Grahame, pedalling her attrac-
tively decadent brand of shop-soiled metropolitan sex, perfect.
She played the boss hood's mistress. Marvin induces terror the
moment he walks, leering and loose-jointed, into the scene. The
menace stems from the mindlessness in this still-young man,
immature and programmed for terror. A punk. Or would be if
he were not a psychopath. The fear comes from our awareness
that confronted with this sadist there would be no reasoning
with him. The IQ is too low. The character too flawed. Here is
someone who could fly murderously off the handle not at a
moment's notice, but at no notice. Marvin's open-mouthed,
piscine-featured appearance – not ugly in a turn-on way as is,
say, Jack Palance – underlines the quality of mindlessness. (For
a man of Marvin's sensitivity, his pulses racing at the sight of a
rare bird, this glazed-eyed dumbness is harder to portray than
it seems. A restricted nasal passage certainly helps.)
When he throws scalding coffee from a Cona jug disfigur-
ingly into Gloria Grahame's face – a famous footnote in movie
history – the act of violence is absolutely right in its savagery,
and in its totalness. It was not the kind of spaghetti violence of
today which lacks any kind of human scale and plausibility.
The violence in *The Big Heat* shocks because it erupts from
credible, humanly recognisable types. But a leading critic,
Penelope Houston, wrote, 'The main impression is of violence
employed arbitrarily, mechanically and in the long run,
pointlessly.'

Maybe, but for Lee Marvin the poison had beneficial side-effects – notably a leading role in *The Wild One*. A sullen, sadistic movie, it told the tale of hoodlum motor-cyclists who roar through a small American town terrorising the locals, one of whom is killed. Marlon Brando, a pallid monster beneath the jaunty peaked cap, plays the vicious chief motorcycle thug, challenged by the leader of a rival gang, Lee Marvin. The role required a fair skill at bike-riding. The original choice for the character who provokes Brando was Keenan Wynn. He was not only a good actor – then under contract to MGM – he was a bike fanatic as confident in that saddle as he was on a horse. (He and Lee could probably still ride rings round Steve McQueen though the latter, virtually a bearded recluse now in Hollywood, is unlikely to agree to the jousting.)

When Harry Cohn, Columbia, approached Louis B. Mayer, Metro, to hire Wynn for the part, according to Keenan, 'Mayer wanted more for me than the whole picture cost. So the director (the Hungarian Lazlo Benedek) who knew I hung out with actors who were bike nuts asked me if I could introduce him to some of them. That's how Lee got the part.' You hardly required an MD in psychology to understand Lee's obsession with motor-cycles and their macho concomitants of solid leathers, steel-tipped boots, and the surging power between the thighs. No question but that he once saw the bike as the answer to the challenge, 'Does this guy have any balls?' As he put it, 'The sound of the pipes obliterates the world around you. And there is the throbbing and slamming of those pistons between your legs.' (On his last ride – a spectacular pratfall coming down a mountain – Lee compared it to the flight of Icarus, surprising all who did not instantly associate Greek mythology with the fastest gulp in the West.) With the sun glinting on the silver studs in his leathers, coked pretty good on the liquor inside him, Marvin came on like a 90mph stud.

'Perfect,' Lazlo Benedek said when he inspected Marvin for the first day's shooting.

Meanwhile the bets were on that when Brando started work he would soon chop Marvin down to size. Marlon, nurturing his own brooding, T-shirted image at the time, no doubt considered that one hell-raiser on the set was as much as the movie could take. He was deep into the Method then, a form of dramatic self-indulgence unlikely to square with Marvin's need for helpful feed-backs. 'Brando slaughtered it for the actors,' Lee told me once. 'He'd go off, rub his eyes, keep everyone waiting twenty minutes, and they would think he was concentrating. Actually he was having a nap. But he would be secure and everybody else insecure.' When the shooting began both were wary, tending to circle each other like predators protecting territory. Marvin respected Brando as an actor. 'To have associated with him in those days – still is – was a real tip-of-the-hat,' Lee conceded.

He has this great depth as a performer. But the competition was there, whether on my part or his, I imagine mine. I remember there was a scene just between the two of us which we'd rehearsed. But when it started I realised he wasn't reaching me. He just projected this far but it would fall and collapse before it got to me. Then I thought of something. These guys have a system of playing through something, some device that they make work for them. Lee J. Cobb did it in *Boomerang* when he's crushing a guy but it's the ring on his finger that hits the focus. So I looked around and saw this cigarette butt. Well they started rolling the cameras and half way through the scene I went over and kicked the cigarette out of the way. Brando said, 'Why you sonofabitch.' I said, 'Well up yours too pal,' then WHAM! he was giving me all of it and I could make no mistakes.

But most of the time the two actors stayed out of each other's orbit. One evening the two actors met in a bar, a confrontation which revealed the level of their repartee at the time.

Marvin said: 'I'm thinking of changing my name.'

'Yeah?' Brando said. 'To what?'

'To Marlo Brandy,' Lee replied.

Brando gave that masterpiece a few seconds' thought.

'I'm planning to change my name too,' he said, 'to Lee Moron.'

Neither gibe was exactly calculated to cause a permanent vendetta. They meet rarely but when they do they look back on that third-grade jest with shared grins.

The Wild One ran into censor trouble, particularly in England where it was not given a certificate for public showing until 1968. The ban was based on two counts; one, the film's absence of any kind of retribution; two, it's possible influence on Britain's own marauding teenagers. When finally it was shown in Britain critics considered it tame compared with the prevailing standards of real-life violence. 'The Mild One' was how one reviewer put it. All, however, noted Marvin's competence against Brando. One of the film's rare comic scenes, where Marvin in a drunken rage falls off his motorcycle, received a burst of spontaneous applause from the crew when it was shot, and from audiences when it was shown. It stayed in the mind of director Elliot Silverstein. Years later, when he was casting around for the man to play Kid Shelleen in *Cat Ballou*, that scene triggered Marvin's name in his mind – and his selection for the role.

You win some. You lose some. Lee's reward for *The Wild One* was a key role in a monumental dud called *Gorilla at Large*. All you need to know is that a circus gorilla is used as a cover for murder. Lee Marvin drew favourable comment for his role as a cop. Anne Bancroft, Lee J. Cobb, Cameron Mitchell, Raymond Burr and the gorilla would like to forget the whole thing. What Marvin wanted, and most experts thought he had earned, was a part in *The Caine Mutiny*. This effective if lightly-sketched movie from the best-selling book which also became a hit play, had a prodigious cast; Humphrey Bogart in the major role as the neurotic Captain Queeg who cracks; and supporting muscle from Jose Ferrer, Van Johnson, Fred Mac-Murray and E. G. Marshall. Lee Marvin was cast as a crewman as much for his knowledge of ships at sea as for his talents as an actor. He had paid his dues with Marlon Brando. He was about to get a lesson in star power from the supremo in the art, Humphrey Bogart.

Marvin studied and revered this lightly-built Hollywood giant the way Richard Burton, Peter O'Toole, Albert Finney and other top British performers genuflect to Larry Olivier. Bogart was projecting charisma long before John F. Kennedy made it the cliché of the decade. Bogart's impact on Marvin – as it was to be on the film – was total. From the first day's shooting at Columbia, Lee saw Bogart's lisping despotism in action, notably against the film's producer, Stanley Kramer and its director Edward Dmytryk. How well Marvin learned the steely routine is indicated by this choice recollection.

I was lying in bed one night with my wife thinking about a

role (well what else are Hollywood movie actors supposed to do in bed with their wives?) when I said suddenly, 'I've got it.' She said, 'What?' I said, 'I'll pull a Bogart.' She said, 'What do you mean by that?' I said it means I'll just go on the set, ask where are my marks and 'let's go!' You see the thing about Bogart nobody ever *saw* what he'd really done. All his work was done some place else. He knew the part, he knew his lines, and he came on the set ready to go, and screw anybody who wasn't ready to go with him. You never saw him on the set rehearsing. None of this 'let me try that again' kind of crap. Just BOOM, WHRRR . . . Jesus it was spooky the way he hit. His technical exactness was frightening. Almost mechanical. But when you saw it all tied together up on the screen, it was marvellous. Nobody could really gel with him as a person. He could be sore, and rough. Once he was there on the set ready to hit the marks you couldn't go in for the social chit-chat asking him about his boat or his Jaguar. That way you got nowhere. But I respected the hell out of him. Not only as an actor, but as a guy. He'd served his apprenticeship and took no shit from anybody right to the end. In the beginning, I suppose, he must have taken some. But once he'd hit it, Bogie did it Bogie's way.

We were in Hawaii for two weeks before he arrived, doing all the little shots, presentations to the captains and so forth. In some ways I knew more about the action than the experts. I'd made some of these raids and Kramer thought it was a bonus using me as a kind of unofficial technical adviser. Sometimes he'd outline a shot and I'd say, 'That's not the way it was, Stanley.' He'd call the captains from the Department of the Navy telling them, 'This man says so-and-so . . . ' and the captains would say, 'Oh, yeah, we forgot.' I was playing one of the deckhands, 'Meatball', doing these dumb sailor things. We were all ready on the ship, Eddie (Dmytryk) and Kramer when Bogart arrived to work. Well something must have been wrong because he kind of walked right through the shot. Eddie said, 'Bogie, you walked right through that shot.' Bogie said, 'Well you can shoot it again, can't you?' Which made him my kind of guy because I wasn't in that position. Then they said, 'You'll be in the next shot so if you'll slip into your rags we'll . . . '

Bogart said, 'Where's my dressing room?'

Stanley Kramer said, 'Well this is the Navy, Mr Bogart, we don't have any dressing rooms.'

'Well I'm not in the Navy, so where's my dressing room?' Bogart said again.

So they all started walking round the ship, up and down. I
was there. I wanted to see the fight, right? Finally Bogie said,
'Whose room is this?'

I said, 'This is the Captain's room.'

'Okay, I guess it'll do,' said Bogie.

So then he comes on for the shot which is sort of 'Let go
Number One', and 'Let go Number Two' stuff. He has a
khaki shirt on and there's a wet spot on it. They want to go
again but Bogie says, 'Let me have a clean shirt please.' They
said, 'That's the only one we have here' – and brother, he
drops another deck. Two minutes later he has a clean shirt. I
thought to myself, Jesus – I've got a long way to go. But the
scene went and he was dead on. Just marvellous! He was not
just being a star. He wasn't just playing being a character off-
stage. He was in a position to control the way the work came
out and he was going to exercise it. And he was always right.
His style was 'Okay let's get on with it. We'll drink at my
house later if you want to, but don't let's fuck around here.'
No actor ever came on a film set better prepared. I loved that,
and the man inside it.

Bogart also loved the sea. To Marvin, that would redeem a
rapist or galloping axe-man.

There are few careers more volatile than those of Hollywood
actors, character actors in particular. Like buckets in a well they
whip past each other, going up, or down. A determining factor
in which way that go is the kind of movies they're in. There's
luck too. And it helps if their talents have a dimension unique
to its owner. Good heavies were fairly thick on the ground
when Marvin went into *Bad Day At Black Rock*. The most
interesting of these was Robert Ryan, a complex, highly watch-
able baddie with whom Lee Marvin was frequently compared.
What was the score?

Marvin had come to *Bad Day At Black Rock* from an absorb-
ing action drama called *The Raid* based on a true incident of
the American Civil War. Robert Ryan, offering a touch more
finesse than Marvin, had picked up some classy rolls such as the
fellow who wins Greer Garson in *Her Twelve Men*. With a
better-looking screen face, crinkly-eyed smile and a hint of bedroom tenderness, Ryan could cross to the sympathetic side of
the tracks far more readily than could Marvin. Ryan's villains

suggest the past – sour, embittering memories of old failures which inform and colour his present-day prejudices. Fuels the violence. Marvin's heavies on the other hand, tend to be of the present, displaying an urgent animal need – food, sex, and the crude means of grabbing them. Anything that gets in the way is going to be slammed. Though both actors offered degrees of intelligence, Ryan had the advantage of being able to convey emotional complexities stemming from a subtly-warped mind.

Matched together in the market place, each offering his own exclusive breed of bully, it was Marvin however, who eventually soared upwards with Ryan observing him quizzically from that descending bucket. And the reason seemed to be that audiences preferred villains it could identify with. They could do that more easily with Marvin's characters and their slick, surface, tough-guy hardness. Ryan's 'thinking-man's hoodlums' were too disturbing for comfort. He had starred in the big success *Crossfire* as the mean and murderous anti-semite, was to do equally well in *God's Little Acre* and (with Marvin) in *The Professionals.* Several other major films followed. But despite his considerable acting resources and sureness of touch he rarely carried a movie entirely on his own. Yet Ryan had the edge on Marvin in *Bad Day At Black Rock.* His billing in the credits was second only to Spencer Tracy's.

The film, a suspense thriller of pace and fine craftsmanship, presented Tracy as the one-armed stranger who comes to a dead-end hamlet in the desert to uncover a killing. It was the first of those cliché situations – hostility and a conspiracy of silence in a small town trying to bury its guilty past. Credit has to go to Spencer Tracy for giving plausibility to the notion of a bulky amputee, one empty sleeve tucked into his pocket, taking on a group of sadistic brutes, literally single-handed. The fight in which he chops Borgnine to a bleeding mass on the barroom floor induced in audiences the feverish, blood-lusting reaction of Nero's Colosseum. Marvin's portrayal of one of Robert Ryan's band of cold, mindless thugs, struck critical gold with John O'Hara writing in *Colliers.* 'By the time he (Marvin) gets his head bashed in you hate him so much that you could supply a supererogatory kick in the face.'

Music to Marvin's jumbo-sized ears. It demonstrated beyond question that *The Big Heat* was no one-off performance. He was no great actor then, of course. But the graph was rising, the money increasing, and the liquor intake was ahead of the field. The high summer of Lee Marvin's professional contentment was matched by a similar euphoria at home. Betty Marvin, happy in those heady years to play the dutiful, feather-dustering wife, had now born Lee a daughter, Courtenay, named after Lee's mother. (In fact all her four children, Christopher, Courtenay and the two daughters to arrive at two-yearly intervals, Cynthia and Claudia, had Christian names beginning with the letter 'C'. Lamont Marvin's wife, Courtenay, was certainly no self-effacing mother-in-law.)

The first epoch in the marriage between Lee Marvin and Betty Ebeling, hilariously sealed and delivered in Las Vegas, was relatively tranquil. Despite their contrasting interests – Lee's were booze, boats and bikes, Betty's art, music, and the peaceful life – no explosions shattered the first seven years. Living with a movie actor in Hollywood, where the inmates are about as supportive as your average snake-pit – is never easy. When the actor suffers from the emotional fallout of World War II, dreaming of killing Japs and pining for his old Marine Corps buddies, you may have problems. They're tougher still when the said spouse turns to the bottle for instant solace. Boilermakers, Bloody Marys, Screwdrivers, Vodka Martinis, Tequila, Margueritas, and just neat old-fashioned Scotch – Lee Marvin could never be accused of showing favouritism. The more demanding the role and the more febrile his involvement in it, the more he craved his 'lubricant'.

At this stage he was not drinking at work. That horror-comedy was still to come. But he was juicing pretty well after-hours. At their most benevolent – as the former Betty Marvin describes – these bouts did little more than make sensitive hostesses blush and write 'NEVER AGAIN!' or 'loved her, loathed him' against Lee's name in their guest books. At their worst they boisterously rewrote the scenario of Hollywood hell-raising, adding an extra furrow in the brow of the LA Police Department. By then they may have been tempted to use dip-sticks instead of breathalysers. Which may be the right moment to introduce Doctor Tristram Coffin Colket the Third, MD.

We are talking in the beach house of writer and fashionable party-giver Edna McHugh, daughter of the late Eddie Cantor.

This is Malibu and along the coast highway are the joints, the bars, and the restaurants which like Ypres, Mons, Verdun and Guadalcanal sustain the legend of Marvin's blistering one-man campaigns. Tristram Colket, a former neuro-surgeon, psychologist, and a most articulate member of Alcoholics Anonymous, is reminiscing to the gentle murmur of the Pacific breakers. He is a tough, sharp-featured extrovert who turned to songwriting when he felt drinking did not hang too well with major surgery. His strongly-carved head is scarred from old, unexplained accidents. And he is speaking of Lee Marvin with rueful respect and affection, as one Mexican bandit may speak of another. The good doctor's comments, and diagnosis, are presented verbatim.

I came out here in the early fifties and ran into Lee almost immediately. I was living in Charles Laughton's house but don't ask me how this happened. The next thing I knew I met Lee and we kind of teamed up. He was tough and looked as ugly as hell. He was living over on Latimer road with Betty at the time and boy we did some crazy things. You want to know how crazy? Jesus where the hell do you stop? I mean take this; he had a little bell over his bar and from the other side of the room he'd whip out a .45 and fire a couple of slugs at it, especially if one or two of us were sitting kinda close to it. The closer the better. Sometimes he'd sit under a dartboard and after about the eighth or tenth drink he'd say, 'Hey baby, why don't we play a little darts?' We'd do it if someone else was in the room, and we'd do it if someone wasn't in the room. It got real spooky. 'Bet you can't hit the bullseye,' he'd say. I'd throw the dart and if it hit him in the head, all the better. He'd just smile and say, 'Hey, you motherfucker, you're shooting pretty good!'

Some nights we'd repeat the act with arrows from a 120lb bow. You also have to remember this guy slept with a Hudson Bay axe behind his bed. Still does. It's as sharp as hell. Like everybody else in this community he was scared of prowlers and things that go bump in the night. And he had these guns, the Gatlings, the semi-automatics, and the .45s. I figure there was a little paranoia going there. Lee always said, 'You run from a knife and you crowd a gun.' I mean there's no fucking way you're going to run from a gun, right? He could swing that axe like an expert but he never took it into any of the bars. He often went to a place called The Raft. They don't call it that now, but the bartender there used to be the one to make the calls. You know – 'you're friend is having a little noisy fun, can you come and pick him up.'

How violent could he be? Tristram Colket coughs on a sudden laugh which sends a lone gull shrieking off towards the breakers. What about the occasion my good friend walked across a bar and hit a paraplegic? Do you get that? Well all the bartenders used to call me. I don't know whether it's because I'm cunning, strong, scary, clever or just because Lee likes me. But when the call came I'd go over to the bar, take one of his arms across my shoulder and say, 'Hey baby, we're going bye-byes.' Now there was this dinner party right here in this house where he got so loaded and disoriented he couldn't negotiate any distance on foot. He was supposed to make a left turn outside the door but his locomotive machinery was all fouled up. He tried to make a turn, got all twisted up, and fell right on his head.

The next day he was due for a publicity session taking photos for his next film. And here he was with his head cut open. He'd have looked like Frankenstein's monster if it hadn't been done right. We get him in the car and over to the local clinic. Lee's looking up at me smiling. And I'm smiling. But this doctor is nervous because he sees it's Lee Marvin. And he gets more nervous because he knows I'm a neurosurgeon. I should tell you Lee has a deep forehead laceration down to the skull. Everything was ready to go but Lee won't lie down. So the doctor grabs this strap and says, 'This is just a restraint.' WOW! If he had only said, 'This is a cock, or your mother's come to see you,' fine. But a *restraint*! I knew he wasn't going to get as far as the buckle with Lee. When Lee heard that word, he came up off that stretcher, head bleeding, knocking the equipment over, the surgical trays, and everything else. He was wild-eyed. 'A WHAT?!' The doctor said it again. 'Just a restraint.' Lee shouts, 'What the shit are you going to do to me?' The doctor opened his mouth but I stopped him. I leaned over the patient. 'Listen Lee,' I said calmly, 'don't worry. We're just going to put an electrode in your brain and change your behaviour.' He said, 'Oh' and just lay back absolutely co-operative.

I mean this man can be so damned ornery and the next minute he's as sweet as Christmas. We had him in a Cadillac once, bombed out on the back seat. These cars would come by with their occupants recognising him. There was this real lady passing by and she lowered the window of her limousine and said, 'Oh Mr Marvin could I please have your auto-

73

graph?' And before I could get in there, Lee shouted, 'up your ass' or something like that and it's really hostile and no joke. And every other autograph hunter who stops alongside gets the same treatment. It's hairy and I tell Lee. And now he's remorseful. So he walks out into the middle of the street. And now he's flagging cars down. They jam on their brakes. 'I'm Lee Marvin,' he's announcing, 'would you like my autograph?' Even if they don't want it they get it. He's prepared to stand on that highway till the end of time flagging down cars and signing autographs. But then this same guy who decked a paraplegic – I wasn't there but I know it happened – is the same guy who gave a $7,000 cheque to a hustler in a bar. This was a fellow called George, who turned out to be a murderer and an arsonist. I gotta tell you about George. At eleven o'clock one Saturday morning in his office on Sunset Boulevard he took sixty bullets from his nipples to his head, and that was the end of George.

And what about this function at a friend's house where Lee came with Betty? There was this marvellous girl, an opera star, who was pretty well endowed. Attractive as hell. She had a Martini at the bar and Lee happened to be standing next to her. It was a formal affair. Betty was across the room talking to somebody else. Lee happened to notice that this lady had quite inadvertently allowed her right breast to pop out of her extremely low-cut dress. It had almost dropped into her Martini which probably had points over a twist of lemon. Before she could do anything Lee upped to the rescue with 'May I dear lady?' and very delicately elevated her breast, reseating it neatly into its little nest. And that's all that was said. Oh, I think she thanked him. [Note: From here on the first Mrs Marvin's version of the incident is slightly at variance with Tristram Colket's which continues.]

About a half an hour later when they were leaving in the car, Betty said, 'And just what in hell was that all about?' Lee kinda shrugged and said, 'Well that's show business.' Betty's hand flew up, caught him across the mouth and knocked out two front teeth. He had this seven o'clock call the following morning and he sure needed those teeth. Well, they got out of the car and he and Betty started looking for them. At one point Lee said, 'My God we'll never find them.' And Betty said, 'Oh well, that's show business.' Eventually they did find them and Lee went to a stunt man, boot black or someone and had the teeth cemented back in. He had them stuck in that way for three days.

Now comes the second epoch. This is when I start bring-

74

ing this girl Black Cloud over. Lee knows I'm in love with her, want to marry her which as a matter of fact I do. I called her Black Cloud because after things started breaking up I said she behaved like a black cloud. Also she looked like an Indian. I think she once said she was part Cherokee. Now this girl was a very sexy, crazy, wild lady. She was just erotic, hard-core pornography. She was like a libidinous nun. Everything a guy could ever want. That's why I married her. In fact that's the only area where I think there was an estrangement between us. Over Black Cloud. I know Lee was kind of fond of her too. Now it was Lee and Betty who gave the party for our wedding. Lee was best man. It was the wildest wedding to end them all. Like the theatre was a shambles even before the play started! I was leaving work that day at the Ryker Laboratory where I was director of chemical pharmacology, tremendous authority, tremendous responsibility. It was the night of my wedding to a girl who if my father had found out she even existed he would have disowned me on the spot. Anyway just before I was leaving to get married I suddenly realised I hadn't got a preacher. So I told my secretary, 'Call a preacher and send him along to Mr Marvin's house on Latimer Road by eight o'clock.'

Well before I had gotten there Lee had taken Black Cloud into the games room and got her drunk out of her mind. Lee's pretty ripped up too. Around 7.30 we get this call from the preacher who says his car is blocked in on a pile-up on the Freeway. Lee says, 'I'll go get him.' He brings the preacher back. The guy has silky hair, frail, and looks like if you blew on him he'd disintegrate. And I get the impression he's a little juiced too. Lee gives Black Cloud a few more shots somewhere upstairs. I'm downstairs where all the polite people are. Finally Lee appears at the top landing with Black Cloud and she can hardly make the stairs. Well she sees the preacher who's a little more evangelical than I'd hoped for. He starts booming off like a Hot Gospeller. 'AND I SAY TO YOU IF THE GODS COME DOWN TO EARTH AND FINDS THE SINNERS . . . ' all that kind of stuff and Black Cloud is rolling and yelling 'A . . . MEN! A . . . MEN!' And then we all start going at it, 'A . . . MEN! A . . . MEN!' And the preacher is sounding off 'THE GOOD LORD IS GONNA SAVE YOU ALL!' and Black Cloud is crying and hollering 'A . . . MEN!' and Lee is stoking it all up pretty good. And all this is going on at the home of Lee and Betty Marvin, and that is just for openers.

My third epoch with Lee was when things started getting

really fouled up between me and Black Cloud. Somehow or other the story had got around in the newspapers that I was gonna kill Lee Marvin. This was bullshit. I loved the guy. It's true Lee kinda liked her but there was no way any man could resist her. This story got out because one day I got back from the Ryker Laboratory and couldn't find Black Cloud any place. Now I wanted her. I mean I just wanted to get laid. I'd worked up a whole twelve-hour number where I was practically intraorgasmic by the time I got home. My place was on the ocean with these stairs outside that are raised ten feet off the sand. Well I ran down these stairs, leaped from the bottom step to the beach and looked around. And under the house I find Lee and Black Cloud with a whole bunch of wine. Lee had been run out of his house or maybe he'd come to see me. I don't know. Anyway he was asleep. Black Cloud had shifted a table right on top of him. She was asleep beside him. I thought, 'that's okay' and went to bed. Then she told me afterwards that she'd heard from somewhere I was going to kill Lee so she interposed the table between me and Destiny. It was as spooky as that.

We had a good laugh over it. But then there was always plenty to laugh at with the Marvins. I mean take his brother Robert. We went up there once when the family were living outside New York. It's hot and I'm there with Black Cloud sleeping outside in a sleeping bag, that is me, Black Cloud and the ants. I'm telling you we were right in the path of the major west coast line of ants from here to Chicago non-stop, right? We're swimming naked at night and the water was fluorescent, and the whole thing is beautiful and the more gin you drank the more beautiful it got. And up there Lee's brother Bob is on a rocking chair in the vestibule and for forty-eight hours he sat there going 'WHEE . . . OOOH! . . . WHEE . . . OOOH!' He'd wait twenty seconds and then go again, 'WHEE . . . OOOH . . . WHEE . . . OOOH!' I said, 'What's he doing?' They told me he was doing a foghorn. I said, 'Why?' They said, 'We don't know. He always does.'

So I tell you you're into something when you team up with Lee Marvin. By the way did Lee ever tell you of the dream he keeps getting? He and I are walking in the desert, right? There's a bitch of a sun overhead and we're as parched as hell. Suddenly the sun dies. It is cold, a chill wind gets through to our skins. A darkness comes down and it is ominous and frightening. There is an urgent need to find a place of safety. A haven. We stumble along in the gloom when suddenly Lee notices a stick on the ground. He picks it up and very slowly draws the outline of a motel in the sand. He draws the door. Then we both push through it and end up at the bar. Ten people have repeated this dream to me. So it must have some significance to Lee.

It does. And to Tristram Coffin Colket the Third, MD. He now has dreams – would he get over immediately to bounce these two guys who are causing trouble in a new motel in the desert . . . ?

Chapter Six

'No broads, no mother, no sleep, no eat, just a dumb, fair cop.'

Lee Marvin of M-Squad

Lee Marvin was now battling for recognition in a Hollywood whose star system was fading rapidly like a dying galaxy. He had come in on the tail-end of the global worship and the glittering prizes. Like other actors low in the batting order at the time, he looked upon those craggy, age-mottled idols, Spencer Tracy, Clark Gable, John Wayne and Humphrey Bogart marvelling at their indestructibility. Marvin knew, as Hollywood itself predicted, that they were irreplaceable. To be sure new superstars would be born – Streisand, Redford, McQueen and the rest – but these could all curl up in one pair of those legendary footsteps and still leave room for a Jagger or Travolta. Lee's mate, Ernest Borgnine, who shared the hoodlum quartet on *Bad Day At Black Rock* also shared Marvin's awe of the big stars, Spencer Tracy in particular. On the last day's shooting Borgnine declared reverentially, 'It was a truly inspirational experience. Mr Tracy . . . (the 'Mister' endorsed the homage) . . . was the first actor I'd ever seen who could just look down in the dirt, say nothing, and totally command a scene. Bob Ryan could've stood on his head, zipped his fly open and the scene would have still been Mr Tracy's.' Marvin's variation on this theme was:

I'll tell you who was a star, Clark Gable. What a man! And what a build. I'm no midget (6ft 3in) but when I tried on one of his overcoats the shoulders came down to my wrists, I

swear it. One day some people were visiting the studio. When
finally Gable came out of his dressing-room wearing this
terrific dressing-gown, a girl in the group fainted clean away.
Gable bent over her and held her head. When she came to
he said, 'You okay, sweetheart?' She looked up at him bending over her and – guess what? – she fainted clean away
again. That's a star, pal.

But whatever other reaction Marvin's thick-eared portrayals
induced swooning wasn't one of them. He knew that success
would have to come the hard way, that he'd have to carve his
own niche, sculpt his own image. What emerged was a laconic,
sometimes sadistic, mean tough guy of indifferent intelligence.
In *Bad Day* as the hard-nosed, red-necked, jeep-driving cowboy
he was not that unattractive to a large section of American
males who would see in his stranger-hating bloody-mindedness
the 'virtues' of loyalty and virility. But Marvin now needed films
to prove he could think his way into deeper, more complex
characters. An interesting though minor movie, *A Life In the
Balance*, gave him that chance and he clinched it. A Mexican-
American low budget co-production, the film has Lee Marvin
as a US killer on the run in Mexico City, who grabs a Mexican's
young son as hostage. The part required a display of sub-
normal intelligence, with the killer needing psychiatric attention.
There is the quality of softness, even pathos, clouded over by
the menace stemming from the psycho's morbid unpredictability.

In that year – it was 1957 and Betty Marvin had three children and several bullet marks over the bar – Lee Marvin fairly
raced through a whirr of assorted movies. Some good. Some
awful. But none of them bad for Lee Marvin. He was a
benzedrine-sniffing thief in *Violent Saturday* allegedly playing
second fiddle in the billing to Victor Mature. When the film
was rereleased ten years later (December 1965) the distinguished critic Judith Crist wrote in the now defunct *New York
Herald Tribune*

If you just ignored Victor Mature, the nominal star, you
could concentrate on Marvin . . . catch his every nuance,
watch his perfect pace, revel in a superb monologue on the
skinny broad he married whose perpetual contagious colds

gave him the benzedrine habit. And you realise, watching this performance, that Marvin stood distinct and apart from the maudlin melodrama swirling around him. A pity we had to waste ten years watching any number of 'stars' do ineptly what he had clearly mastered long ago.

'Bullshit' was Marvin's response to that, his way of concealing the self-admiration which by his lights no man should ever reveal. Central to this Marines-inspired conviction was the notion that it is a show of weakness for him to expose what he really cares about, put his emotions on parade. So we get the wild histrionics, the ZAP and KAVOOM and the crotch-oriented black humour, all to camouflage that he *does* care, *is* emotionally stirred – though he'd pee on your porch to disprove it. Well that's okay for Lee Marvin. But as he lurched from mild horseplay to gabbling barbarism, nobody cared to stay around to probe his motives. To be fair, when things got really rough and he himself couldn't take Lee Marvin at full belt, he did haul himself off to a psychiatrist. The sessions lasted six months. Lee took the shrink back through the Marines, Saipan, a dozen school expulsions, to his first audible kavoom from the cradle. It set Lee back $6,000. He learned nothing new about himself but emerged a mildly better-integrated monster.

Man cannot live by dread alone. Meyer Mishkin and Lee Marvin put their unsymmetrical heads together after *Violent Saturday* and resolved he, Lee, was ready for some cinematic honeysuckle. Would audiences take this mean but compelling thug in a switch to more sympathetic roles? The answer was, they could take him, and leave him. As a medical student in *Not As A Stranger* with Robert Mitchum, and in a band with Jack Webb in *Pete Kelly's Blues* Marvin merely threw off a couple of pointers to the rich comedy to come in *Cat Ballou.* The films did little for themselves, nothing for him. It was back to the old menace again in *I Died A Thousand Times.* (So apparently did the picture – a heavy-going, over wordy gangster tale of a robbery that gets fouled up.) There was more mileage for Marvin in *Shack Out On 101* a spy melodrama in which he plays a cook-turned-secret agent. What he gained there he lost on *The Rack* a tedious film version of a TV play about the court-martial of a US soldier for collaborating with the enemy under torture. It starred Paul Newman who was more beautiful then than ever, the contrast to Lee Marvin's palaeolithic features being the joke of the production.

For all that, Marvin's next movie was a landmark, enabling him to command a better table in the studio commissary, get the furnished dressing-room, have his portrait up in the executive corridors. He achieved a star billing at last, opposite the mature if not downright saddle-sore cowboy hero, Randolph Scott. It was a Western, *Seven Men From Now*, in which the well-honed theme – sheriff seeks revenge for the murder of his wife by the baddies – is directed well by Budd Boetticher. Marvin learned plenty from the veteran Scott, whose silken kerchief and whole range of two expressions had hallmarked a record number of Westerns. Marvin noted that behind Randy Scott's boyish, sun-creased smile, was a shrewd understanding of publicity. The story goes that when Scott, a keen golfer, asked to join a famous Los Angeles golf club he's told 'Sorry we don't admit Jews or actors' So he says, 'I'm not an actor and I've made twenty-five films to prove it.' (He was not all that off-beam either.) Later Marvin improved on the anecdote. He is stopped by a passer-by on a London street who says, 'Mr Marvin would you please shake hands with this woman – she's my wife and she's seen all your pictures.' 'All of them?' Lee frowns, 'D'you want an apology?'

The Scott Western (more than the Jeff Chandler horse opera *Pillars of the Sky* which followed it) convinced director Robert Aldrich that Marvin was spot on for a major role in *Attack*. And Marvin, who can fill a military uniform with stylish authenticity, is unerring as a senior US Officer in World War II. Typical of many of those films which Robert Aldrich both produces and directs, *Attack* is high on melodrama, veering towards the simplistic. It is in every sense, black and white. Set in Belgium during the Battle of the Bulge in 1944, it homes in on a squad of GIs dependent upon a spineless colonel, a role well-handled by Eddie Albert. The colonel, emotionally flawed by the beatings and expectations of his (off-screen) US senator of a father, is incapable of coherent leadership under fire. Jack Palance (near the crest of his wave at the time) plays the squad's leader and hence the film's lead.

Marvin comes late on the scene. A senior officer with the edge of rank over the colonel, the character is as calculating and cynical as his hoodlum in *The Big Heat*. He knows what's going

81

on. He knows he should instantly relieve the colonel of his command. He does not. For he knows too that the war being won, comes the peace, a plum Washington post is on the cards for anyone who held the senator's son's hand tightly enough to establish a long-term hold. The plot detail is given to emphasise that in this particular characterisation Marvin, though no less hardnosed, is all intelligence. He is the long-term career opportunist calculating the percentage play behind those sneering eyes. So though in those days Jack Palance took home the larger pay cheque, Marvin, as the devil, had all the best tunes. And with Aldrich to orchestrate them, Marvin couldn't fail. It was the beginning of a profitable partnership between Marvin and the teak-tough Bob Aldrich whose credits punch-card the man: *The Big Knife*, *Attack*, *Whatever Happened to Baby Jane?*, *Hush Hush*, *Sweet Charlotte*, *The Flight of the Phoenix*, *The Dirty Dozen*, *The Killing of Sister George*, *The Emperor of the North* and others, like the lustily explicit *The Choirboys*.

It was a stroke of near genius to switch Marvin straight from *Attack* into the lavish multi-starred epic, *Raintree County* for which Montgomery Clift, as the hero of the story, received an Academy nomination. In this movie Marvin plays nothing more vicious than a small-town braggart-cum-dandy who bested by Clift in a foot-race behaves with commendable good grace. The film, Metro's lame attempt to outdo its *Gone With The Wind*, produced some sizeable competition for Marvin to beat. Elizabeth Taylor, Eva Marie Saint, Agnes Moorehead and others combine to grind out this Civil War tale of a southern belle's dilemmas of love. Marvin went to work on it and encountered the same sort of problems with Clift as he had done with Marlon Brando. The star wouldn't look him in the eye. I mean shit! I gotta know what he's thinking right? I gotta react to it. But on the set, for the two-shots, Clift kept his eyes locked in on Marvin's forehead. He did this apparently with all his co-stars. Lee Marvin wouldn't have objected to Clift staring at his forehead if there had been a lump on it, a cross on it, or a bullet through it. But having those dark, tormented eyes angled high above his own eyeline, threw Marvin, as he told Millard Kauffman, who wrote the script. Said Kauffman:

Some thought it was Clift trying to throw Lee off, but I

doubt that. Clift had his own problems, the biggest of which was the doubts about his own ability. Lee Marvin understood this and didn't ride Monty Clift hard as a result. But then Lee, though an actor, has always led a rich life off the screen, always his own man. Most actors are actors because there is a banality or a parched quality about their lives. Lee Marvin is a hell of an actor, but that's just one dimension in a can-full of others. There is an astounding scene in *Raintree* which nobody notices in an otherwise generally unastounding picture. He has this foot-race with Monty Clift. Now Monty was many things but one thing he was not was physically co-ordinated. He couldn't run a yard without stumbling on his own feet. In a 100-yard dash, Lee could give him a sixty yard start and still stand there waiting at the tape. But from beginning to end in that race (and there were many, many takes) he made it look as though Monty was outrunning him. It was phenomenal.

Not to those who understood Marvin's thinking at the time: 'The job of an actor who's playing number two is to make number one look a hell of a lot better than he is.' So though Marvin has made a ton of movies with co-stars of class, there is no evidence to show he ever tried to 'throw' them. 'Marvin? A regular pussy-cat to work with,' seems to be the purring consensus, though all qualify the compliment with, 'unless he's been drinking, in which case, forget it!' More significant accolades come from the extras and the stunt men, for whom Marvin always had unlimited respect – proving it by preferring their company at the bars to that of his fellow 'artistes' (Marvin turns the word into an exquisite insult). His role in *Raintree* called for a kind of frontier bravado, the choreography of the dare. In a particular scene Lee has to take a running jump at a round column in a bar, swing round it three times before landing. As Kauffman recalled it, the man who was stunting for Lee, was not hitting it right.

Lee told him he could do it himself. I said, 'well for chrissakes, go ahead and do it and let's get out of this damn scene. I mean, he's a stunt man, he's supposed to have an educated body, if he can't and you can, let's get moving!' But first Lee had to take this guy on a side and clear it with him. He was not going to leave that fellow with egg on his face. Then Lee did the stunt, perfectly, first time. That was Lee, the actor, and the man.

Though the film, despite Clift's Academy nomination, generated little enthusiasm among the critics, there was some warm praise for Lee, notably over his final scene. Shot in the back by a sniper, he takes a long time to die, roaming deliriously over the paradise lost of his young manhood in Raintree County. It is a soliloquy which is totally moving, demonstrating that Marvin's expressive vocal resonance could be harnessed to more than just a menacing threat or hit-man's obscenity. It led to a loud, if not standing, ovation in Hollywood – and the television series that was to give him world-star status and, with some peripheral assistance, pull the roof down upon his marriage.

It was 1957, the dear dead days beyond recall of the thirty-minute crime series on prime-time television. The giant NBC, raring to corner this market with its enticing spin-offs overseas, was playing around with a proposed series called *M-Squad*, the élite section of the Chicago Police Department. They needed an actor to play Lieut. Frank Ballinger, a tough no-nonsense cop, hard-nosed but with a brush-in of compassion. Lee Marvin was seen, tested, and approved. He had no notion then that the series would make him rich almost to the point of uncontrolled laughter. No idea that the said meal-ticket would be renewed year after year with his dependents, notably Betty Marvin his wife, lapping up plenty of the cream. *M-Squad* did not merely become the highest syndicated TV show in the world. Its 117 episodes over a three-year span, pioneered the cop hero, created the prototype, which, like the Great American Cowboy, became a permanent implant in the anatomy of screen entertainment.

But *M-Squad* differed significantly from the overblown, mannered samples of the breed which were to succeed it. It made no concession to stardom. There was none of the modish mugging-and-hugging of *Starsky and Hutch*, or the head-scratching and studied afterthought shtick of *Columbo*. And a grimacing police lieutenant sucking lollipops in public would have been run out of Chicago. Marvin took to the Ballinger character the way Marlon Brando thankfully grabbed the Godfather. Lee liked this hard, seldom romantic, workday cop. He dug deep into the forensic tricks of the Chicago Police Dept, went out on arrests, listened in on the briefings. Maybe the show was kind of hokum, but even its critics conceded that *M-Squad* compelled interest, pulled no punches, neither whitewashing dubious police methods nor romanticising the thugs. All the stories were tightly-structured, the plot-lines neat.

Reading through the combined pages of all 117 scripts offers a grand tour of dope-peddling, swindling, hijacking, kidnapping, forgery, and fifty-seven varieties of sudden death in the 211 square miles of Chicago. Some of the titles do less than justice to the stories – *Street of Fear, Face of Evil, Neighbourhood Killer, The Frightened Wife, Killer in Town, Lovers Lane Killing, The Black Mermaid, The Executioner*, and *The Terror on Dark Street*. But premiered in the autumn of 1957 on a Friday evening 9pm time slot, *M-Squad* topped the ratings against stiff competition from the other networks. The show attracted the best creative talents. Major writers like Jack Laird and directors of class such as Don Weiss cut their teeth on *M-Squad*, helped to take it, in 1958–9 to third in the Nielsen ratings of the top-ten suspense dramas, beaten only by *Perry Mason* and the *Alfred Hitchcock Hour*. What kept the millions enthralled was the ingenious plots, and the authentic Chicago backgrounds. But Lee Marvin was the show.

He began, as with every role, by 'psyching-in' into the part with such intensity Betty Marvin rarely knew when Ballinger had left off, Lee Marvin taken over. Invited to describe his part Marvin flipped, 'no broads, no mother, no sleep, no eat, just a dumb fair cop.' For all that modest dismissal, *Variety*, sometimes described as 'the bible of the trade' noted, 'What distinguishes this production is the class performance of Lee Marvin – his cop is soulful without being sentimental, clinical but not cynical, and as smart as they come.' And later, 'He's a good actor who gives the role an air of authority. He looks the part of a tough cop perhaps more so than any other TV policeman.' They did not mention John Cassavetes' *Johnny Staccato*, Lieut Ballinger's TV rival, being screened around the same time.

This was a good show though *Staccato* was lean meat compared with Ballinger. It went from the New York night-time atmosphere in a *Naked City* sort of key with Cassavetes playing, would you believe, a Greenwich village jazz pianist who doubles as a private eye. Despite such a hokey premise, *Staccato* got by on Cassavetes's charisma, up-market casting and poetic approach. *M-Squad*'s strength was its taut, no-bull brusqueness. It is almost the difference between Cassavetes and Marvin. The movies they made together confirmed it. Cassavetes was chilled by Marvin in Don Siegel's remake of *The Killers* and got close to stealing the acting honours from Lee in *The Dirty Dozen*. But *M-Squad* coasted home far ahead of *Johnny Staccato* both 'domestic' and world-wide.

Though after the first thirty-nine segments, Lee Marvin relished all the money and the fame, he began to weary of the weekly grind. A maverick down to his treasured service boots he hated being imprisoned inside the network bondage. When the top brass at NBC studied *M-Squad*'s high ratings and joyfully announced 'we go on and on', danger signals jangled inside Marvin's head. He was drinking doubles now. And his bar-room brawls weren't funny any more. Don Weiss, who directed Lee in a couple of the earlier *M-Squad* shows, has a lively recollection of a well-primed Lee Marvin.

> We went to Chicago to do some background shooting and the biggest mistake of my life was sharing a suite with him. I mean I love him, but . . . well our lifestyles are different. He's really rough and he gets drunk. But I'll say this for Lee he does his work and he survives anything. I used to go to lunch with him to see that he didn't drink, kind of hang on to him which is a thing I rarely do with actors. But I did in his case because I was afraid he might not come back or something, which happened once or twice. But as I say, when he drank . . . well I'll tell you. There was this bell-boy who'd been bugging him ever since he'd got into the hotel, saying 'Hey, Mr Marvin, y'know Chicago's my town. Anything you want, anything at all you might want, come and see me'. So one night Lee got drunk and he calls for him and says, 'Come on up here, Joe,' or whatever his name was. Joe got up there and Lee said, 'We want a couple of broads,' I said, 'Lee, Jesus, don't start, you can't do that, it's not cool here.' It was the best hotel, the Ambassador East. So the guy starts to make a couple of enquiries and he can't find anything. Lee says, 'Here, wait a minute, you're the guy who says Chicago's your town and you can get me anything and everything.' The guy says 'I'm terribly sorry I just can't Mr Marvin', and starts to back towards the door. Lee says, 'Now just you wait a minute. Take down your pants!' The guy turned white, and ran. Marvin, when he's drunk he's drunk, and he gets really bad, I mean bad. No doubt about it.

The point is, as an actor he gives you everything you ask for, and more. Every time I see him he's great. Some guys just take the money and run. There is no way Lee is going to do that. He spends a lot of time thinking, though making damn sure to create the illusion he isn't. I don't know a director who works with him who isn't impressed as hell. There are a lot of actors wandering around this town [Hollywood] who are constantly complaining about having to work with lousy directors. One day I'm going to run a course for actors called 'What To Do When Faced With A Lousy Director'. These characters should watch Lee. He's flexible but no one can hurt him. And the secret, as I read it, is that whatever hazards you throw at him, he makes them work, adding something you didn't expect but are as glad as hell to use. That kisser in itself – it's a great face. But the rest is entirely physical. He's got a system. He says there's the mental actor [Mr Weiss pointed to his head] and in-between actor [finger on the midriff] and an all-physical male man, [Mr Weiss stabbed at his crotch]. Everything with Lee is here. The way he walks, the way he talks, the way he slings a gun – it's all in the crotch with Lee.

So now we know.

They were harmless enough, Lee's convention-style japes in bars, hotel suites with his cronies. But at home with Betty and the four children, the joke was wearing perilously thin. 'When I think back, the most difficult period of our marriage began with *M-Squad*.' There's no doubt about that in the former Mrs Marvin's recollections.

It just went on and on. With a film, even if it means separation, you know it is only temporary. There is always an end in sight. But a series is different. Lee's co-stars, the crew, the grips and so on all became his family. And when he came home weekends it was like coming home to strangers. I was married to *M-Squad* not Lee Marvin [She smiled]. Yes in a way an actor marries a series whereas he only has affairs with films. Two things frightened me most of all, Lee's powerful capacity for violence, and his obsession with guns. It's funny now in retrospect, but I remember when Lee, unable to handle a great rage within him, was so frustrated he took a gun ran out and started firing at his own house! Shot up his own home! Just total hysteria, not wanting to kill anybody but needing to release this tremendous frustration. There really were moments of incredible violence, usually when he had been drinking. The guns around the house made it worse. I detested them. We had all kinds of guns there right up until the time of our divorce. It was very frightening to me. They were never properly locked up. And remember there were four children in the house. And of course there would be these childish games of shooting at the glasses on the bar. It caused me great anxiety especially when Lee and his friends had been drinking.

The traumas did not end there. The social pattern of their lives swung between the mildly raucous and the totally ruinous. 'There was no specific routine to Lee's behaviour. When we went to parties I used to watch and think, "Oh God . . . there he goes again, he's going to pee in the hostess's plant, he's going to upset the dinner table," or whatever bizarre act occurred to him at the time.' With Lee frequently away on location in Chicago, his wife, an honours graduate strong on wisdom and understanding, had time to analyse the motivations of the man she still loved, regardless.

I was always fascinated by Lee's capacity for acting at home like the character he happened to be portraying. It could be good or bad depending upon whether he was a heavy or playing a fun role. At times he could be four or five different men. Remember he had come from a home environment where violence always seemed to be simmering under the surface. I don't want to be negative but I think being Lee Marvin was terribly painful to him. He could be very aggressive and it disturbed him. The closer you get to someone who doesn't really love himself the greater the animosity towards you. You know too much. You are somebody who is walking around harbouring secrets. All this to a self-destructive person can cause considerable conflict.

The point is confirmed by Lee who once said to me, 'I don't like actors. I don't like myself. How can I like them?' Many women suffer if they feel there is an estrangement, when they are not communicating with their husbands. Often their first concern is, 'Is there another woman? Is he playing around?' As she sat alone each evening, playing a classical disc, or painting an abstract, the very-together Mrs Marvin suffered no such torments.

Oh sure, Lee was very remiss about coming home many

times, she smiled. But frankly I was much more concerned about his drinking and its possible repercussions. If I could generalise I'd say Lee's basically an anti-woman man. He's happiest hanging around bars talking with other guys. He feels comfortable doing that. Not challenged. He can get away with a great deal more. Naturally there would be times when he would end up in the company of another woman. There is a certain type who makes herself available to these kind of men. So maybe after a number of drinks Lee was happy to go off. But frankly, I've never found that alcohol and sex are such great partners. So I was never terribly concerned that he would fall madly in love with another woman [she corrected herself with a laugh]. Well not at that time. Nor was I jealous. There was just this growing feeling of rejection. The fact that I was willing to hang in there it couldn't help but make it a sadomasochistic relationship. But here was a man who loved me as much as he was capable of loving any woman and who could be sweet and generous to me and the children to an almost overwhelming degree.

If Betty Marvin had been a different breed of woman, unwilling to 'hang in there' when Lee Marvin went ape, his relationship with the four children might have been dangerously troubled. As it was Lee had, still has, an extraordinary rapport with the son, Christopher, the three girls, Courtenay, Cynthia, and Claudia. Betty Marvin kept things cool. It was 'business as usual' during altercations. Lee might deliver the ritual put-downs against children, and marriage, in public. It was all part of the dedicated-bachelor act. But whenever they needed help or he heard a whimper in the night, Marvin was there with ready cash, or a Hudson Bay axe to swing at the world. But his drinking, and the Rabelaisian freak-outs that came with it, was running out of afficianados.

He said to me once that he used to drink the way one wandered close to the scraggy end of a cliff. 'You know you walk along the edge to see how near you can get without falling. The more you have against you the better you think you can operate.' Fine when it's just a spree between a well-loved buffoon and his buddies. Back home in Santa Monica, Betty Marvin grew tired of pulling Lee Marvin back from the edge. She had the artistic talents to make a career of her own. She had all the drive and spirited inclinations that would have put her on the national committee for Women's Liberation. But she knew that Marvin's work and accident-prone lifestyle couldn't encompass a competing wife. 'His ego-needs were such that any other career in the marriage would have just been too unwelcome,' she said.

So they had their first trial separation, a matrimonial device that was bound to fail with a couple who found it just as painful to be apart as together. The pattern of their lives seems to have been: Lee gets drunk; Lee makes big scene; Betty remonstrates with him; Lee accepts the reproof but is stuck with his problem and himself. Another trial separation. Don't miss the next devastating instalment. From where Lee sat – drinking apart – his marriage problems revealed the familiar ambivalence, a strong need for something that he instinctively resisted. He loved the notion of a wife and kids, loathed the 'ball and chain' that came with the package. He felt confined. Getting home for dinner, being friendly to the neighbours, PTA meetings, it was all a scenario for the Death of the Male of the Species. To him. A chip off the block of the Marvin who went to the North Pole with Admiral Peary. Lee's restless, maverick spirit died somewhere between Hollywood's Farmers' Market and the first mandatory visit to Disneyland with bubble-gum on the car seats and candyfloss in his ear. He put it sombrely in an interview, 'To me, marriage symbolised the end of the road. I was still a dreamer but I saw myself marking time until I fell into a ditch.'

Yet in his own aggressive, wild, sometimes boozily-incomprehensible way, Lee worked hard at his marriage. But the chips stacked against the Marvins got higher all the time. Try almost any of the Hollywood clichés on for size and it fits. Maybe the one that comes the closest is – Star gets reputation for being a raddled hellraiser. Star bibulously raises hell to keep said reputation on the boil. Great for publicity, bad news at home. So Betty Marvin must have had internal tremors as she saw her volatile mate's liquor intake always a lick ahead of his triumphs as an actor. And these were becoming impressive. *M-Squad* with its multi-million audiences at home and abroad, made it possible for his agent, Meyer Mishkin to ask for – and get – superstar money for film contracts. In tandem with his television series, Marvin did some great guest specials on TV with the *Dick Powell Theatre, Schlitz Playhouse, Route 66, Twilight Zone, Suspense Theatre* and *Desilu Playhouse*. In a short hiatus from *M-Squad* he made a forgettable movie called *Missouri Traveller* though a critic declared that his sardonic bully was 'a relief from the general atmosphere of pastoral sentiment.' What was memorable was his portrayal of Ira Hayes, the American Indian who became a legend at Iwo Jima. Having soldiered there Marvin required scant directorial arm-jogging to express a marine's feelings during one of the most brutal battles of World War II. A year later he was cast as a psychotic veteran in *People Need People* for an *Alcoa Premiere* on ABC-TV. It was a stunning performance, sensitively constructed. The piece won him an Emmy nomination.

The day they wrapped 'Prod. No. 13340' at the Revue Studios, Hollywood was writ large in Marvin's professional life. It was the 117th segment, the last *M-Squad*, 'end of the frigging line'. As director David Cahn took him through the closing set-ups Marvin felt like Dreyfus preparing to leave Cayenne. If the crew, assistants and others mourned this cancellation of their three-year meal ticket, Marvin didn't share in the tears. Some of the bars on the Chicago locations were not exactly weeping either. But there were other pressing reasons why Marvin found it tough to grind out the last TV scenes. Meyer Mishkin had gone down to Twentieth Century Fox and negotiated a star role in *The Comancheros* while Paramount had inked his name in for *The Man Who Shot Liberty Valance*. Both put him in major league movies alongside John Wayne. And *Liberty Valance* meant working for John Ford.

To be roped into Ford's exclusive band of actors who had better be his friends, was a career landmark for any performer. Against all this heady action, the last in the line of *M-Squad*, a routine thriller called *Fire In The Sky* demanded more than a drink or two to get Marvin through the day. (Perhaps it's uncharitable to sell the final TV episode short. The plot – bomb put on plane to collect $200,000 insurance money on which the villain and his luscious playmate can live sexily ever after – has been honourably reworked for many a subsequent large-screen thriller. There were too some deft touches to it as Lieut. Ballinger finally nails the murderer through some give-away traces of toupee-glue and dental casts.) That Friday evening when they finally dowsed the lights, the studio hands were genuinely sad to see Marvin go. NBC would go on to do bigger and better things. The stockholders would note with satisfaction the residuals and the reruns that would keep the Marvin Tele-epic alive for years.

Lee Marvin flew to the Mexican location for *The Comancheros* glad to exchange the reconstituted air blasted out of studio grilles for the real McCoy of the rugged countryside. Betty Marvin waved him goodbye with the customary mixed feelings – relief and regret. Marvin probably felt the same way. He was going to be roughing it with the boys. He could stand there, a grinning saturnine threat of a man, flinging out f - - - offs in all directions, unzipping his flies wherever the need took him, without having a wife or other critics bleating in protest. Catching an unsuspecting iguana in the jet-stream was more rewarding than hitting the bullseye in the creamy porcelain of the Beverly Hills Hotel. He knew he would win no Oscars from this new film, a lively, thick-eared Western directed by the Hungarian Michael Curtiz who fractured the English language with the same panache that had produced scores of money-making pictures.

The Comancheros was all blood and guts with John Wayne as a Texas Ranger who teams up with his gambler prisoner to search out and kill a band of renegade gunmen. It was interesting casting, Lee Marvin as 'Duke' Wayne's adversary. Strategically set apart, the two men sat around, their egos glinting off each other like the desert sun off a gun-barrel. Wayne was The Star and he spelled it out unmistakeably to one and all, especially to Marvin. If Marvin had sardonic views about Wayne's reactionary postures and Hollywood-confected war heroes, he kept them to himself. Even Lee grudgingly conceded that not every American actor should have served in the Marines. Anyway, as the cameras rolled on the first sequences Marvin acquired some respect for Wayne's style and aggressive professionalism. He also noted that 'Duke' had the shortest fuse around, capable, when driven to it, of being as mean as Marvin on a good day. He admired this uncompromising American folk hero whose attitude to wives and women was like a page torn from Marvin's own male-chauvinist book.

It was as hot as Hades on the Mexican location. Joined by the film's writer Jimmy Grant – Wayne's special buddie who was known to shift a litre or two before the serious drinking began – their combined liquor intake had Mexican onlookers speechless, on one part admiration to two parts tequila. One brief off-the-set exchange between the two rough-cut actors had Wayne rising unsteadily to his feet, squinting at Marvin through his lidless, overhung eyes. 'Lee, he growled, his all-weather face an inch or two from Marvin's, 'you bin drinking?' Marvin leered back, 'When you're this close friend, why don't you just shut up and smell!'

The film did little for either actor's reputation though their fight scenes were finely orchestrated by Curtiz; critics praised Marvin's portrayal as the drunken, half-scalped agent of the Comancheros, hinting that he was as much a match for Wayne as an actor as he was for the lawman in the film. What Wayne could, and did, do for Marvin was to mark his card on the subtle art of working for John Ford. The Wayne-Ford partnership had already produced *Stagecoach, Fort Apache, She Wore A Yellow Ribbon, The Long Voyage Home* and more. Wayne promised Marvin that at the close of *The Man Who Shot Liberty Valance* Lee would never be the same again. Ford was an already ailing and ageing sixty-seven, still competent and highly personal, but living on the reputation of his much earlier classics.

Marvin was excited as well as apprehensive when he drove into the film's Utah location. In fact he declared to me once, 'No matter how tough the old bastard was to me I couldn't wait to get to the day's work.' Lee had heard all the stories about Ford: the 'Irish egomaniac', the merciless needler who, the consensus had it, 'will cut your balls off if you don't give him five hundred per cent of your attention'. Marvin confirmed it with a minor anatomical adjustment: 'Oh Jesus, he'd tell you exactly what he wanted, I mean in theory, and if you didn't immediately pick up on it he'd pull out that club and beat the shit out of you!' So actors with sensitive souls or low threshold of truth-endurance trembled when Ford strutted on to the set. On *Liberty Valance* he arrived as usual in a chauffeured limousine with an entourage that would have done justice to a presidential cavalcade or arrival of a Don of Dons.

Lee felt mildly short-changed when he noted that 'Pappy' had not brought his accordionist friend Danny Borzage to serenade his arrival with 'Bringing in the Sheaves'. But mood music apart, lackeys still ran in all directions bringing coffee, pipe tobacco, script pages or nervous assistants while Ford launched into his ritual insults or mischievous torments. Marvin recognised the withering putdowns for what they really were – a shrewd manoeuvre to get everybody stirred up and involved with the production. Every Ford movie had to carry his own personal imprint. 'Sure he worked from a script,' Marvin allowed, 'but on the day, at the actual moment of filming, you and he had to construct something new, something that came from the gut not the pages.' In the event, however, the old wizard did not pull it off.

The movie, a free-ranging treatment of a legend about a lawyer's fight to protect homestead land against villainous cattlemen, starred James Stewart along with Wayne and Marvin. Wayne as the honest cowhand kills Liberty Valance (Marvin) leader of the greedy cattlemen. While Ford brought some lovely touches – a grotesquely-funny John Carradine as a carpetbagger type, and a beautifully poetic final landscape shot – the director seemed to have been out of touch with his actors. The reviews confirmed it. 'A heavy-spirited piece of nostalgia,' is a summary of Judith Crist's bland reactions. Significantly, Marvin's performance is hardly noted, a rare event in his career. It is arguably the one film in which he comes close to failing as an actor. Though Ford's own brash self-indulgence must have nudged Marvin over the edge. There was a brief flickering of the old man's fire, and Lee's swift comebacks, when Marvin's last scene is shot. As he pitches, satisfactorily dead in the dirt, Ford snapped 'Cut' then announced to everybody, 'Well ladies and gentlemen, that wraps up Mister Lee Marvin.'

Lee pulled himself to his feet and said just as loudly, 'You mean this wraps up *the whole picture?*'

Ford wheeled on him. 'You can talk, but do you know how to write?'

'Enough to cut twenty pages from the script and save you $25,000.'

Wayne listening to it all, chuckled his approval. Taking no horse-dung from Ford was basic to a fruitful relationship with him.

Maybe the lingering euphoria of returning to the big screen from the postage-stamp confines of television explains Marvin's going over the top in the film. The script's demand that both Stewart and Wayne start off as much younger men than their known years, added another embarrassment. Meanwhile Marvin, dressed like a Texas rodeo singer never ceases to

resemble an actor as he rants and raves under uncertain direction. It was a sad piece for John Ford who was to do no better
helming *Donovan's Reef*. Ultimately he was the man who shot
Liberty Valance. Right between the eyes.

Chapter Seven

'I was told they sent for a nurse and she came at
me with a needle so I grabbed her by the breast
and threw her on the deck.'

Lee Marvin

The Marvin's home in Latimer Road was in an area called The
Uplifters, an old avocado ranch on Santa Monica Canyon. It
was not listed on the tour-bus route whereby gawping out-of-
towners may catch a glimpse of, say, Cary Grant tossing a
script into a trash-can or a pop star wiping the obscenity of the
day off his gate. But bartenders, police patrolmen and other old
campaigners knew the house and its traumas only too well and
never passed it without a smile. The fun, specifically in the
years 1963 and 1964 was noticeably not shared by Betty Marvin.
'Frankly I was furious, tired of the whole business,' she says
now though without bitterness. 'I was just so in despair at
seeing him being such a buffoon. I really didn't find it
funny . . . ' She became weary too of the gleeful commiser-
ations of her friends, 'You poor darling, we heard last night
Lee got quite stewed and . . . '

And what? Betty Marvin could have written the catalogue
(with a little assistance from Tristram Coffin Colket the Third)
and have to update it immediately after as almost nightly the
new incidents came lurching up to the door. There was that
morning on the freeway when the police patrols caught up with
Lee driving too fast to the airport. It took a little time for the
cops to recognise the character who beamed at them from

96

behind the wheel. He was wearing a hairnet, a red-black-yellow striped bathrobe, a fifth of whiskey in one hand, a pistol in the other, and, reportedly had been shooting up mailboxes along the route. He was locked up at the station, and then released. The police always gave points to Marvin for impeccable behaviour under interrogation. Marine-trained, he was intuitively disciplined in the presence of uniformed authority even if he was a shade unsteady on his feet. In bars it was a different story. The behaviour pattern then was dangerously unpredictable. Whether he was going to be brash, boorish, affably obscene, or just a good, honest garrulous drunk, depended upon what he was drinking, with whom, why and how much. On a good night it might be a raucous scene; there'd be some tactful manoeuvres by studio muscle or well-trained friends, and incident closed. But when it was bad, the asphalt forehead, cement-mix face and low-slung jaw all geared for belligerence, then Mister Marvin was not the best company around.

One night, after winding up on *Sergeant Ryker* a television drama about a soldier accused of being a traitor in Korea, Marvin went drinking in a San Fernando bar with an assistant director. It had been a hard piece of work for him and his need for a few laughs and a lot of liquor was urgent. As they stood at the bar horsing around a stranger barged in on them. It was no new experience for Marvin. Like Kirk Douglas, Marvin relied upon the old and trusted antidote – slapping loudly on the bar and announcing, 'I'm a coward and I bet anybody in this bar can lick me!' But as the stranger nudged and baited the ex-Marine, it became clear that he was not carrying his audience. Marvin turned his back on the man. The stranger just walked round the other side. The assistant director tried to push him off. No dice. Marvin's sand-blasted features slowly took on a smile that might have fooled everybody except your friendly neighbourhood sadist. At hand was a banjo the ownership of which was never officially established. Marvin picked it up and crashed it down on the idiot's head. There was blood on the floor. And teeth. And nobody, certainly not Lee Marvin, would deny that it was the kind of brutish overkill you'd expect from an adolescent thug. Lee's explanation in an interview: 'The man represented some anxiety that I was working out and he just happened to be in the way,' found few takers. The fact that the man received some money and a new set of teeth does not entirely get Marvin off the hook. Put him in the company of some of Hollywood's more colourful tipplers and Lee would give a performance to out-wreck them all.

The wrap-up party on *The Losers*, a Four Star special made for television, was the definitive example. The situation presented Marvin with classic casting; Keenan Wynn as his bottle-scarred mate, Sam Peckinpah the prime target of the day. A day Lee Marvin recounts with total recall and an occasional wince between the lines. Not surprisingly. When it was over, the debris cleared, the armistice signed, apologies accepted, the consensus nominated it as the brawl of the decade. (Marvin's explanatory monologue gets a little fouled up on syntax but by then he'd loosened up pretty good that well-lubricated morning on Malibu.)

Keenan and I had been drinking all during the show. This was the last day and we had bottles stashed – you know. We went across to the Blarney Stone and had a couple there. Then I said, 'You know Keenan, we'd better stop by the drug store and pick up a jug because it's gonna be a long hot day.' So we bought the jug and hid it in the dressing room. They didn't need us till nine o'clock on that last morning, so we started licking on that. At eleven o'clock when they got around to us we're in a good mood, right? We didn't have much to do in the shot, just sit at a table or something, no dialogue. When it was over I was sitting outside the sound stage in a car. Then Peckinpah comes out and gives me his little flat moustache look. I said to him, 'What's up, Sam?' He said, 'That scene, it was awful, Lee, just fucking awful!' So I said, 'Why don't you shoot it again?' But he couldn't, we both knew that.

Well by then Keenan and me are pretty drunk and they keep stealing the bottle from the dressing room. I told them, 'I will not work if the bottle is not returned.' But they kept stealing it anyhow so we'd go across the street, get another jug from a joint called The Stage Door and we're buying and kinda gulping pretty good. At around 4.30 somebody came over and said, 'Hey, they're going to wrap in about five minutes and have a big spread over at the sound stage, a party.' By this time Keenan and me were really shit-faced snockered. I said, 'Well, what are we waiting for?' and we went over. I have to repeat Keenan and me are really out of

it and as we walk in I see these tables of hors d'oeuvres and
people standing around.

So standing there looking at this lot – one guy looks worse
than the other, you know how it is – Sam Peckinpath absolutely pulled the trigger on me. I mean he takes a look at me
and he says, 'Don't you think you ought to have something
to eat.' He says 'something to EAT!' WHAM goes the table.
and thirty-feet of hors d'oeuvres are kissing the floor and
then, I don't know, Sam says something else so I grab him
and have him up against the wall with his feet off the ground
and I say, 'Sam – I hope you know what I mean, Sam!' He's
looking at me and now he's in a tough position, right? He
says, 'That's okay, Lee, now forget it,' and he gives a little
sag, goes limp and I let him down. Then it's all a kind of
blurr. I was told they sent for a nurse and she came at me
with a needle so I grabbed her by the breast and threw her on
the deck. It was a sedative or something. Anyway I knocked
her down on to the hors d'oeuvres. Then they got some
muscle to hold me down and finally cleared me and the rest
of the debris off the premises. I eventually woke up in the
back of somebody's car on the way home.

The next morning I had the guilts pretty bad. Then I
remembered I'd left my own car at the studio. I called my
business guy down town. He said, 'Okay I'll swing by, pick
you up and take you there.' It was Saturday and the gates
were closed. A cop comes out, sees me and he says, 'Well,
well, well, you really did it, Mr Marvin, didn't you.' I said,
'That's what I'm told.' He said, 'Well I'm going to tell you
something, Mr Marvin, I haven't seen anything like that since
1936.' I said, 'No kidding,' although I didn't know what the
shit happened in 1936. So there it was. Sam and me, we've
fought a few rounds in our time, but we're still amazingly
good friends.

As a token of that friendship it was to Peckinpah that Lee
gave his collection of guns when Betty declared, 'You're going
to have to choose between me and the Magnums.' Lee must
have felt he owed Peckinpah something.

Overturning a table-load of goodies at Republic Studios was
part drink, part an acting-out of a public persona which
Marvin's movie roles and the image-machine had given him.
The liquor was becoming a problem but he didn't duck it at
home. He confronted it honestly, whether with Betty or the
children. One evening, during a worrying hiatus in his career, he

sat in his den, heavily into the bottle. His son Christopher, then around ten years old, came in, looked at Lee and said, 'Are you drunk, Dad?' Lee said, 'Yes.' 'Okay, then I won't bother you,' the boy said, quietly closing the door behind him. For them, the four children of his marriage to Betty Ebeling, Lee Marvin could rarely do wrong. When the situation at Latimer road became rough, they rallied round their mother. But they were only one step behind their father in pleading mitigating circumstances. The relationship between him and them – tested white-hot on the anvil – remains true, open, and with much mutual respect to offset past misdemeanours. They were proud of him too. Loved to read about him. Eagerly followed his every success.

He had come out of that lame John Ford comedy *Donovan's Reef* critically unscathed. He was now joining forces with the director Don Siegel for a remake of the Mark Hellinger classic *The Killers.* (It was the second time Marvin and Siegel were to work together. Marvin had played a small part in *Duel at Silver Creek*, the Audie Murphy film which Siegel had directed.) *The Killers* was intended for television but on completion it was considered too violent for the times – *circa* 1954 – and hastily reshaped for the cinemas. The original Mark Hellinger film, based on a Hemingway story, was similarly controversial. *Variety* declared at the time (1964), 'Seldom does a melodrama maintain the high tension that distinguishes this one.' But a respected British critic, the late Richard Winnington, dismissed it as 'About one part Hemingway, the rest is Universal International.' Curiously, Don Siegel, then eighteen years younger, had been approached to film the original version. 'But Jack Warner, hating me and loathing Mark Hellinger, wouldn't let me do it. Then I find myself many years later,' Siegel mused, 'being asked to redo it.' The film was a perfect vehicle for Marvin and was arguably the most villainous role he's ever been hired to play. There were a couple of more vicious samples to follow but nothing he's done since matches *The Killers* for his cold-blooded, calculating, sonofabitch hoodlum. He is one of the two hired killers in this story of cross and double-cross between gangsters.

When work began, Don Siegel, who also doesn't shrink from a stiffener or two, remembered Marvin's reputation for being more thirsty than most.

But our relationship was very good because obviously he liked the job. And when Universal, idiotically, and typically, insisted that we shot the ending first, not only did Lee not know what he was supposed to be doing, neither did I. So I could understand his getting drunk and carrying a bottle of 7-Up which was full of straight vodka. He doesn't know to this day but when I saw how he looked I made that shot as uncomplicated as possible. But we never made it. He was that rough. Then later on in the picture came a day when we were shooting, on the stage, the interior of a garage and he was just too low to make much sense. So I took him off the set and said to him, 'Look, it's very easy for me to chicken out of this but you cannot act when you're this loaded. We're going back on the stage, we're going to do one more take and we're going to call it quits for the day.' However, when I pulled the plug he said, 'How about joining me across the street?' I said, 'Sure.' So while I had three screwdrivers he had about ten boilermakers, (three ounces of gin in a pint of beer times ten) and he said, 'Listen, I appreciate your taking me off the set and talking to me.' And from that moment on he didn't touch a drop. There was a scene on a train where he and another character order drinks. To test Lee I had the props man fill his glass full of straight Scotch. But Lee wouldn't drink it. It was one of the major victories I ever had with an actor.

Yet when he worked, Marvin gave Siegel both barrels. The violence in the film, even by current standards of acceptance. seemed pretty sick. Marvin's own summary of his part has the edge on the official version.

In the opening me and my partner sidle into a blind home looking for a double-crosser. I get behind the head blind dame, grab her by the throat and push her to the floor. 'Where's Johnny North?' I breathe into her ear. So she tells us. I barge into the room knocking the blindies over – we used real ones – and I say, 'You Johnny North?' He says, 'Yeah.' So we take out our guns and we put ten bullets in him straight down his middle. It's great. And everybody out front is getting their vicaries ... (pronounced vie-care-ease, Marvin verbal shorthand for vicarious thrills). Playing against John Cassavetes, Marvin is mean and powerful. He calls the shots. The delivery of his last line in the movie is memorable. Bleeding to death from a bullet wound, he has driven across town to take revenge on the Mr Big who has double-crossed him.

He kills him (Ronald Reagan's last, and very good performance), and then turns to Angie Dickinson, cast as the boss-
man's mistress. She has been a pivotal character in the film
as a 'con-woman' setter-upper. She now turns on all the
plausible charm and double-talk on Marvin. He shakes his
head. 'Lady,' he says, 'I just don't have the time.' Then he
shoots her. Eugene Archer, then critic for the *New York
Times* was impressed by the film and Marvin's 'laconic
authority' in the killer role. Rejected by the TV networks for
its brutal, sadistic content, nevertheless it did well on cinema
release and is still one of the most popular bookings in the
film libraries.

One of the first to congratulate Lee was Stanley Kramer who
had seen him come a long way since his 'young protégé' days at
Columbia Pictures. He sent Lee forty-seven pages of the script
of *Ship of Fools*. It was a complex scenario, bound to test the
muscle of even the most experienced directors. A kind of *Grand
Hotel* at sea, placed on a German liner in 1933, it fairly reverberated with the talent Kramer had already hired. When
Marvin heard that Vivien Leigh, Simone Signoret, Oskar Werner, Jose Ferrer, George Segal and Heinz Ruhmann had already
signed for Kramer who was both producer and director, he was
flattered and scrutinised the script more closely. He called
Kramer up. 'I've gotta do this Stanley,' he said. He was less
terse, more revealing, to Howard Thompson of the *New York
Times*, explaining his reasons.

> In essence Bill Tenny is the Ugly American. He's an ex-ball
> player, a has-been, a wash-out, a drunk who has spent his
> life pursuing Mexican whores. He's childlike, a little afraid,
> a man trying to work out values in his own way. He's a little
> like me. He's a horrible man. A bigot. Though a bigot I'm
> not. He was a man who had to be exposed. I had to play him
> because he is a facet of me. A part of me I don't like at all.

Few actors scalpel that deep into a part. Most count the
number of scenes they've got, insist on the correct billing, take
the money and run. But as director Don Weiss said, 'There's
no way Lee can do that. You can't get him to tamper with bad
material for the sake of an extra dollar.'
Stanley Kramer knew that *Ship of Fools* just had to be a
rough passage from day one to wrap-up. Vivien Leigh was

seriously ill relying upon brief and merciful respites to carry her through. It was her last film. She died three years later. Marvin would drink. No question. Simone Signoret, France's radical movie queen, would erect a subtle Maginot Line against Oskar Werner the outspoken Austrian actor and her fellow passenger on the *Ship*. While Jose Ferrer would also be around to toss in his own sardonic ten cents. But the most eagerly awaited confrontation was the first meeting between Marvin and Vivien.

The executive enclave at the Columbia studio commissary was abuzz when these two manifestly diametric opposites faced each other across the basket of crackers. It was more than Beauty and the Beast. Feed this pair into a computer-dating machine and the contraption would blow up in a confusion of screeching metal and burnt wire. Here was the delicate and distinguished flower of the British theatre, the former Lady Olivier, elegantly face-on to a leery eccentric who relied heavily on Mexican obscenities, and his crotch, for his more incisive metaphors. And that when sober. When drunk, Kramer feared, he would fling the 'shee . . . eet', the 'ass-holes' and the deafening 'KAVOOMS!' to her presumably unamused ladyship. Kramer need have endured no such apprehensions. Each read the other like experts. Marvin sensed that this butterfly could easily double as a praying mantis, while Vivien's large candid eyes indicated she could see much tenderness to the beast across the table. With both public images kicked out of the way, the chemistry between them spat and bubbled like a witch's brew. Kramer lit a celebratory candle in his mind. With Marvin, at least, he was home – if not dry.

The filming began on the Monday morning at Columbia with all parties trading the expansive smiles concealing sensitive egos. But after the first week the curtain came up and the cast reverted to type; Oskar Werner revealed a volatile, abrasive style behind those correct Alpine courtesies. Vivien Leigh was difficult and unpredictable, largely due to her illness, though the discipline that had made her a star had cast and crew ready to jump through hoops. Marvin as usual began to take on facets of the character he was playing – the clapped-out baseball player, Bill Tenny. One afternoon after a well-juiced lunch he sauntered on to the set where Vivien was rehearsing a scene. It was a tough sequence. The actress, accustomed to working on a closed set could see Marvin grinning at her from the shadows. Now and again he closed one eye aimed a finger at her and went 'Phwtt!' If he was not drunk it was a convincing imitation. Finally Vivien had had enough. She called across to him, 'Lee remove your bloody drunken hulk from the set. I can't work with you standing there, you gaping idiot.'

Lee reacted like a reprimanded schoolboy. Or a repentant drunk. 'Yes Miss Leigh . . . Yes . . . Ma'am,' he mumbled, shuffling away. Kramer rarely knew what Marvin, in an unscheduled freak-out, would do. Rehearsing a scene with him in a stateroom, Kramer, crouched behind the camera, said, 'Okay, let's go.' Without warning, Lee reached under a pillow and came out with a gun. Nothing in the script called for it. Kramer recoiled with a startled, 'Christ, what are you doing with that gun?' Lee grinned back at him. 'Just thought I'd try it on for size, Stanley. See what it looked like.' Working with Vivien Leigh however, Marvin kept his caprices down to a minimum. And clean. Internally, he may have felt some unease playing against experience and ability of such a high order. But it didn't show. The scene where she is assigned to his table on the ship, the cool lady and the drunken ex-ball player, is a gem. He looks at her. 'You an American?' 'Yes.' 'I just come up from teaching them greasers how to play baseball – I dunno, I ate something or drank something – I've had the runs for four days.' Vivien responds with steely delicacy. 'Really . . . I'd like to hear more about it.'

Superstar confrontations were no new phenomena to Kramer who has shuffled a large pack of egos in his time. The problems on *Ship of Fools* were considerably lightened by the evident respect, in some cases affection, between him and the leading players. And between some of the players themselves, recalled Kramer:

We sure had our difficulties. Vivien wasn't well, she was really in her last days. Oskar Werner was volatile and sometimes impossible. But she thought he was wonderful. An oddball, but wonderful. But then I'm sure she had seen plenty of odd ones in her career. Lee worshipped at her shrine and would take from her what he just wouldn't take from anybody else. She belaboured him with choice invective in front of the whole crew. But he was a ready mark. What was he going to do? He couldn't hit her. So he took it. I know for certain Lee has crashed his fists through side-walls of dressing-rooms in company with a whole group of guys. I find certain parallels in this respect with Bob Mitchum. Both of them are violent enough to kick down dressing-room doors. Punch things. I've worked with Lee more than most and to me he's a pretending extrovert. He's really as introverted as hell. And what bugs an introvert with standards, is anybody who is a poseur. With that kind of character Lee goes into his whole act. If he gets a director who is, in effect, directing from a horse, that's a signal for Lee to come staggering in and say, 'Well what kind of bullshit are we doing today? I mean what the hell's all this . . . Jeezus!' Then we get the whistling, the blowing, and the KAVOOM. It's the wall. All it means is he's closing down. I can't tell you exactly why I'm really, really fond of that galoot. But I am. I'm not his psychiatrist. I don't know whether he has one or needs one. I'm only saying that to understand him, one needs some help.

Director Don Siegel, taking Kramer's point, offered an interesting theory.

There is something feminine about being an actor that offends a man like Lee. The fact that whenever you pass a mirror and have to worry about how your hair is combed, is your make-up smooth, is so narcissistic, a guy as manly as Lee is bound to detest that aspect of it. So he has to offset it with the whole machismo act.

The theory sounds good when one thinks of the flawless Paul Newman's obsessive passion for racing cars; Steve McQueen's supercharged motor-bikes and Russian wrestler's beard; and Robert Redford's lone, heavy-booted safaris through the forests of Utah.

What Lee Marvin loved about Vivien Leigh was not merely the whole tease act, the direct, flirtatious gaze, and the genial expletives which spilled from her ladylike lips. 'I mean, just to be in her presence, that talent, Jeeze it was almost spooky!' From where she sat (pretty close to him between takes) Vivien saw a sensitive, complex man behind the clowning. If both had been free from other commitments there's no knowing where their jaunty relationship might have taken them. She watched him one afternoon working with the dwarf actor Michael Dunn who was to die eight years later. It is the sequence where

Marvin, with the dwarf as his audience, launches into a boozy, savage soliloquy of a written-off ball-player. The fact that it is to this misshapen monster that he reveals himself, compounds his self-disgust. He begins:

'I never forget a curved ball on the outside corner . . . ' The words sound like a graveside oration.

'I see,' murmurs the dwarf.

'No you don't see! You don't see at all . . . you don't know what it's like to be out there and the crowd yellin' . . . all you see is that curved ball on the outside corner . . . so you've had your big chance *and . . . you . . . have . . . muffed . . . it!'*

It is an epitaph, delivered by the corpse.

Vivien told Kramer afterwards that Lee's performance was as perfectly judged a piece of acting as she'd seen at any time in her career. That accolade tended to overshadow the perform-ance by Michael Dunn. Toting an enormous cigar, strutting with that rolling gait from scene to scene, he produces sequences of rare insight and sensitivity. His personal tragedy is thus made all the more poignant. The bond between Marvin and Vivien Leigh had the additional strand of experience. Lee had had a grandstand view of death in the Pacific. Vivien Leigh must have known that death was too close to her for comfort. Both reacted to the contingency with characteristic graveyard humour, matched by the obscenity of their choice. (Pity Vivien wasn't around to hear her roguish friend on the subject of transplants; 'How would you like to be walking around with a seventeen-years-old broad's heart in your chest? You wouldn't know whether to menstruate or ejaculate!'

What Lee did not talk about was the problem of his fourteen-years-old marriage now teetering perilously close to the edge. The crisis which finally sent it hurtling on to the rocks is a matter of fine argument. There was that party of course where Betty Marvin saw her husband obligingly replace an opera singer's wayward boob back into its cup. 'The incident was one of many,' she said with a case-hardened shrug. 'I was outraged by it, but then I had been outraged by so many things before. It was during *The Ship of Fools* when I reached the point when I had really had enough. I was totally exhausted with marriage, with ourselves, with life generally. It was just too much.' What turned out to be 'too much' for the first Mrs Lee Marvin was the arrival on the scene of a petite, frisky young singer named Michelle Triola.

The result of a union between a French mother and Sicilian father she was, predictably, dark, attractive, with a steely respect for honourable retribution. What nobody could predict, however, was that this sexy, large-eyed 'chanteuse' at the smarter supper clubs might one day threaten to revolutionise the entrenched laws of marriage and divorce in the USA. Further, the same diminutive Amazon seems set to establish a 'rights for mistresses' charter which could make the cost of clandestine love even more punishing than your good old-fashioned alimony. So when the writer Abby Mann invited his friend, Michelle, to play a minute role in *Ship of Fools* it hardly occurred to him he could be making history and threatening what straying husbands cheerfully call 'the action'.

Chapter Eight

'Doctors told me Lee's never going to stop drinking as long as he wakes up in the early morning between clean sheets and you feeding him minestrone soup.'

Michelle Triola

Michelle Triola arrived on the set of *Ship of Fools* with a problem. Sleep. The lack of it. At night, until the early hours, she sang at The Little Club, a smart and smoochy night spot in Beverly Hills. Soon after dawn an alarm call jolted her awake. Minutes later she yawned her way into a studio car taking her to Columbia Pictures in Hollywood. She craved sleep, and partially solved the problem by wearing enormous sun-glasses behind which she slumbered peacefully between takes. Even behind the shades the face was peachily attractive. Oval-shaped beneath chin-length soft, dark hair, it contrasted almost virginally with her clinging silk dress whose neckline plunged provocatively to reveal a masterpiece of Italian sculpturing. The crewmen who passed, paused, and whistled 'get a load of those!' summed up the general reaction to this arresting creature who contrived the neat trick of looking undressed though manifestly she was not. She generated a kind of erotic tension, with a teasing confusion of demureness and lust. As though a nun scheduled for Lourdes had been mis-routed to Las Vegas – and stayed.

So that morning at Columbia, as Michelle slept behind the sun-glasses, characters on the set sauntered over to chat. They found her unusually attentive. But curiously uncommunicative. To Lee Marvin this cuddly creature who sat Garbo-like behind the dark glasses offered a tantalising challenge. 'Who's the broad?' he asked a production assistant. 'Michelle Triola,' the man said. 'She's some kind of blues singer who's playing one of the dancers in the party scene.'

'Go and ask her if she'll join me for lunch. '

The emissary sat beside Michelle. 'Excuse me miss, Mister Marvin would like you, if you can, to have lunch with him.'

Silence.

'There'll be a whole group of us going,' the envoy pressed on. 'It'll be real fun.'

Deep sigh.

'Okay ma'am, have it your own way,' the character shrugged, moving back to rejoin Marvin.

'What d'she say?' Marvin enquired.

'Not a damn thing.'

'Shit,' Marvin growled. 'What does she think I wanna do, rape her?'

So the ex-marine launched himself into the attack. Lowering his long lean frame into a chair beside hers he played his part in the ritual.

'Hi, the name's Marvin. Yours is Triola, right? I hear you sing pretty good.'

Michelle Triola's soft lips parted slightly, and dreaming pleasantly, a faint smile brushed across her features.

'Jee-zus!' exploded Marvin, and he reached across, raised the sun-glasses. Michelle was profoundly locked in sleep. Marvin shook his head, walked back to the cameras. 'I've been talking non-stop to a broad who's out cold behind the shades. When she wakes up tell her I want to talk to her. She owes me some answers!'

What Michelle Triola, awake, could have told the inquisitive Mr Marvin was that she was a singer who had hit big in Las Vegas pushing the intimate blues stuff at the Sands, the Riviera and other plush casino hotels. She could have added to the credits a record contract with RCA and another film slated foɪ her after the winding of *Ship of Fools*. Given that this preamble fell upon sympathetic ears, she might then have told Lee that she too was going through the torment of a busted marital relationship. Her marriage, to actor Skip Ward had lasted a year. The divorce, painful enough in itself, was the more shattering to a girl with a strict Roman Catholic upbringing. As Michelle saw it, neither she nor Skip Ward had been ready to cope with the responsibilities of marriage. They were both embroiled in separate careers – his by day, hers by night – and the result was as gloomily familiar to Hollywood as smog.

Following the divorce Michelle moved to Rome where American artists were much sought after in the then-flourishing café society which milled around the Via Venito. But the separation hurt the singer and the actor more painfully than either had anticipated. They wrote frequently to each other. The idea of a reconciliation was mooted eagerly by both parties. Michelle Triola, a tour of personal appearances for RCA over, flew back to Los Angeles with that one thought bobbing on the surface of her mind. 'I felt a sharp twinge of conscience,' she said, 'a tremendous sense of guilt. A feeling that somehow I really hadn't given the marriage my all. When I got back home I told myself, "By God I'm going to try to make a go of that marriage if it kills me!" '

Maybe if Lee Marvin had been aware of her burning urge to be reunited with her former mate, he would not have been so persistent towards the sleeping beauty on the set. (In fact Michelle had seen him at close hand once before. But they hadn't spoken. It was at a benefit where Marvin and his buddy Keenan Wynn did some comedy act together. As Michelle remembered it, 'They both wore those slim suits in fashion at the time, with thin ties, and Lee combed his hair forward. The whole effect, especially with that lean body of his, made me think, "Oh my God . . . Lee Marvin is a fag!" ' Prudently she didn't unleash that intelligence until their relationship was well forward into the shared-breakfast-cereal stage.)

It was early in June 1964 when she returned from Rome to receive the call from Abby Mann, who'd scripted *Ship of Fools* offering her a small part in the picture. They had known each other for some time. He regarded her as a 'good-luck' person and figured a touch of good fortune wouldn't come amiss on that production. Michelle jumped at the chance. For that good old-fashioned reason. She needed the money. Blues singers in the mid sixties in America were getting crowded out by the Beat revolution. Her marriage on the rocks, Michelle felt vulnerable and insecure. When Marvin finally managed to get through to her on the set, he found a warm though initially guarded response. As one of the most famous litigants of her time, Michelle Triola has astonishing recall of events that occurred, let's face it, some fifteen years ago. It seems that:

> Lee asked a bunch of people including me to join him for lunch at Naples, Columbia studio's famous lunch joint. I said, 'No, I have to go into the dressing-room and sleep.' Lee said, 'Oh, c'mon,' I said 'No' again. Now you have to know Lee Marvin. He doesn't pursue. He stops. He doesn't come on like the average man.

Yet, according to Miss Triola's unflagging recollections he persisted finally into getting her alone at a lunch table. And it was there, apparently, that Lee Marvin and the chanteuse traded heartaches. Miss Triola asserted that 'Lee started telling me he was an unhappy man, unhappy in his marriage; and I was saying how unhappy I was, and that by God I was still going to give my marriage a try even if it killed me'. The effect this had on Marvin, if Michelle's memory can't be faulted, was to stoke up his sympathy to the point that they lunched together almost every day. 'Then we'd have cocktails in the evening followed by dinner together.' Hanging over Michelle was the knowledge that one day Skip Ward would fly in from Paris (where he was working on *Is Paris Burning?*) and that as per their ardent exchange of letters, they would attempt to put their broken marriage together again. When that moment came – Skip was due in on an evening arrival at LA airport, Michelle murmured to Lee over her cocktail, 'You know I have to go there.' Marvin stared back intently. 'You happy at the idea?' Michelle blushed. 'Oh yes,' she lied. Thinking back on it she rationalises with: 'But what else could I have said? Here I was very involved with this man. I guess everybody knew we were madly in love except the two of us. We hadn't been intimate then. I think the only reason we hadn't been was I guess because we never really found the time. Or the place. Also,' she laughed, 'as I recall I had a room-mate I didn't trust.'

But in the event, she never made that trip to LA airport. Marvin, ever the astute romancer, coaxed her with, 'Well just have one drink before you go.' By the fourth double, Michelle Triola was entranced by this 'beautiful, handsome, cultured

111

man'. And Mr Skip Ward was searching the faces at the arrival gate at the airport with that sinking feeling that Michelle was reconciling some place else. The following morning Michelle awoke at her home in the Hollywood hills, blissfully hungover and decidedly in love. Whether Betty Marvin suspected that a third party was milling around in the ruins of her marriage, was purely academic. It would not have mattered either way. It was the end of the line. She says now:

> I don't happen to believe that any one person comes in and destroys a marriage. Lee and I had had a lot of fun together. I have to say that in all our early years together Lee could be quite the funniest man to live with. Life could be gruesome. But never a bore. It was only later with the drink and the violence that I decided I couldn't take any more.

Their cooling-off was matched by some heavy pyrotechnics between her husband and Miss Triola. Working on the same film, though Marvin was one of the stars, Michelle way down on the list, they could be with each other constantly. Came the moment when the film wrapped, they'd have to find an alternative playground. The film closed in October of that year. The stricken, though still vivacious Vivien Leigh returned home to England, to die some three years later. The dwarf actor Michael Dunn, whose scenes with Marvin are some of the more effective moments in the movie, also left – to die in 1973 at the age of thirty-five as his condition foreshadowed. He and Lee had forged a friendship based upon a total candour between the two men, the one towering grotesquely over the other. Marvin, characteristically hostile to any 'unmanly' display of sentiment called the dwarf over to him after their last scene together. Said Marvin:

> I guess I sort of laid it on the line. I remember saying to him, 'Well what's wrong with you, why are your legs like that?' kind of stuff, and he said, 'Well it's a genetic thing that comes from so and so . . . ' because with it all he was a real bright guy. Not as bright as people would like you to believe but he was learned and naturally he'd been through all the tests or whatever they do in childhood. He'd been pinned out on this graph stating the kind of midget he was, so he knew well enough and he had that old go-to-hell spirit which was good, because, what the hell, he did go didn't he? His life expectancy

if I recall him correctly was thirty-two. He made it to thirty-five. So that was something I guess.

Ship of Fools completed, Marvin and Michelle exchanged formal goodbyes knowing that this was merely a holding pattern pending urgent rearrangements. Michelle Triola remembers:

I didn't start screaming, 'Oh my God I'll never see Lee Marvin again!' But around ten days later I suddenly thought, 'Where the hell is that MAN.' By that time I'd moved into an apartment hotel with a set plan to go to New York to make a career there. I'd given Lee the phone number of the place but I guess he never wrote it down. Lee is like that. He never makes a note of anything. He gets other people to do it for him. All he ever carries is his money and his pocket knife and that's about it. Well apparently he'd been searching around for days trying to find me. One day he was driving around Beverly Hills when he saw me driving down Sunset Boulevard, make a turn and pull into my hotel. By that time I'd convinced myself I never was going to hear from that person again. He was just somebody telling me things. You know how women are. I went to my room where I had my telephone calls screened. A minute later the operator came on and said, 'We have a Lee Marvin on the line. Do you wish to speak with him?' I've always thought of that day, wondering what would have happened if I had said, 'Tell Mr Marvin I'm not in.' It might have changed my whole destiny.

'Well . . . ?' the operator persisted, 'what do I tell Mr Marvin?'
Michelle Triola ensnared by that old frisson, the spirit willing, the flesh weak, dismissed a momentary hesitation with a firm, 'Please have Mr Marvin come up.'
There was a tap on the door. Their meeting indicated that the short hiatus following their last farewell, had whetted mutual appetites. Or, as Michelle Triola described it,

We were back where we'd been ten days before, only this time it was much more intense. I knew we were in some kind of trouble. We were very attached by then. I had never truly been involved mentally with a married man before. We just knew that we couldn't be away from each other. There is a side to Lee that the public hardly knows about. They see the drunkenness and the rowdiness. But that doesn't really come from Lee's heart. He is a terribly handsome, attractive, sauve,

beautiful man, with beautiful taste and a gentle soul and I
like to think I helped to bring it all out.

This process began that day in her apartment. The flame
rekindled, Michelle promised Lee that she would not move to
New York, thus shelving the plan she had nurtured for some
time. He had to go away for ten days. She was due to go to work
on *Synanon* a film starring Alex Cord and Stella Stevens. 'He
phoned me constantly,' she said, 'but all I could think of was
that he was a married man.' Lee Marvin had to be thinking that
too. He was finding marriage intolerable but he had a monumental regard for Betty and the children. Hurting them was
going to crucify him. He knew that. But as he explained years
later, 'There was total incompatibility. We just couldn't communicate in the same house.' The ideal marriage, a life contract
with no options, did not, he was convinced at the time, fit into
his scheme of living. He suffered an emotional ambivalence
that would send most wives or other playmates screaming into
the hills. Or, as he put it once, 'When I love, I love; when I
hate, I hate. I'm guilty of both sins.'

Marvin is less superficial than he sounds. His thesis is that to
love somebody might be just as selfish as hating them; both are
equally limiting, great for the guy, cruel on the broad. Michelle
Triola was something else. She slid into his field of view when
the landscape of his marriage was already a heap of rubble. She
had all the fire power that makes for the archetypal 'other
woman'. Her sexiness had a resonance to it, and the large
Sicilian eyes made Marvin offers he couldn't refuse. He knew
this a week after Michelle left for the *Synanon* location. He was
preparing for *Cat Ballou* but thinking of Michelle. One day
during a lunch break on the beach she looked up and saw him
standing over her. She felt embarrassed. Marvin was already a
star, she had a minor part in this movie. And people were
already gossiping. Marvin called over to Richard Quine, the
director, 'Dick, will you be needing Michelle for a couple of
hours . . . ?' The director waved his consent. 'Let's go and eat I
want to talk to you,' Lee said to her. 'We walked for a while,'
Michelle recalled, 'then he turned to me. "I'm going home to tell
Betty I'm leaving. I just can't go on living my life the way it is."
And I'll say this for Lee. Whatever he said he was going to do,
he did.'

Well, not that night. 'He came to my home instead,' Michelle
Triola said, 'and we spent five days together. They were wonderful days,' she murmured nostalgically, 'but nagging at the back
of my mind was the knowledge of his own situation.' She told
him finally, 'Lee you just have to go back home. Everybody
there, your wife and children, must be worrying and wondering what's going on. Nobody gets lost for five days – not even
Lee Marvin.' He agreed, she said, and reluctantly went out to
her car. It was late at night. She drove him over to Latimer
Road and left him, ostensibly to walk right in and tell Betty
he was leaving. But it seems that fatigue, drink, or a laudable
desire not to drop this bombshell late at night, prevented Lee
from going right in. Instead, says Michelle, he quietly slid into
a heap on the front porch and went to sleep. He awoke the
following morning with his dog licking his face – and Mrs
Betty Marvin, standing there smiling the weary smile of long
experience. Lee rose to his feet and went into the house.
According to Michelle he wasted no time on softening-up preliminaries. He told Betty he was in love with another woman
and was moving out. Michelle Triola's version of Marvin's
announcement had a not unfunny twist to it.

Once, for some reason or other, he had called me
'Monique' instead of Michelle. He just couldn't get that
name out of his mind. So when he went home what he actually said was, 'I'm in love with Monique Triola.' Betty said,
'Who . . . in . . . the . . . hell . . . is . . . Monique?' And then she
called me on the telephone. She said,
My husband told me this evening that he was in love with
you . . .'
I said, 'Who me? . . . don't be ridiculous!'
'I understand you've been all over town with him . . .'
'You know how it is,' I told her. 'Lee's got to have company
after filming. You know that. He's got to get away from the
scene. You really have got the wrong girl.' I couldn't admit it
because Lee had never expressed himself that strongly to me.
To hear Betty say 'he says he's in love with you' came as a
shock.

Marvin's former wife, Betty, remembers it differently. Judg-
ing from her tone as she spoke I'd say that, to her, who called
who that evening hardly added up to a row of beans. By then
her marriage was finished bar the paper work. Michelle Triola's

arrival as 'the other woman' was merely an annoying sub-plot. With impressive frankness Betty said:

> I really don't know whether it was a case of innocence or repression on my part, but I truly did not know about Lee's relationship with Michelle. I was obviously shocked when she called on the telephone, introduced herself, and proceeded to tell me that I did indeed know who she was. After all whatever the circumstances, Lee and I were still together. It was all very bizarre. As I remember it she said that I was making trouble in her relationship with Lee! 'Really?' I said. 'Who is this?'
>
> 'You know who this is,' she said. 'This is Michelle.'
>
> In all honesty I was so overwhelmed that I called Lee's agent, Meyer Mishkin, because I truly didn't know her. He told me about her. I must say it was humiliating to have discovered the affair that way. Yet though Lee moved out he kept reassuring me that he certainly never left me for Michelle. That that relationship had nothing to do with our not being together. He said he didn't love her and was not planning to marry her, which was one reason we didn't divorce for a long time. But I don't blame Michelle. As I said, I don't think one person comes in and destroys a marriage.

But if Lee Marvin was not in love with Michelle he was giving a fair imitation of it. In November, six months after they had met on *Ship of Fools* he moved in with Michelle at a rented house perched up among the tall palms behind the Beverly Hills Hotel. The Marvin-Triola affair was now in the open. The gossip writers who had tantalised Hollywood with oblique references to 'Marvin's secret playmate' found themselves up the creek without a scandal. Still, they put the details in the 'pending file' from the coming divorce action which on the face of it promised some juicy revelations. The scenario took an exotic turn when Michelle joined Marvin at San Blas, a small, colourful Mexican town below the Sierra Madre Mountains.

Lee had gone there alone to compete in a tournament of big game fishing. Like Bogart on his sleek sailing yacht the *Santana*, Marvin at sea, his silver-white hair whipped by the wind, was a whole universe away from Hollywood and its charisma-machine. With Bogart it was a three-cornered love affair between him, his hand-picked shipmates, and the boat. Marvin had his chosen buddies too. But they were the bit-players in the

major drama – his personal battle with a fighting fish. He has
hauled in more than one 1,000 pound sea monster. He has
hunted the big black Marlin off the Great Barrier Reef, the blue
marlin off Hawaii. He knows the migratory habits of the big
game fish better than he knows which actor's 'in' this week, or
who's balling who according to the gossip of the day.

Marvin summed up his contempt for the *Confidential*-style
exposures in the magazines with:

> I met them all in my time, but I wasn't going that route. All
> they wanted to know was who was I fucking and I didn't feel
> I had to oblige them. Sure I'm glad to get away from the busi-
> ness once in a while. But you can never escape the bullshit.
> That never disappears. Bullshit came before the planet
> formed. I don't have any feelings for that, the old Hollywood,
> or the robber barons of the studios. And I don't know
> whether I'd care if Metro sunk right into the fucking ground.
> I was never that involved with the third floor of the Thalberg
> building. They blow you full of smoke and say what a great
> guy you are – the most important guy in the whole frigging
> world. And if they lay it on hard enough some of it is going to
> stick to your fingers like the guts of a fish you've just opened
> up. Well you come away from the boss, look out of the win-
> dow, you see the ocean and you say, 'Jeez, it's still there!' *It*
> hasn't changed so why should anything else? And you settle
> down and let someone else swallow the horseshit.

So when the line whirrs out into the sea, then cracks like a
gun as the rod whips and the reels groove in, to Marvin it's . . .
well, orgasmic was his word, not mine. The pre-battle duel as
the stubble-chinned seafarer coos encouragement to the hooked
but defiant sea-beast far below, is straight out of *The Old Man
and the Sea*. Only the dialogue is different. 'Shit baby, I know
you're gonna run, but you'll be back . . . okay you beautiful
cocksucker, you've had your turn now it's mine!' And then
there is the killing. Not with a matador's finesse. No time for
that. Marvin and his mates lay about the flailing creatures with
heavy clubs in a mêlée of blood, spray, and tangled lines. Once
Marvin helped to club a giant marlin to death. 'He was wrecking
the boat so I just lit into him and didn't ease up until he was
dead.' That way, Lee admits, he gets rid of his blood-lust at sea
instead of taking it back ashore with him (he omitted to explain
what happens to his blood-lust when the weather's too rough

for sailing.) But after a week of this happy carnage, the sun, the sea, and the tequila, Marvin phoned Michelle and in his own inimitable way, instructed her to 'get her ass down there right away'.

Michelle took off for San Blas as thrilled as an eloping adolescent. The thought of steering their love affair through old Mexico, alone on a boat together under the stars, made the Sicilian share of her blood tingle. The French connection didn't drag its feet either. She telephoned Lee first – San Blas Numero Uno wouldn't you guess – to tell him to pick her up at the nearest airfield, Mazatlan, two hundred miles south. It was blazingly hot when she arrived but she looked coolly delicious as she stepped from the plane into Lee's arms. They stayed the night together at Mazatlan. In the early morning they motored north to San Blas checking into the Hotel Bucanero. She signed the register as 'Michelle Triola'. Later that night, assisted by a cascade of margaritas and the music of Spanish guitars, the couple walked, unsteadily, through paradise.

'I think it was there in San Blas,' Michelle declared, 'when I really knew I was deeply in love with Lee. I knew I cared for him more than anyone in my life.' Marvin gave her a ring. In fact over the years he seems to have given her several. It was a Marvin habit. That aside, any resemblance between him and the conventional lover, was a joke. Not that he didn't know how to pull a chair out for a lady; smartly produce a cigarette lighter, or stand up at the right time. But the Marvin women could get that kind of ritual from other guys. They expected – and were treated to – the caveman touch. A mixture of tenderness, explicit love talk, and animal by-play wrapped in a bear hug with a faint aroma of after-shave and fish-gut floating on the air. Michelle Triola had plenty of that in the fourteen days the lovers spent in Mexico. They flew back to Los Angeles in late December. It was the first Christmas Lee spent away from Betty and the children. He felt the twin pangs of sadness and guilt. For all his public scorn for children he missed his, the Christmas hearth and the candlelit Christmas tree. Bourbon with a liberal lacing of Michelle proved a powerful antidote. When they moved into their beach house on Malibu a couple of months later, Michelle, now assuming Betty Marvin's role of 'casualty sister', informed bartenders on the Pacific Coast Highway of the new address and phone number for 'emergencies'. It was not long before they were on the line. Remembered Michelle:

They were always kind. They'd just say, 'Listen Michelle, you'd better come down and get Lee. He can't drive. He's really out of it.' But they left him alone. He had his own sort of language which could never really be insulting. The only problem arose when people tried to help him up. The moment anybody tried to get hold of him he struggles. And when big Lee struggles you need plenty of muscle on hand to cope. Strangely, Lee's drinking patterns carried a particular signal. For instance I knew if he wore something yellow, a scarf or a pair of socks, we were going to be in big trouble. The colour obviously held some kind of meaning to him. Whenever I saw it, I thought 'Oh oh . . . here we go!' He would disappear without telling me where he was going and eventually some bartender would ring up, I'd make the pick-up and it was 'here's to the next time'.

Michelle discovered, as Betty Marvin had done before her, that Lee's drinking took him into bizarre situations. 'Once Lee phoned me in a real stew. "You're not going to believe this," he said, "but I'm in this motel room with this crazy broad . . . I don't know how I got here . . . but you just come over and get me out of here!" Women were always doing this sort of thing to Lee, he would panic and look to me for help.' What sort of things? Students of Hollywood's tribal rites and customs may be fascinated by Michelle Triola's samples of the female species at work – on Lee Marvin.

We were together at a hotel bar in Las Vegas one night when this tall blonde came up and sat next to Lee. She looked like a showgirl and was very definitely making a pitch. Lee looked at me and I just said, 'Listen sweetheart, you're a big boy now.' Well this girl was drinking a Tom Collins and as Lee watched she took the cherry out of the drink, ate it, and then actually tied a knot in the stem with her tongue! It was supposed to be some sort of come-on. Lee laughed so much he nearly fell off the bar stool. I was so impressed I asked her to teach me how to do it. But she just moved off. I don't think she liked the audience reaction.

No cause for jealousy there. There can't be many blues singers can tie a knot in a cherry stem with their tongue. Michelle

was less indulgent about an incident which froze all conversation at Mateo's, a much-favoured restaurant of the movie
crowd. Onlookers assert that this one exquisite cameo expressed
women's sexual independence more effectively than a short
course of Masters and Johnson. Michelle Triola's lively version
of the affair is as intriguing a revelation of the mistress, as of her
mate.

We were having dinner with a dear couple we knew from
Honolulu. As we walked in Lee recognised a girl who had
once had a small part in a picture he'd done years before.
She looked at him, smiled and said, 'Hi, Lee.' He smiled back
and we walked on to join our friends at the table. A few
moments later she sent over this note asking, 'Can we join
you after dinner?' She was with a man. Lee who was used
to this sort of thing, didn't answer the note. He always feels
embarrassed when a woman is making a play for him in the
presence of her escort or husband. But they joined us anyway.
She sat next to Lee and everybody's talking, and she's going
on about films as though nothing else is happening. But I
notice Lee is going kind of pale and looking nervous. But I
know what is going on – and it's going on under the table.
It would have been obvious to any woman – and man – that
she has her hand on his crotch. Well you know me, Sicilian
and all that. So I didn't care if the restaurant was crowded. I
turned to this girl and in a very loud voice I said, 'Listen,
whatever your name is would you kindly remove your h· ·
from Lee Marvin's crotch. And I may not have said crotch.
She sort of choked and brought her hand up. 'What do you
mean . . . ?' I said, 'Lee's crotch darling, you know what I
mean!' Well the restaurant crowd who had been stunned at
first just broke up. Lee paled right out. The girl's escort got
up and walked away. She went after him. Our friends from
Honolulu said they'd never spent an evening like it.

Marvin could have entered a 'not guilty' plea on the grounds
that all men, especially movie stars, are vulnerable under the
table napery. Ali McGraw's priceless grope in *Goodbye Columbus* came four years too late for Marvin to cite it in mitigation.
    Like all love affairs where both parties finally end up under
the same roof, the Marvin-Triola saga ran into the usual
hassles of marital bliss. They fought as passionately as they
loved with Michelle's Sicilian heritage giving her an edge. She
talks of magnificent combats followed by idyllic surrenders.

Alert-eyed members of the Malibu set might just have spotted Marvin chasing after Michelle along the beach snorting like an enraged bull. It seemed that after 'one of those little moments couples have' she clobbered him with a broom. And then ran. It is no way to settle an argument with Marvin. Michelle's father being Italian and a restaurateur, her mother French, she could cook like an expert. If Lee didn't show up after she had prepared some special delicacy, she blew her Mediterranean top, tossing the masterpiece out on to the Pacific sand.

I have a terrible temper. It wasn't unusual for me to throw an entire meal out of the window. Neighbours walking by the following morning would laugh and say, 'Oh oh . . . looks like Lee and Michelle had a row,' because sometimes there'd be a whole roast there, with the garlic bread and the salad lying untouched, for the birds.

Michelle handled these 'dumb unnecessary fights' as best she could. Lee's post-tippling behaviour patterns were something else. Anxious to be clued in with some effective help she went to meetings of a Los Angeles organisation for the relatives of heavy drinkers. She made friends, but no headway.

Doctors told me, 'Lee's never going to stop drinking as long as he wakes up in the early morning between clean sheets and you feeding him minestrone soup.' But I was entirely devoted to this man. Ours was a deep relationship and I worried with him, worked on his scripts, cried with him, and enjoyed all his triumphs.

When Betty Marvin heard about The Marvin Follies, now under new management, she could be forgiven for reacting with a knowing smile. She'd been that route and had finally decided there was no going back along it. In March 1965, nearly fourteen years after their Las Vegas marriage, she sued Marvin for divorce in a Santa Monica court. She charged that the actor 'had destroyed the legitimate aims of matrimony and had caused her great anguish and mental suffering'. She asked for $5,000 monthly alimony, $3,000 for child support, and $1,200 legal fees. It was a modest claim by Hollywood standards and Lee reacted swiftly with characteristic generosity. His former wife remembers the discussions about the settlement as being almost loving.

> Lee would say, 'I want you to have everything.' I'd say, 'I don't want everything.' It was a total reversal of the conventional Hollywood roles. I can talk easily about it now because at this stage of our lives all the rage has burned itself out. We were both very hurt at the time. There were so many sharks in this town who were dying to handle the divorce because of the publicity and the scandal. We kept in touch after the separation. He was always extremely generous. If he felt I wanted or needed a change, or a vacation, he insisted on taking care of the bills. If I was going through a bad time through ill health or whatever, he always took charge. Once during the holiday season when I somehow couldn't face taking care of the children on my own, he packed us all off to the Sun Valley for a skiing vacation and picked up the tab. He is that kind of man.

So the run-up to the Marvin divorce was kept pretty clear of the scandal sheets. Which was just as well. It had not been Marvin's happiest year. No sooner had the lawyers become busy planning the finale to his marriage, when they were also engaged bailing him out of a drinks charge. In late September two Highway Patrol officers hauled him in, following a collision between his car and a motor scooter in West Hollywood. The rider of the bike, an actor Robert Hathaway, was taken to Westside hospital, fortunately not seriously injured. The officers told the court they had arrested Marvin on a plain drunk charge after they detected signs that he was 'under the influence of alcohol'. Lee's lawyer, Louis Goldman, however, said that Lee had shown no signs of being intoxicated when they talked before his release. Marvin could hardly afford to indulge in that kind of misdemeanour at the time.

Ship of Fools had opened to mixed reviews. Richard Roud of the *Manchester Guardian* (22 October 1965) who dismissed the film as 'absolute trash' thought it was redeemed by some of the acting including 'Marvin's bravura performance'. Some of the critics were unduly harsh on the movie. It was a shade heavy on the moralising and one or two of the performers, notably Jose Ferrer as a bone-headed Nazi type, went over the top. But there were fine performances from Oskar Werner and Simone Signoret. Vivien Leigh, Lee Marvin and the sad little

Michael Dunn gave the film class, over-shadowing the film's remorseless platitudes.

But Lee had had enough of punching his way out of a multi-talented arena. He felt he'd paid his dues, had earned the right to pitch for top-billing in a major movie. It was his good luck that others thought that too. Specifically Eliot Silverstein who had filed for future reference Marvin's very funny scene falling off a motorbike in *The Wild One*. In the event, the making of *Cat Ballou* must be seen as the making of Lee Marvin. That name in the records of the Motion Picture Academy Awards is there for all to see.

Not on record, is the juicy power-game that was played backstage by the main contenders in the multi-million dollar production. What follows, first time ever, is the Silverstein File on the making of *Cat Ballou*.

Chapter Nine

'He's very worried . . . why don't you twitch for
him a little today . . . '

Eliot Silverstein

On the night of 18 April 1966 at the Santa Monica Civic
Auditorium, Lee Marvin won the Oscar for Best Actor of the
year for his dual roles in *Cat Ballou*. Laurence Olivier and
Richard Burton had both been heavily backed to capture the
coveted bauble. But it was Marvin's lyrical performance of the
sloshed-out gunfighter which transcended the two mighty talents
of the British theatre. As he leapt to the rostrum to accept the
statuette, Lee Marvin broke with the tradition which required
him to thank the producer, director, writer, crew and anyone
else in the pecking order. Instead, in one of the shortest and
most quoted acceptance speeches in the history of the awards,
he mumbled, 'Half of this (Oscar) belongs to a horse someplace out in the Valley.' It stopped the show. So would have
this one-liner by screenwriter Frank Pierson had the millions
heard it. 'The half of the horse in the Valley was the head . . . !'
Few will miss the inference, that therefore it must be the horse's
ass up there on the stage. It was an expression of mild irritation
by one of the two writers on the film who felt that characters
who toiled to put the movie together deserved at least as much
praise as that horse in the Valley.

The traumas behind the scenes in the making of the movie
centred mostly on Eliot Silverstein who directed it. He talked
about them, manifestly more in sorrow than in anger, at the

Screen Directors' Guild on Hollywood's famous Wilshire Boulevard The events had taken place ten years earlier. But like any ex-con who has served a term of hard labour, there are certain experiences which remain permanently chiselled into the subconscious. Silverstein, whose quiet delivery conceals a steely independence as a film maker, remembered with some irony that he was not the first choice for *Cat Ballou*.

It had apparently been turned down by some twenty-four different directors. A number of them had suggested that because of my own particular way of looking at things I might be the appropriate choice. So the producers called me. In fact they had also talked to a man for whom I had worked as a director here. His name was Frank Pierson and I knew that the producers were in contact with him to discuss writing the shooting script. It had already been scripted by Walter Newman, I believe, but they wanted some additional work done. I don't know why Newman wasn't available to do it. Frank and I got together and compared notes to see whether we, as colleagues, could work harmoniously together towards the same almost surreal end, which we both eventually came to. We presented, individually, our notions to the producer. He agreed that we seemed to be in harmony and we were both hired.

Then the subject of casting came up. Jane Fonda had been in the producer's mind for a while and she at that time was virtually at the beginning of her film career. She had done a number of films. She was in no sense a neophyte but in the commercial world she had not yet, as I recall, done that blockbuster that had made her (in the argot of the financial community), bankable. Now somebody was needed to play the role of Kid Shelleen which was being expanded in Frank's shooting script. The producer had had a past relationship with Kirk Douglas and I was asked to speak to Kirk. Although I had a lot of respect for Douglas's work as an actor, this was my first film and I did not want to deal with what was known at that time as rather a consummate ego. Consummate is not the right word . . . [Silverstein said carefully. He fished for the right adjective and pulled in;] 'huge ego. I felt that because of what I had in my head, I couldn't ask anybody to take it on faith.

It was going to be a very strange adventure indeed. A star, with few exceptions, is cautious about making any theatrical venture outside his accepted commercial range. It's a long fall from the mountain top and not quite as much

125

of a fall from a chair – so the bigger the star the more reluctant, I figured, he would be to go way out. The more he would try to preserve his commercial image. I much preferred someone without a past, or who had nothing to lose. Which [Silverstein said with a ghost of a smile] was my own position. But I was pressured and I agreed that I would make an ethical best effort to talk to Kirk Douglas. We had a long phone conversation and his position was that the role of Kid Shelleen, in the version he'd read, was not large enough for a star and not small enough for a cameo. Those were his words. And I remember thinking to myself, 'Aha, I'm off the hook'. So I made some other suggestions as to how we might expand the role a bit more. But no, nothing I said no matter how hard I tried – and I did try – persuaded him.

I became more hopeful and more confident that any suggestions I made to Douglas would be rejected. And it was merely a harbinger of what I'd originally thought might be the case once we got on the set. Only now, the film had not begun and we were not yet bound at the hip. So I was able to report, with chin on my chest but smile as wide as Sunset Boulevard, that Douglas did not feel the role was appropriate for him. The company now was in a quandary because they really did want someone of substance to play that part. But because of the nature of the part and how it was going to be played – it was almost a musical comedy-type treatment, a kind of vaudeville structure – most of the standard stars also seemed conservative, personality actors. So there was some bumpiness in the vehicle as it moved towards the shooting date. It didn't seem as if there was anybody on the horizon.

Well, I had seen *The Wild One* and recalled Lee Marvin coming off a motor-cycle in a kind of horizontal striped shirt, and that he seemed, well, mad. We were going to start the film, we hadn't got anyone, so I said, 'Hey, I'd like to suggest Lee Marvin.' At that time he was quite an accomplished actor and also a respected television leading man. He'd done a series called *M-Squad*. It was not a prestigious series but it was highly commercial, and a continuing one. People looked at me as though I was crazy. How dare I make the suggestion that a hard-nosed cop – the Telly Savalas of his day – could play this comedic part? My own background was in the theatre and I felt at that time that there is a certain mysterious, undefinable quality about a trained actor. That making demands of someone who is not a familiar, everyday personality, could breed unexpected results. I had a difficult time because Lee was not a bankable actor at the time and because he had this hard-headed cop image. I remember feeling peculiarly confident about it though because there was nobody else, and I asked the company (Columbia Pictures) to see that film and see that scene. I can't recall now whether they made a special effort to do so. But I do remember there was a discussion about how I could take that scene and extrapolate it and assume that character was Kid Shelleen, when clearly it was not. That's the difference I suppose, between a director and other people. You can't really communicate except on the final film. Whatever a director knows can't be described in words. If it could be described then you'd write a book.

So eventually they agreed to send the script to Marvin. And I remember one of them talking rather giddily two days later, about Lee going around cocktail parties quoting from some of the speeches. Then my guess was right and Marvin was signed for the part. And we had two weeks during which his wig was set and the 'Suit of Lights' was designed and set, and an inspection was made of the rehearsals. There was a good deal of apprehension about Lee. Lee is a highly professional actor who believes he's paid to perform. And he wasn't giving very much. However, actors have a way, in rehearsals, of signalling that they understand what you and he have spoken about and that goes into their internal computer and it takes a certain amount of training to read those signals. If you don't understand those signals you will say, as was said to me, 'But he's not doing anything.' At any rate, the concern rose to the point where I was told, instructed, ordered by the producer to tell Marvin 'to do something' in the rehearsals so that the producers could judge. The producer was very nervous. So I went on to one of the stages where they were rehearsing and sat down with Lee at a table – a big banquet table with no cloth on – and I remember saying to myself, 'How the devil do I communicate to a professional actor that the producer wants to see a performance? If he's willing to give a performance, am I not in danger of ruining his ultimate performance? Because he reaches his concert pitch too early?' This was a strange part – there'd not been a part like this before and it wanted gradual building. He could probably come out and do something great and that would be the end of the development . . . and the movie.

So I finally decided to take the most cynical attitude possible and said, 'Lee he's got a problem.' Lee said, 'Oh yeah . . . what?' I said, 'Well, he's very worried . . . he doesn't see any development here. Tell you what we'll do. Why don't you twitch for him a little today – do something that looks like you're doing something. But don't do anything that you're going to do in front of the cameras. Keep that secret for a while.' He said, 'I gotcher. Know what you mean.' That was communication. He knew that what I was asking him to do was to seem a little more vital and maybe throw a shoulder up, or literally twitch or – anything. That was to be my weapon, saying, 'You see, he's doing something for you.' The producer would say, 'That isn't right.' I would say, 'Well of course it isn't right – that's what we have rehearsals for.'

So at another inspection rehearsal Lee twitched a little bit – that's all – not very much. He looked over his shoulder at the producer with a baleful look, which really said, 'What the hell are you doing here? Let me work.' Now that wasn't enough because a scene of some anxiety followed in the producer's office. We were leaving for Canyon City, Colorado in a couple of days to begin shooting and the nervousness expressed by the producer was that Lee was not doing anything. He might be doing a little more, but he seemed uncertain of himself and the producer wanted to replace him. I was dealing with a man who was concerned about the casting for very legitimate reasons, as seen from his point of view. He couldn't see and couldn't understand that the casting was right, until the film came out. That's the kind of high-rolling which is involved in this kind of film. But I was damned if I was going to ask Lee to spill all his secrets before he got on camera. I knew what some of them were going to be, because I'd agreed to them. And I knew a lot about the things he was going to do because he had talked with me and I knew I could call upon them in the middle of shooting. So I decided to handle this instruction rationally in the hope of cooling it. Well, we were within a couple of days of leaving for Colorado where we'd start shooting.

I said to the producer, 'With whom will you replace him?' He said, 'Jose Ferrer.' I said, 'We've had two weeks of rehearsals and all the costume fittings and you can't expect a man to come in within two or three days, even if I thought he'd be right which I don't. Although he is a respected actor, you can't expect him to achieve much when you haven't been happy with the ten or twelve days we've been rehearsing. Secondly, the company has a new Production Head, Mike Frankovich. I don't know that he's going to look kindly on the fact that two or three days before production starts there's a major disruption on this film.'

The producer said, 'Well, he'll have to.' I said, 'I want to

Top: Lee Marvin, the track champion (sixth from left in back row), St Leo College.
Left: Lee Marvin, PhD.

Top: Lee Marvin, all bad, with Gloria
Grahame in *The Big Heat,* 1953.
(Courtesy Columbia Pictures)
Above left: Hoodlum on a motorbike.
Marvin in *The Wild One,* 1954
(Courtesy Columbia Pictures)
Above: Marvin, mean and menacing: *Bad
Day at Black Rock,* 1959. (Courtesy MGM)
Left: Marvin — without malice.
Facing page top: Happily married to Betty
Marvin, née Ebeling, on holiday with
their children.
Right: Marvin, the definitive police
lieutenant, in *M-Squad,* 1958-61.
(Courtesy Universal)
Far right: *M-Squad,* one of the most
successful TV series on record. (Courtesy
Universal)

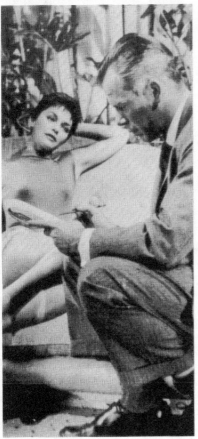

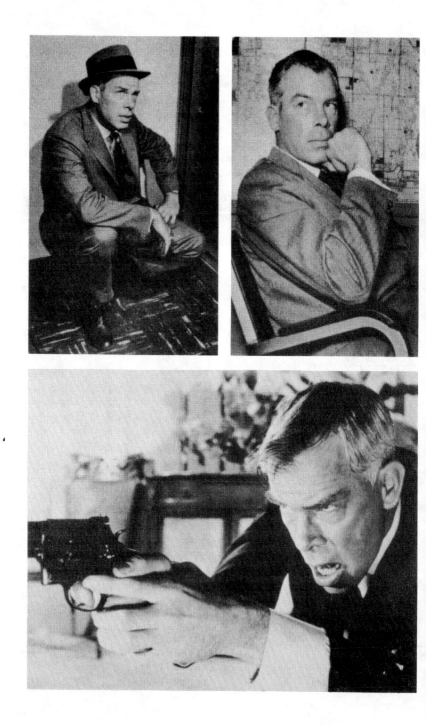

Facing page top: Lt Ballinger — 'just a dumb fair cop'. *M-Squad.* (Courtesy Universal)
Facing page below: A sadist is born — Lee Marvin in *The Killers.* (Courtesy Universal)
Left: The Classic shot from *Cat Ballou* (1964) — and an Oscar. (Courtesy Columbia Pictures)
Below: Kid Shelleen. Marvin's price goes to $1 million. (Courtesy Columbia Pictures)

Above: *The Dirty Dozen*
(1967) — both Marvin and
the movie go in with the
boot. (Courtesy MGM)
Top right, and left: A
memorable performance
with a rare perception
behind the muscle. Marvin
in *The Dirty Dozen,* 1967.
(Courtesy MGM)
Facing page top: The bully
is back. Lee Marvin in
Point Blank, 1967.
(Courtesy MGM)
Facing page below: Lee
Marvin and Japan's
Toshiro Mifune. The war
is over but the friendship
persists. A scene from *Hell
in the Pacific,* 1969.
(Courtesy Cinerama)

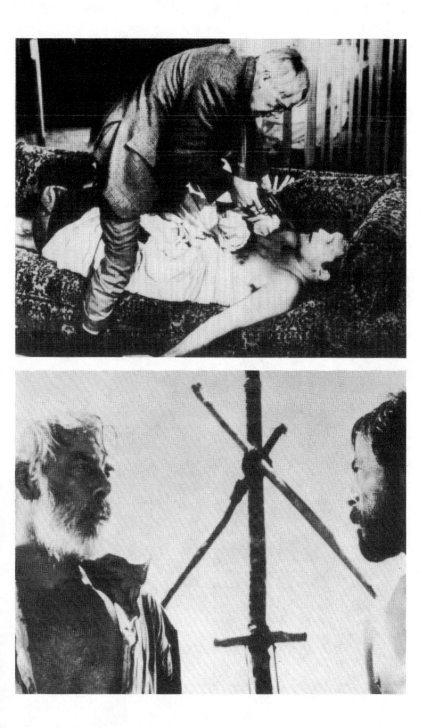

Far left: Another boozy gem — and a no.1 single ('Wanderin' Star'). Lee Marvin as the hard-drinking Ben Rumson in *Paint Your Wagon*, 1969. (Courtesy Paramount)
Left: *Paint Your Wagon:* exquisite lunacy and no deodorant on an Oregon location. (Courtesy Paramount)
Facing page, bottom left: Marvin and his famous mistress, Michele Triola, at the premiere of *Paint Your Wagon*. (Courtesy Camera Press)
Facing page, bottom right: Happier moments — Michele had changed her name to Marvin. (Courtesy *Daily Mirror*)
Below: The Doctor of Philosophy, 26 April 1969.
Above: Lee Marvin with the other recipients of St Leo College Honorary Degrees. Third from left is the Hon. Melvin R. Laird, US Secretary of Defense.
Bottom: The birdwatcher. (Courtesy *Daily Mirror*)

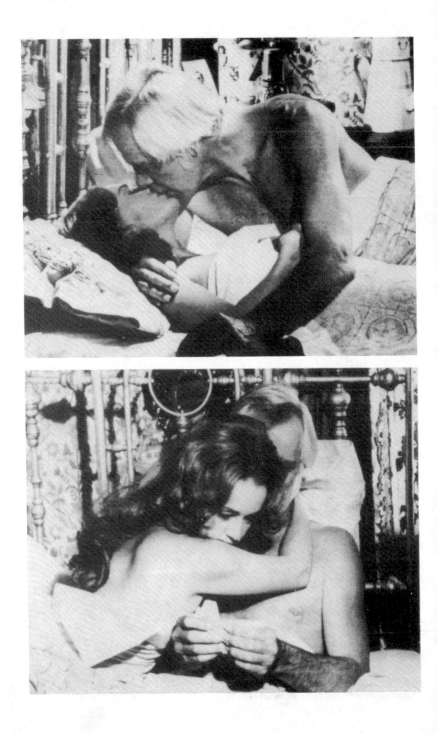

Facing page: The much-discussed love scenes on *Monte Walsh,* 1970. Lee Marvin with Jeanne Moreau (Courtesy Cinema Center)
Left: Lee Marvin and the second Mrs Marvin, Pamela Feeley, eat the wedding cake in Las Vegas, 18 October 1970. (Courtesy Popperfoto)
Below: The nastiness lingers on. Marvin with Angel Tompkins in *Prime Cut,* 1972. (Courtesy Cinema Center)

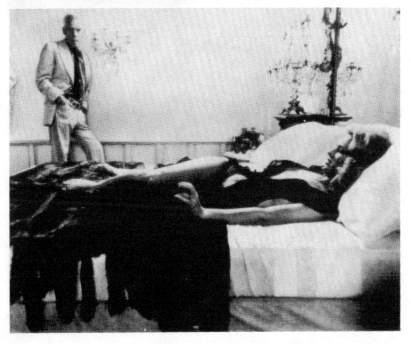

Right: Lee Marvin as Dixie Sheriff. *The Klansman*, 1974. (Courtesy Camera Press) Below: Let's be friends! Lee Marvin and Elizabeth Taylor on the set of *The Klansman*. (Courtesy Camera Press) Below right and facing page: Marvin and Burton: the blind leading the blind. Though both actors had their trouble during the shooting of *The Klansman*, they both bounced back. Oroville was less resilient. (Courtesy Camera Press and Paramount). All photos by Terry O'Neill

Top: Marvin and gun in *Great Scout and Cathouse Thursday,* 1976. (Courtesy Universal Pictorial Press)
Above: Lee Marvin (with Pamela) arriving at an LA courtroom, 9 January 1979, to face (right) Michele Triola's historic court action.
Facing page: Marvin on the set of The Big Red One, 1979 . . . Now on the longest dry-run of his career. (Courtesy *Daily Mirror*)

Above: 'That craggy decency' — Lee Marvin the actor and the man. (Courtesy *Daily Mirror*)

add one more ingredient. If Lee Marvin doesn't go to Colorado, I don't go. So you don't have a star and you don't have a director and this film will be closed down within twelve hours, and you know it.' To this day I don't know whether Lee knows what took place.

The first real scene he had was with Jane Fonda, Micky Callan and Swayne Hickman, as he tries to shoot the side of a barn door. Poor Kid Shelleen is so hungover he hits the weather-vein instead, and he gets called drunk by one of the kids. He then launches into an aria which was one of my favourites, about the Old West and how men like him had been respected. It is a defence against what he considered to be slurring attacks on his character. I bought a boat and called it *Take Eight* because of what happened that day – which was the third day into shooting. Lee was coming out inch by inch, which was the right way to do it – going into unknown territory. I was the only audience he had and I was uncertain at what point the character would emerge . . . I was waiting for that instinctive bell to ring.

We were up to Take Five. The producer, who was watching, called me over and asked me to take a break. He told me he was very nervous, that he was right and Lee wasn't doing anything. I said, 'He is, he is.' I had to try explaining again, that we were going into space – you didn't make that jump with absolute conviction. It would take a little time to get built up. He said, 'I think Lee's magnificent.' I said, 'That's a contradiction. First you say he's not doing anything, now you say he's magnificent.' He said, 'Well you're a half-a-day behind.' I didn't take the time to try to analyse that just then. If they would take away the picture from me because I was a half-a-day behind, then they would take it away from the producer too. I said, 'I can't trouble myself with that at the moment.'

Take Six worked rather well for the crew, they all laughed like crazy. I didn't laugh and that worried me somewhat. The crew, who were aware of the personal aspects of an actor's character, will see him working at it and will laugh. It's very bad. It doesn't really do what it's supposed to do. I didn't find it very funny. I therefore had to take the bit in my own mouth and say, 'Well, you know they laugh at anything.' I suppose that's what they call being difficult. So I was again called over by the producer. I said, 'I'm not going to come next time you call me.' He said, 'You've got to come.' I said, 'Lee, who is going out on this unknown territory – he's going to get very insecure if he sees on every take that you're calling me over and talking to me.' He said, 'I'll throw a stone and that'll be a signal.' I said, 'No, I'm sorry. There isn't any more time for doing this.' So again he persisted. And again I said I can't be bothered.

We went on to Take Seven. Everything was still pretty tough. Lee was still more of a typical Western hero than an a-typical Western hero. He was a strong man. We weren't reaching the level of inanity that we both hoped for. I was beginning to get worried a bit and so was Lee because it wasn't coming. Now the Production Manager came over and I recognised I'd been out-manoeuvred by the producer because I'd said I wouldn't talk to him again, so he sent a surrogate and the Production Manager threw his arm around me and said they'd just received a telephone call and that either I moved ahead or I was going to be fired. And I said, 'You're lying, number one. And number two, I'll take the challenge and I'll give you my reasons, and whoever told you to take this message to me, you tell him what I said. If they take me off the set right now, it'll be three days before another director can get up here and I defy anyone else to make sense of this material at this point, with the wigs and costumes and music and preparations all laid out. So that is going to cost you five, six, seven, ten times as much as allowing me to continue. So I'm ignoring you. You take that message back.' He said, 'Listen kid, I'm trying to tell you something . . .' Now Lee was waiting very patiently. I never asked him, but if he was getting annoyed he had every right to be. Every time he'd do something there was a major conference of some kind.

On the way back to the set I was headed off by the pro-ducer who was practically pleading with me now. I had done seven takes and I could see that the result of this was de-moralising. It was demoralising to me so it had to be demoral-ising for others too. So I struck a faithful deal, saying, 'All right, one more take and we'll see what happens.' He said, 'What do you mean, see what happens? No more after this one take.' I said, 'Okay, one more.' I went up to Lee and all he said was, 'What's happening, kid?' I told him what hap-pened back in the studio and said, 'They don't understand.' He said, 'What are we gonna do?' We were muttering to-gether and I was trying to think fast. Then I decided to take one last shot and go a hundred and eighty degrees in the opposite direction. I said, 'Lee, I tell you what. Let's not try to be funny. Make me cry this time, don't try to make me laugh.' That was the scene where the kids who had hired him to come and protect Cat Ballou from the gunfighter, are mocking him. 'Let's see what kind of a hero you've got there. Let's see what kind of a great gunfighter he is.' He reaches for his gun and he doesn't have any gun. One of the kids says, 'All right, here's a gun, take this one – it's a good gun.' And Lee looks at the gun and looks at the barn as though it is a million miles away, and then he fires at the target which is on the barn door, and the weather-vein spins around and the boys are laughing and Cat Ballou seems despondent, and the insults eventually force him into that aria about how nobody respects the Western heroes any more.

So I said, 'Let's not try to make that funny. Make it sad, make me cry. When they call you drunk, instead of turning round in anger, turn round in great pain and look at them. When you look at the barn door, instead of mightily trying to find that barn door in the target, play it like 'What barn door? What are they talking about, where's there a target, where's there a barn? Where am I?' So he said, 'Okay,' and I remember giving him a slap on the back and saying, 'Go all the way this time.' Neither one of us had anything to lose. He grunted. And he did it. And that was the eighth take. That was the character that he played the rest of the way and the one he got the Academy Award for and the one that got me my boat.

But it was still not all plain sailing for Mr Silverstein. Two things happened after Lee's scene. The production manager came over and congratulated both director and actor. Followed by an instruction that,

we'd got to undo all the make-up because they'd paid X-amount of dollars for Lee Marvin and they couldn't see him under the wig, hair and make-up. You know the old Hollywood thinking. I said, 'No, we can't take the make-up off. We've already shot him in that scene.

'Well, you're gonna have to change the actor or change the director if you don't take off the make-up. We want to see Lee Marvin!'

Again there were threats of firing me, firing him, or firing somebody . . . and I had no choice but to believe that they were bluffing because to accept it would have meant to change whatever I had going for me. To reject it, logic said to me, would cost them more money than I was spending. The film came in pretty close to budget. But Lee had a chance to pay back my protection of him, because I understand that the

producer went around after that, when my professional
demise was expected momentarily, asking individual cast
members, including Lee, whether they could get along with
another director. Lee said, 'No . . . he's got a concept. I don't
know what it is, but he's got a concept.'

Lee was in every sense a leading actor. He established an
atmosphere. He played very well. He was very generous to
Jane. She had a very tough job to do because she was aware
that he was getting a lot of laughs and she had to maintain
this kind of solid, credible centre to the picture and resist
going for big laughs. If she'd tried to be comic too the whole
picture would have gone adrift. I really care about one aspect
of an actor, ultimately, and that is whether he has professional discipline. I'm often told that actors are frightened.
They are frightened. I'm told they're often paralysed with
fear . . . so they are. These are things directors have to deal
with and work with. But the true measure of a professional, I
think, is the recognition that he isn't the only one that's afraid.
Everyone's afraid. And the test is whether he can control it. I
remember I wrote Lee a little message on a photograph I had
taken while we were looping – a photograph of him sitting on
a horse with its legs crossed, and the little legend I wrote
across it was: 'To a Man For All Seasons'. The reference
really was, that I thought he had an enormous amount of guts
to take the kind of chance he was taking. The results weren't
known yet at that time. But he did have an extraordinary
amount of courage . . . and skill! It wasn't simply personality.

In the middle of one scene his pants were supposed to slip
and he was supposed to reach down and pull them up. Well
he was so into it that his pants fell and he didn't pick them
up, and those were the days when there were always these
weird and paralysing questions of taste. I thought it was riotously funny but I was worried . . . 'Pick 'em up . . . pick 'em
up!' I was yelling. He stood there roaring his speeches and
let the pants stay down . . . and eventually I realised he was
right and I was wrong. He just ignored me and he was right.
At that time there were directors who told me they'd had
difficulty with Lee. Production departments told me they'd
had difficulties with him. So what? I've had experiences with
actors who are difficult and strident and egomaniacal and
just plain professionally undisciplined. But I detected a softness in Lee. He knew what I was having to take. Tremendous
loyalty there. Shooting took twenty-eight days. Then there
were two additional days afterwards, at Mike Frankovich's
request to enhance some of the sequences. Mike supported

me continually throughout. That film would not have been half the film it was if it hadn't been for him. I am not the lover of guys who sit in front offices. But I cannot imagine any Head of Production doing more of what a director thinks a Head of Production should do, than Mike Frankovich did for me.

I do remember one notice that I liked – that the film could have gone either into an art house or a commercial theatre. But Pauline Kael? Well she can't laugh too well. She doesn't know how to laugh (Kael, one of the few dissenting voices in the chorus of superlatives, called it 'uneven, lumpy, coy and obvious').

What were my emotions on Oscar night? The same as Frank Pierson's. He was very pained that Lee gave none of us any particular acknowledgement. I've not spoken to Walter Newman so I don't know about him. But I understood. This was Lee fighting sentiment. Trying to hide emotion. That resulted in Frank saying . . . I don't want to misquote him now . . . how did he put it? 'The half of the horse in the Valley that night was the head!'

Well it was Lee Marvin's movie and his triumph. Virtually overnight he was no longer a 'problem actor' but a performer the banks would gladly lend money on – the sacred criterion. Not that the film was the unflawed masterpiece it was cracked up to be. Launched as the 'definitive satire' on the Western, the piece seemed oddly empty at its centre. But it had some richly funny ideas and a few set-piece interludes that were brilliant. Among the gems was Marvin's balletic preparations for the final shoot-out, played like the solemn ritual before a bullfight. Sliding an arm through the 'Suit of Lights', trigger finger extended, was like Manolete being installed inside Alcoholics Anonymous.

If ever a film struck oil by one inspired shot, it was the one of the horse leaning cross-legged against the saloon wall with the seemingly pie-eyed Marvin slumped atop of it. It was an astute idea to freeze it momentarily thus giving added verve to the burlesque that followed. Kid Shelleen's booze-dependency, played here for laughs, is caught by Marvin as to the manner born. It has to be conceded that nobody can quite play a drunk like Marvin. He clinched the point afterwards with his usual candour: 'Let's face it, I've been training for the role for years.'

133

Yet it was more than type-casting. Marvin's finesse as an actor enabled him to time his laugh lines to the split second. His soliloquy on the West that had gone, adroitly, and movingly, counterpointed the film's raucous overtones.

During the production, though they sparked off each other as performers, Marvin and Jane Fonda established little personal rapport. To Marvin, Jane came on too strongly as 'the star'. When her lover-turned-husband, the French director Vadim, visited the Colorado location, Marvin reacted testily.

'Who's this?' he asked a crew man.

'Roger Vadim.'

'What's he doing on the set?'

'Just visiting Jane.'

'Well I think he'd better wait someplace else. One director on the set is enough.'

Marvin was not playing the temperamental actor. It was a show of support for Eliot Silverstein. (There are several examples of Marvin's loyalty to directors under fire which explain why they'll take all his misdemeanours short of Murder One.) 'We were under a lot of heat in the picture,' Marvin frowned. 'They were all over Silverstein's ass which was very unfair. So I wasn't going to see him take anything he didn't need to.'

It is customary for actors nominated for the Oscar to adopt a public stance of faint disapproval. Marlon Brando and George C. Scott are the most celebrated examples. Secretly relishing the professional distinction while publicly disdaining its most prestigious symbol. Marvin didn't go quite so far. When his name was included in the 'Best Actor' nominations, he retreated behind his usual holding pattern of 'Pop . . . wheee . . . and Kavoom!' Privately he was sweating on the top line, never seriously believing he would win but thrilled at the prospect that he might. Michelle Triola remembered that he was 'terribly nervous the evening of the Awards. And when Lee is nervous he sort of does strange things to conceal it. They had put Lee in an aisle seat which is what they usually do for nominees. Makes it easier for them to get out. He was two rows in front of Rod Steiger (nominated for *The Pawnbroker*). As he walked past him Lee said to Rod, "You know why they put me two rows ahead of you? Because when they call your name I am . . . going . . . to . . . stick . . . my . . . big . . . foot . . . out . . . and you . . . are going . . . to . . . fall . . . on . . . your . . . ass!" '

As the ceremony went through the lesser awards Lee became so jumpy he ignored the 'No Smoking' sign and furtively lit up, then bent down to blow the smoke out under Michelle's chiffon skirt. Now and again he came up for oxygen, smiled benignly at a baffled usher, then dived under the skirt again. He was half-way out of his mistress's smoke-wreathed thighs when he heard his name called. He leapt forward with far more eagerness than he accepted his Purple Heart in the Pacific. It was then he made his 'horse in the Valley' speech. The gale of laughter swept him out into a night of celebration which Kid Shelleen would have conceded an all-time record. At home with the family, Betty Marvin shared in the general jubilation. She also discovered with slight annoyance, that she was crying. She had loved, fought, indulged and sustained Lee on the long rough ride to the top. But it was Michelle Triola there beside him to share in the ultimate ovation. There was no trace of hurt in her congratulations, nor lack of understanding in Lee's response to them. He knew how much he owed Betty.

Meyer Mishkin, his agent, radiated the ecstasy that comes with the knowledge that a client's 'going rate' had soared over-night into the half-million-dollar-plus bracket. Producers and studio chiefs who had previously backed off unwilling to gamble on Marvin, would now come running – such is the magic of this cheaply-cast, simulated gold statuette. Mishkin had brought Lee in from New York fifteen years earlier, on a hunch. The consensus then was that Marvin's pug-ugly features and rock-blasting style would take him no further than second heavy in a thick-eared thriller. They were wrong. It was Marvin up on the stage not Olivier or Burton. Mishkin was entitled to his ten per cent of the glory. Perhaps more. But he knew his tippling friend only too well. Marvin fighting his way up was one thing. The same character with the actor's biggest ace up his sleeve and a bottle in his hand was altogether a different kind of onslaught.

The day after Lee Marvin walked away with the Oscar, scripts came in by the score. Mishkin scrutinised them as care-fully as he did the directors who were offered with them. Talent aside, they would need to know how to take Marvin's spectacular liquor intake and the loud-mouthed cussedness that occasionally came with it, and make it all work for the movie. Director Richard Brooks, who could be as easily intimidated as the Boston Strangler, seemed dead on target for this bed of nails. If anyone could take on this one-man fracas named Lee Marvin it was this bone-hard, closely-cropped film-maker. He also had the bonus of a sharp intellect and the insight of a trained analyst. He needed them both on the approaching Mexican adventure with Mister Marvin.

Chapter Ten

'I don't care if they prefer goats, or women or men so long as they stay out of gaol and are in shape to work . . . '

Richard Brooks

With Lee Marvin, plus Oscar, 'hot' as the word is in the trade, Columbia, who were making a packet out of *Cat Ballou*, could hardly wait to get the actor into another movie. They had the story, *The Professionals*, based on Frank O'Rourke's novel *A Mule for the Marquesa*. The script was ready. So too was the man who wrote it and who would direct the film, Richard Brooks. Claudia Cardinale, who may have weighed in a pound or two less than Sophia Loren but not in the essential areas, had already been signed. True she was Italian while the woman in the piece was Mexican. But with those large eyes and frigate-class bosoms the point seemed trifling. She was cast as the kidnapped wife of a millionaire rancher who hires a consortium of mean but skilled mercenaries to bring her back. Brooks had a clear notion of the players he wanted for the film's key roles. He had directed Burt Lancaster in *Elmer Gantry* and wanted him for this meaty epic *The Professionals*. Brooks knew he could count on Lancaster to turn in his usual unerring performance. And as disciplined as the best of the Hollywood veterans, Burt would give Brooks an easy ride on the production. Lancaster read the book and assumed he would play the role which eventually fell to Lee Marvin, that of the leader of the group. Brooks swiftly put him right.

137

'Oh no, that won't work Burt. That's no good at all.'
Lancaster's square-cut smile faded fast.

'How d'you figure that out, Richard?' he asked.

Brooks didn't fool around. 'Because Burt,' he said cheerily,
'when you give orders with your stiff upper lip and all that shit
you're *boring*. This guy (the character Brooks had pencilled in
for Lancaster) he's a dynamiter, he's a clown, he's funny!'

'Dynamiter?' Lancaster said, baffled, 'there's no dynamiter in
the book.'

'I know, but there will be by the time we get to do the movie.'

Lancaster wavered. He wanted to know what his character
was like. 'Like you, Burt,' Brooks said, ladling out the apple
sauce. 'He's funny, and good at his job, and a hell of a pro.'

'Okay,' Lancaster nodded, 'as long as we start by October.
Who's gonna play the other guy?'

'Well they're talking about Lee Marvin. He's under contract
here to Columbia and he probably is good. I dunno. I'll meet
him and we'll find out. But it's all going to be okay.'

Brooks drove off for his meeting with Marvin his thoughts,
he told me, running like this:

He's been around for a long time, playing, until recently,
second banana, the feller who gets shot by the hero. If it
wasn't Jimmy Stewart who was killing him it was John
Wayne, or Marlon Brando, or Tracy or somebody. True he'd
just delivered a delicious performance in *Cat Ballou*. People
were beginning to write about him, and spell his name right
and think about him seriously. And hell, he *had* won the
Oscar for the best actor of the year. Yep, Marvin would be
great if he could fix it.

The two met, Brooks selling, Marvin wary. Brooks remembered Marvin was curiously self-conscious at first.

He had this diffident manner. You know how he plays the
shit-kicker all the time. He has this great physical appearance
and the marvellous voice. But underneath, he's watching you,
wondering why you *really* want him. I mean do you really
care about him or don't you? He sensed something big was
breaking in his career but he wasn't sure what, so he was kind
of cynical. He wanted to make sure he was his own man.
Which was fine by me because I'm in no popularity contest
myself.

Marvin stared hard at Brooks with his all-purpose take-it-anyway-you-like sneer.

'I hear you're very difficult to work with. What are you, some kind of tough guy?'

Brooks let the flak slide past his ear. 'No, not tough, but I have a certain way of making a movie and if you wanna be in it fine. If you don't wanna be in it say so, and stop playing games, because that's a waste of time.'

Round One to Brooks.

'No, I'd like to be in,' Marvin said. 'What do I do, play one of the stooges?'

'No,' Brooks replied evenly, 'you're not the stooge. You're the feller who gives the orders.'

'I like that. Who do I give the orders to?'

'Burt Lancaster for openers.'

Lee Marvin liked that even more. Brooks got him for the picture. But he'd heard all the stories and did not delude himself that life was going to be easy with the liquor-happy Oscar winner, particularly when pitched against Burt Lancaster, Robert Ryan and Jack Palance. But Brooks's capacity to handle tough subjects and abrasive performers could hardly be questioned after a glance at some of his earlier films: *The Blackboard Jungle* (Glenn Ford); *Cat On A Hot Tin Roof* (Elizabeth Taylor, Paul Newman); *Lord Jim* (Peter O'Toole); *The Brothers Karamazov* (Yul Brynner). Brooks's general philosophy on how much hogwash directors should have to take from actors may not be the definitive handbook on the subject but it's worth a hearing.

The first function of a director if he's going to make a movie with a difficult actor is that he's going to have to learn to eat shit and maybe enjoy it. It's not all sitting in a chair and calling through a loud horn telling people what to do. You have to take the crap and you have to compromise. I compromise nine thousand times a day. I won't compromise on the two times it really matters. That is to say you don't change the story or the content or the meaning of the piece to please anybody. But compromise? Jesus you take care of this guy's drinking and that feller's girlfriend; and somebody doesn't want his wife out there; somebody wakes you at two in the morning wanting you to babysit with them – or 'we can't work unless we have a certain jockstrap'; and this guy says, 'if the wife comes in I'm not going to work any more, I'm leaving.' There are a hundred such nonsenses. But you take it because you want to make a movie, and with God's help and a couple of good performances, maybe a good one. So when they told me about Marvin I said I didn't give a damn what he or anybody did from the time we stop shooting to the moment we start again in the morning – as long as they're in shape to work. And as long as they keep out of gaol in between. What their personal habits are, they are. I don't care if they prefer goats or women or men, or are asexual, bisexual or play the whole Freudian book.

So much for Brooks on Directing. But how did it work with Marvin?

Well promisingly enough, with Lee as always studying his part alone until he was sure he knew how the character moved, talked, thought and sweated. And always the perfectionist. At the costume fittings Brooks said to him, 'You can't wear those leggings, Lee.'

'Why not?' Lee snapped back, 'they're legitimate.'

'Maybe, but you can't wear them, you look like a boy scout or a Western Union messenger.'

The confrontation lasted fifteen loaded seconds. 'Okay,' Marvin finally said, 'have it your way.'

Despite that, Brooks allowed that Lee knew more about weaponry than any other actor he'd worked with. 'And I'll tell you something else. He is mentally agile to an extraordinary degree, knowing how to read a script, and how to integrate his role with others – and himself with others.'

So Brooks had high hopes for Marvin and *The Professionals* when the unit moved on to the first location at Las Vegas.

There are certain places high on the playful movie stars' list of favourite film locations. The 'action' in London, Rome, Bangkok, Tokyo and Taipeh is so eager and thick on the ground actors have been known to check the location first, script last. Las Vegas, the hedonist's idea of heaven, is among the top seeds. It brought out the demon in Lee Marvin. The fact that the woman he'd married there was now suing him for divorce couldn't have helped. Moreover a town given over exclusively to drinking and gambling – neither activity unfamiliar to Marvin – was bound to engage his non-working hours. The crap tables, the robot-lines of slot machines, the garish Disneyland casino-hotels, the hookers and the high-rollers; the euphoria as night slides imperceptibly into day and just as subtly into darkness again – no question a Las Vegas movie location was better than shooting *M-Squad* in a grimy backstreet of Chicago. So Lee Marvin, acting out his public persona amused himself occasionally by shooting out some of the twinkling lights on the Strip. Or, the misdemeanour which got him arrested by the police, shooting steel-tipped arrows at a huge animated sign across the street from his hotel. This is the famous one of the giant, fat-mouthed cowboy who beams down to the passing throng with a twenty-four hour non-stop delivery of 'Howdy stranger . . . howdy stranger . . . howdy stranger . . .' To Marvin, one hot and fuddled evening, it was more than any human should have to take. Well any more than Lee could take. He had a long-bow and some steel-tipped arrows. Aligning his aim, he let loose a quiver-full of arrows right into that brash, cavernous mouth. Trouble was, like Kid Shelleen, some of the shots went wide. Passers-by complained that Indians were attacking the Strip. The cops accepted Marvin's plea of 'provocation', collected his autograph and let him go. A slightly different version of this affair was to be heard in Michelle's celebrated court action years later. If Las Vegas could take that kind of jape Richard Brooks, who can raise a little hell of his own, was unlikely to run a sweat over it. It was Marvin's work pattern that mattered. Here, Brooks found, as he had feared he might, that he had a problem.

Now, at the beginning of the picture I never noticed anything wrong with Lee. He behaved like the pro he is, giving me everything I needed, sometimes with a bonus. He had two people who were his constant companions, Michelle, and a big fellow who maybe was a sort of bodyguard. Anyway we were about three weeks into the movie, a difficult area of work, and as hot as hell. We started to rehearse and I realised something was wrong. What was wrong was that Marvin, well, he was tanked up. He was beginning to miss his marks, miss his lines, miss the intention of the scene. I took him aside and we talked for a few moments. He said, 'Oh bullshit! Jeezus, just because I'm not the big star. Are we all supposed to be Lancasters? What is this? Is it because he's the star. Is that what it is?'
    I said, 'You're drunk, aren't you?'
    Lee said, 'That doesn't change anything does it? It's still the truth isn't it?'

I said, 'No, it's not the truth at all. You're being disrespectful to *all* the people around, not just Burt Lancaster because you think he's the star, but to everybody else. And it won't work that way.' He said, 'Well, that's the way it is, isn't it baby?'

We finished the scene. That was about eleven o'clock in the morning. I called my assistant director, a marvellous guy called Tom Shaw over and I said, 'Tom, get this sonofabitch back to his hotel.' It was about a hundred miles away from the location. 'He can't work for the rest of the day.' It was a Friday. I said, 'Get that friend of his to dry him out, get him to bed, otherwise he's not going to be any good on Monday.' I'd heard that usually after a Saturday night and Sunday night he'd be okay by Monday morning. I had never seen him like that and candidly the stuff he'd shot that day was no good. Tom said, 'Well I don't know if I can get him in the car.' I said, 'Well, if it takes more than one guy, get more than one.' And sure enough the moment Tom went over to talk to him Lee came back over to me and said, 'What the hell's the matter with you? I don't want to go back to the hotel. I'm out here to work. What are you trying to do, say I can't work?'

'Yes, that's what I'm saying. You can't work. You're abusive and worse than that, your performance is no good.' Lee said, 'Oh, you gonna tell me about acting!' I told him, 'Your performance stinks, and that's no good, Lee. Go back to your hotel and go to sleep.' [Brooks, narrating the tale in a house on Coldwater Canyon, Beverly Hills, laughed as he recalled the second chapter.] Well they got Lee into the car, back to the hotel, and into bed. He didn't want to stay there. That night after shooting, Woody Strode went there and sat on Lee. Actually it took several people to sit on him. Woody, his wife who is no small creature, Michelle and Lee's friend. They sort of took turns. The plan worked. On Monday morning he arrived on the location. I called him aside. It was about 7.30am, the sun was bright enough for us to shoot. I showed Lee a small can of film, not more than about a hundred feet in it. I looked at Lee, and I spoke to him.

'You know, Lee, in this can is the negative . . . *THE NEGATIVE* . . . of Friday's work. Your work. The sequence you were working on on Friday morning. If anyone ever sees this, if a print is made of it, you know what this could mean. You are at a turning point in your career. If anybody has a chance to go all the way, it's you. You've got it. You've put in as much time as Bogie put in. Bogie played George Raft's brother-in-law for seven years, nothing else, at Warner

Brothers. He always lost the girl. Ann Sheridan always ran off with somebody else. Dennis Morgan got the girl and Bogie was killed in a car crash, eaten by lions, or whatever. He was still relegated, and that was after he'd played *Petrified Forest* on Broadway and in the movie. He had to fight to break out. Well you've paid your dues the same way, Lee. You're just becoming attractive enough to be lovable. That doesn't mean you have to be sweet, because you'll never be that. You'll always be a sonofabitch with that craggy face of yours. But you're interesting. You don't have to prove anything to anyone now. You're good. You're ready. That's what you've wanted all your life. Well you've got it. Don't throw it away. Big guys don't have to hit little guys to prove they're big guys. You know it. I know it. Now you have a problem. If you can handle it and do your work nobody is going to sweat. Now I'm going to burn this film. I'm going to burn this negative right here, in front of you. Don't ever do what you did the other day.'

He said, 'What if I do?' 'Then,' I said, 'you'll have to go.' He asked me, 'What about the stuff you've shot so far?' I said, 'I'll reshoot it. Or I'll find a way to kill you off in the story. But I won't go through this and I won't put others through it either. I can't make a movie this way. It's too tough. It's tough enough if everything is on your side. Fifty per cent of the time you're going to fail anyway. So why stack the deck against us?' Lee looked at me and he said, 'Is that really the negative?' I opened the can and unrolled the film. So the deal was struck. I burned the negative right in front of him. He went to work. Never had another rough moment with him.

Marvin's growth as an actor, he was jettisoning most of the 'sadistic killer' image, shows in *The Professionals*. As the leader of the rescue mission it is he who calls the shots over Burt Lancaster and Robert Ryan, actors not usually given to taking orders in movies. Marvin does it with style, and without the customary show of muscle. The power is all cerebral, relying on deep vocal subtleties, the tone pitched so low at times, it's like a tape run at the wrong speed. His strength and dominance is all in the eyes. That crooked, slack-mouthed smile is all threat and imprisoned violence. To this Marvin adds the bonus of a high degree of skill with horses and with guns. Required to handle a shot-gun for one scene, Lee took hold of it, said to Brooks: 'This won't work. It's not good enough, and it's the

wrong one. I've got the real McCoy back home.' Brooks put
back the scene, had someone fly to Los Angeles, drive to Lee's
home and bring the gun back.

For all that, *The Professionals,* while being visually stunning and as entertaining as the best piece of hokum on offer,
remains a flawed work. The big names barge self-consciously
into the plot with each having to be given equal time to get his
'caper' over. Of the hard-bitten professionals (Marvin, Ryan,
Woody Strode) Ryan comes out the most sympathetic. (As
an obsessive horse-lover preferring to kill men than stallions
he's bound to win points with a large chunk of the audience.)
But he looks less sure against Marvin than Burt Lancaster who
has never had a film filched from him yet. When they weren't
shooting, 'the wild bunch', as Brooks and his players were
called, were amiable drinking buddies. They had the common
denominator of military service. Marvin in the Marines, Private
First Class. Brooks, Marines, Private First Class. Ryan, Marines
Private First Class. Lancaster, the US Army, Private First Class.
The irony of it didn't escape Marvin. 'All those millions riding
on the backs of Pfcs. Makes you wonder whatever happened
to the generals!' Behind the rivet-spitting façade, Marvin displayed the professional's concern for the smaller-fry in the
business. Claudia Cardinale, though arrestingly contoured in the
sunsets and shadows of the Mexican plains was no great
horserider and Marvin was genuinely concerned that she might
get hurt. He taught her the rudiments, led her horse around on
a bridle, and though often not in the shot, stayed around in case
he was needed.

The film had mixed reviews including this withering comment
from Pauline Kael: 'It has the expertise of a cold old whore
with practised hands and no thoughts of love.' Well the old
whore made a mint of money and helped put Marvin among
the ten biggest box office stars of the year. He had also been
named by the British Film Academy as the year's Best Foreign
Actor. Likewise by the National Board of Review and at the
Berlin Film Festival. He had broken through the money barrier.
Marvin was 'bankable'. Come wind, rain, or a crate of Jack
Daniels, he, and Meyer Mishkin, could choose his subjects,
instead of standing in line for what was on offer. If the successful afterglow resulted in Michelle Triola sometimes having to
prop him up, spread him out, or give him the ice-pack-and-

black-coffee treatment, what is love all about? She saw her role as a combo featuring a passionate mistress, Earth Mother, protector and nurse – in short, a wife in everything bar the documentation.

On the Las Vegas location she walked in on Lee during a big game of blackjack and broke it up – not very funny to the spread-nosed fraternity of Nevada. Nor was it the smartest trick to pull on a man whose public image and private inclinations relegated the female to the bed and kitchen-sink departments. But she explained it this way:

When I walked in the hotel Lee was playing wildly with a lot of money riding on each card. Just for the absolute belligerence of the thing he was trying to hit on eighteen, nineteen, even twenty. I mean he had one chance in a million of pulling in the right card. Well I watched it for a while. Then I felt this was absurd. So I went over and put my hands flat out on the table.

In Bugsy Siegel's day they'd have been pinned there with ice-picks. The effect was paralysing. The dealer went into shock. Eyes fixed on Michelle in disbelief. 'Mr Marvin is not playing,' she declared in Judgement Day tones. 'No further cards will be delivered to him at this table.' But she didn't stop there.

I was so bloody mad, I reached over and grabbed the whole pile of chips which I thought belonged to Lee, shovelled them into my purse and marched off towards the elevator. Now there is the manager, four security guards, a couple of the blackjack players all chasing after me. It seems I picked up the pot money and they don't like you to do that in Las Vegas.

As for Marvin, who used his capacity for overkill responses sparingly, he just wrote it all down to the hazards of man-woman relationships. 'It's the commitment that kills you,' he once said to me. 'When they've got you on the hook you're going to be beaten, balls and all!' Typical Marvin overstatement. But challenge him on it and he's likely to deliver anything from his standard lecture on Marriage and the Emasculation of the Male, to a homily to hookers, like this stirring defence of whorehouses, made to the writer Richard Warren Lewis in *Playboy*:

I used to find an honesty there that I never understood before. You pay for your happiness or your pleasure; and in a properly conducted house of ill-repute they make it very pleasurable indeed. There is no sadness involved. There is no going beyond the reality. You know what you're there for and so does the hooker. There is no initial commitment, only a commitment on your exit.

Before *The Professionals* wrapped in the desert, Marvin received a visit from the two men who both wanted him for *The Dirty Dozen*. The producer was Kenneth Hyman, one of the new young lions of Hollywood. With him was Robert Aldrich, a large, gritty extrovert, raised in the 'no-crap-from-anyone' school of directing. He'd had a short course on Lee Marvin in *Attack*. It was he who convinced Ken Hyman that Marvin was custom-made for *The Dirty Dozen*. It was some assignment. He would play Major Reisman, a truculent Army misfit who would take twelve 'volunteers', a hand-picked band of death-cell criminals and life-sentenced psychopaths on a suicide mission to blow up a chateau in Brittany, stiff with Nazi officers. These include a Bible-quoting sex maniac, lasciviously portrayed by Telly Savalas; a black murderer (Jim Brown); and a small-time hood (John Cassavetes). Hyman read the existing script, disliked it, and suggested to the studio, MGM, that he call in someone else to start again.

'Who d'you have in mind?' asked Robert O'Brien, then production chief at the studio.

'Nunnally Johnson.'

O'Brien frowned at his associate in the room. They cautiously registered amazement.

'You have to be kidding. He's a comedy writer,' one of them said.

Ken Hyman reacted mildly. 'Oh? All that funny stuff like *Grapes of Wrath*, *Tobacco Road*, and *The Desert Fox*?'

Nunnally Johnson wrote the script. Bob Aldrich thought it was a gem and saw only Marvin in the leading role. In the limousine on the highway out to the desert, he marked the young producer's card, on Marvin's form. 'Look, this feller is a pretty good boozer, he's got a short fuse, but he can be handled okay.' (Sending out storm warnings about the actor was becoming the standard exercise before every Marvin picture.)

Ken Hyman, born into the business, raised to the sound of clashing egos, remained unperturbed. He too had served with the US Marines. As a corporal. He reckoned he could handle Pfc Marvin. L. Their conference in the bar was quick, friendly, and successful. 'I have to go to England to make a picture,' Lee told Michelle that evening. She felt a brief tremor of uncertainty. She was due to leave for Hawaii on a ten-week singing engagement, Lee insisting that she carry on with her career. They parted, one going east, the other west. But when both had checked into their respective hotel rooms, the phone lines between London and Honolulu pulsated with 'I miss you, do you miss me!' endearments. The cost of these long, trans-Atlantic-Pacific love calls were astronomic, even to Marvin who was now on a hefty percentage of his films' profits. But all the vested interests, Metro, Aldrich and Hyman, were eager to keep him happy. Marvin, without Michelle around to sweeten the beast, posed problems.

A fortuitous piece of casting, of American actor Bob Phillips, in *The Dirty Dozen* allayed most of their fears. Apart from being a talented actor, Phillips had the advantage of being an ex-cop, was built like a tractor, and was said to have written a book called *Sixty Ways to Kill a Man With Your Bare Hands.* Whether that was true or not, Phillips was much in demand for Westerns, war movies, or gangster roles. As Damon Runyon said of Dave the Dude, 'He is certainly not a man to have sored up at you.' As a result of this happy coincidence, Ken Hyman knew he had hired a package deal of an actor, plus drinking partner and unofficial bodyguard to his unpredictable star. The reasoning was that Phillips would accompany Lee into a bar and in the event of Marvin being insulted or insulting somebody else but being too smashed to raise his hands against a punch, Phillips would catch the other guy's fist in mid-air and while not actually breaking it, might render it harmless for a week or so. 'Actually Bob is a very nice guy, a good actor, and a very useful character indeed,' Ken Hyman emphasised. 'In fact he did bale Lee out of a lot of pubs on several occasions.'

But there were certain 'Marvin incidents' early on in the production, over which neither Bob Phillips, nor the US Marines for that matter, could have had any control. Describing them, Ken Hyman wanted it to be understood that the incidents in no way diminished his admiration for Lee Marvin the actor. That posy delivered, the producer began:

> Lee is never vicious, but he can certainly be outrageous. There was this party one night in Belgravia. It had been on for about an hour-and-a-half when I arrived. The room was full of people. Lee was sort of sprawled out in a chair, you know, eight sheets to the wind but smiling. I must say Lee is a very happy drinker. He's not mean, never violent, never a bully, but . . . oh boy! Across the room from him is an elderly lady, seventyish, a real English lady. Sean Connery is there. Sean and I know each other, he made *The Hill* for me. And suddenly I hear – I mean almost everybody in the room hears – Lee saying to this lady across the floor – 'I bet you got the prettiest pink little clittie in the room'. He can't help himself. He's being outrageous. Well it turns out that this poor lady is a friend of Sean's aunt or mother or someone who had arrived with Sean. Connery turns white and starts to move across the room at Lee. I remember jumping up – Sean's half-a-head taller than me – grabbing him around the body and holding him, though we're still moving, and saying, 'Please Sean, we've got close-ups, hit him in the body! Don't touch his face. Please, not his face, Sean!' Maybe my panic not wanting Lee's face marked transmitted itself to Sean. Suddenly he starts laughing. I'm laughing too, and Lee is sitting there with a big smile on his face, not realising how close he'd come to having his face altered a little that night.

The records show that while everybody else at the party momentarily went into shock, no complaints verbal, or written, were made by the lady, who must have been in her seventies, at the centre of it all. While Ken Hyman, Bob Aldrich, and other film-makers were inclined to indulge Marvin's soused-up eccentricities, actors who did not hit the bottle on the same scale, felt no such obligation. Typical of these was Charles Bronson, a curt, taciturn character who had no taste for fooling around between takes. Divorced, miserable without Jill Ireland whom he later married, Bronson's tolerance of Big Star horseplay was fading fast. The climax of the film – the blowing up of the Nazi-held chateau – involved a night shot. Said Hyman:

> Bronson was in the sequence where he and Lee, in a giant weapons carrier, go across the bridge after the big explosion. Well Lee didn't show up. I left the studio and drove to

London, straight to the Star Tavern in Belgravia. Lee was hanging on at the end of the bar apparently as drunk as a skunk. Now he is the man who has to drive that vehicle across the bridge. I get him into the car, and feed him like a child from a flask of coffee. He's singing, telling punk jokes, like a big adorable kid, which would have been great if we hadn't got this big night shot waiting. We arrived on the set and got out of the car. Bronson was standing at the back of the chateau where he'd been waiting for Marvin to show up. We pulled in and Lee sort of fell out of the car. Charlie says, 'I'm going to fucking kill you, Lee!' or something like that. And I go through my routine again, 'Don't hit him Charlie – please don't punch him!'

Well I have to tell you Lee did drive that vehicle across the bridge. He always came through. There were several moments in the production when he probably couldn't have articulated his own name, but you'd never know it from the sure way in which he moved. He could always take direction regardless – look straight at the camera, hesitate, make a terrific exit – he never let liquor interfere with that. The other actors may have been wary of him, but they always allowed he had great professionalism. He never detracted from anybody else. He gave them as much as he gave me. It was when he was alone, lonely, that he'd take the old antidote. That's why we were glad when Michelle flew in to join him.

It was no sudden whim on Michelle's part. Lee phoned her in Hawaii, she said, with the ultimatum. 'You're going to have to make a decision, Michelle. I want you with me. If you're not here by July 15, forget the whole thing.' She took the first plane out to Los Angeles, then London. Their reunion began 'ten days of absolute bliss'. He took her to London's prestigious store, Fortnum and Mason, to buy her gloves, and 'afternoon tea', a ritual which Marvin muttered sent him into shock. They took time off to visit the ailing Vivien Leigh at her home in the country. She teased him mercilessly as she had done on *Ship of Fools*. And flirted with him too.

'Now if you talk about an attraction between a man and a woman, that was really something!' Michelle said. 'I wasn't jealous because I really loved her too. She had a room stacked with her awards, tributes, and signed photos from some of the most distinguished people in the world.' To Vivien, used to the Noel Coward-style adulation, to be told by Marvin, 'you're not a bad broad,' was a delicious turn-on. They drank, and played cards. In one wild, zesty moment, Lee grabbed the pack and ripped it in half. Vivien said nothing. Marvin learned afterwards, to his acute distress, that he'd destroyed a pack of rare seventeenth century playing cards. He and Vivien parted with a kiss, Michelle smiling approval from the sidelines. Lee Marvin knew when he left Vivien that day it would probably be for the last time. She died less than a year later. 'She was just one of the greatest . . . that's all,' was Marvin's sad comment. 'That face, that talent, Jeezus, I was grateful just to share the same planet with her. Oh hell, I guess we've all been robbed.'

They had of course talked about Laurence Olivier, once married to Vivien Leigh. Marvin shared every 'physical' actor's admiration for the world's most distinguished performer. They met not long after Vivien's death on a flight from London to Los Angeles. The scene, as Marvin told it to Roderick Mann, went like this:

We were in the lounge of the plane having a coupla drinks and there he sits wearing this Rolex watch. I know it's a Rolex because I have the same watch. Well, I tell you, I must need to relate to greatness real bad because sitting there sipping my Martini I find myself taking off my watch, my goddam expensive $350 Rolex and dropping it into his drink. 'Now you've got two of them,' I say. He kept it too.

Whether this account of the incident is as accurate as the watch has never been tested. No one is going to walk up to the world's finest actor and say, 'Excuse me, my Lord, do you happen to be walking around with Lee Marvin's watch?' In spite of Lee's irresistible attraction towards disaster, there were several bartenders in London genuinely sorry to see him go. Lee shared their regret. He felt a contentment in the London pubs he experienced nowhere else. 'Jeezus, they even pass out in a civilised fashion!' He said this over a lunchtime interview in Beverly Hills. That lush environment with its crisp napery and round-the-clock smiles from the black-tied gauleiters at the door, was not his scene.

I'm worse at the Beverly Hills Hotel. That's an area I don't want out of life. I mean I could never go to that place *without* getting drunk. Hell, you can find some real hustlers there, male and female. When the lunch hour is over and the wives

150

remain – wow, you have to get out of that bar because there ain't any good going to come out of it. And any man who is drinking there at three o'clock has obviously missed his trick for the day. So there's nothing healthy in it. And the dialogue isn't going to be about the ball game, the fish they caught, or civil rights, or anything like that. It's about conquests. Any kind of conquest. A chick, a deal, or a lawsuit. Winning is the name of the game. If you're losing, you better get out of the joint!

On those terms, Marvin was in particularly good shape. *The Dirty Dozen*, though it offended some critics – 'over-violent . . . basically meretricious', 'unlikeable slice of wartime thick-ear' – grossed $20 million in the US and was a similar blockbuster in Britain. *Time* Magazine was generous to the movie, even more so to Marvin. 'The film works . . . largely because of a fine cast and a taut plot . . . Director Robert Aldrich gets convincingly raw, tough performances in even the smallest roles. Marvin comes off best with his customary abrasive humour . . . ' The humour, however, is peripheral to the thrust of Marvin's performance which derives its impact from thoughtful underplay. Using little more than a twitch of an eye or cheek muscle, he transmits a chilling, below-the surface hint of authority and brutality. Few actors ever wore an army uniform with such steely assurance. If body language is basic to dramatic articulation, Marvin's has an eloquence all of its own. Projecting anger, he even contrives to drive the blood up into the back of his weather-creased neck. But even before the good word had got around about *The Dirty Dozen* several studios were jostling for the current Academy Award winner. There was an interesting approach from Toshiro Mifune, the legendary Japanese actor. This slightly-built but powerful, almost hypnotic star of *Rashomon* and *The Seven Samurai* was now a major figure in the world cinema.

Rashomon, first shown at the Venice Film Festival in 1951, made a stunning impact on Western audiences. Most of the filmgoers were seeing a Japanese film for the first time. The film won the Grand Prix of Venice and also the Oscar for the best foreign-language film of the year. It's director, Akira Kurosawa was thrown into the forefront of the world's film-makers. Ferociously handsome, revered as a national hero as well as a screen idol. Mifune had already tested the water a couple of

years earlier in Hollywood, playing the Japanese owner of a
racing-car team in John Frankenheimer's *Grand Prix*. It was
a limp, unsuccessful debut for the great warrior of the Japanese
movies. It was a compliment to Marvin that when the dust had
settled on that one, Mifune was ready to try again, this time with
an actor pitching the same kind of heroic masculinity.

He flew into London with a prodigious entourage of lawyers,
businessmen, and personal aides, and invited Lee to a dinner
discussion at the Dorchester Hotel. He spoke scant English.
Marvin had to speak through interpreters. Mifune knew that
Marvin, and the rest of the US Marines in Saipan, had killed
Japs with a passion. And Marvin knew that Mifune, born in
China, then switched to Japan and ultimately into its army, was
not about to apologise for World War II. But each intuitively
knew he was the other's kind of man. Or as Marvin said, 'Suddenly the dinner was over. I took him out and we went down
Curzon Street and hit a few of the clubs and gambling joints
and he dropped all the money he had and we got a little pissed
and that was that.'

As darkness fell outside the Dorchester Hotel the exaggerated
courtesies exchanged between the juiced Jap and his canned
American buddy was like an old silent comedy. Given a sharp
ceremonial sword and a steady eye and they'd have sealed their
comradeship in blood. But it was to take a year before that
heady, mutual admiration could be translated into *Hell In The
Pacific*. In the meantime Marvin was to announce to one and all
that Mifune was 'just about the most gutsy, honourable chunk
of talent in the whole frigging world'. Toshiro would like to have
been similarly eloquent. Trouble was, the English that Marvin
taught him that boozy night in Belgravia sunk without trace.
Somewhere between the crotch, and the big 'KAVOOM!'

Chapter Eleven

'You realise you have Lee Marvin on the roof
of your car?'
'Of course.'
'Well drive carefully.'

Back home from England in their beach-house on Malibu,
California, Lee and his resident mistress, Michelle Triola picked
up the threads again of the Hollywood life, Marvin-style. For
Michelle, this meant not batting an eyelid when the handle of
the Hudson Bay axe behind the bed would occasionally tap her
on the noggin during their love-making – a small price to pay,
Marvin grinned, for security against prowlers and things that
go bump in the night. If now and again he and his drunken
friends shot bullets at the bar glassware of the Pacific moon outside, it was usually all tidy and peaceful by the dawn's early
light. True, being half Marvin's size, she found lifting him, un-
aided, from the prone, pie-eyed position hard on her delicate
vertebrae.

But when you're Lee's woman that's what you have to do.
Unless you're very basic, earthy, able to listen to all the
profanities and have a great sense of the ridiculous, then
forget it! Lee always laid it on the line. Either you say 'Oh
my God!' and leave the room. Or you join in and have fun.
I joined in and had fun. You have to remember that Lee
could be enormously tender too.

She meant by this that he knew everything about butterflies,

153

birds, the fishes of the deep, and the wonders of nature. She remembers sitting on the sun deck watching the sun dancing on the Pacific waves when a butterfly settled on her dark hair. 'Don't move,' Marvin whispered, 'that is just about the most beautiful picture ever.' Then he gave her a brief rundown on the insect's short, bitter-sweet life, from the chrysalis to the final flutter. The tears welled in her eyes. And why not? It proved that the man who could urinate in a party hostess's favourite plant could still have a hint of poetry in his soul. But such reveries did not float too frequently into their Malibu scene. In this respect they were no different from several other celebrated twosomes, married or otherwise, along the beach. ('Gunshots, boozing, and everybody with someone else's wife – that's Malibu, brother,' said the colony's prime performer at the time.)

At night, when the empty bottles and the odd house-guest had been stashed away, Marvin and his mate would be lucky to have an uninterrupted sleep. Often around 2am there would be an assault on the house by the night drinkers eager to share their bottles with the all-time champ. The taxis would screech up to the driveway. There'd be a hammering on the door and, 'Hey Lee, what's goin' on man, let us in.' If Marvin was due to work early that morning he'd come to the door with that axe in his hand, towelling robe fluttering open in the breeze, the combined effect of which was daunting – and sobering. Then he'd give the cab drivers twenty bucks to take the callers back from whence they came. The incidents began to pall on Michelle as they had done on the first Mrs Marvin. 'I would have done anything for this man. I had such total belief in him and a very deep love,' Michelle says. 'But I have to admit there were times when I was totally exhausted. He literally ran me out.'

If Betty Marvin knew that Lee's affair was having a rough ride, it was to make no difference to her plans for divorce. Any hope of a reconciliation was killed the moment Lee and Michelle moved in together. On 5 January 1967, at Santa Monica, California, she divorced Marvin on grounds of extreme cruelty. He was ordered to pay her $6,000 a month alimony and $1,000 in child support. Betty was given custody of their four children, Christopher then fourteen, Courtenay eleven, Cynthia nine, and Claudia seven. It was a gloomy day for them all. No consolation that a Hollywood divorce was about as unusual as collecting a police ticket on the highway. No particular comfort that it had been a quick clean fight in the court-room. Marvin was lucky in this respect. A less worldly, more embittered wife, could have pinned the judge's – and Holly-wood's – ears back with lurid tales of her life with Doctor Jekyll and Mister Marvin. But she chose otherwise. No mud was thrown by either party. As Lee Marvin said afterwards:

> I thought the divorce settlement was extremely just. I found the courts to be overly fair, almost detrimental to the woman. When a guy's been balling a chick his responsibility towards her should be up to him. I knew what I had to do and did it. I made my ex-wife financially secure, as she had been in the past thereby allowing her the freedom to seek other interests in her life.

No question but that Lee Marvin did all that. It had been more than fifteen years since that wild wedding ceremony at the Wee Kirk O' the Heather in Las Vegas. 'There will always be scars for both of us,' Betty says softly, 'but two people don't stay together for all that time unless the good outweighs the bad. Anyway four children is a pretty good example of together-ness!' The divorce left Marvin free to marry Michelle. They discussed the possibility frequently, with Marvin displaying an even greater reluctance to 'stumble into the big ditch'. His argument according to Michelle, appears to have been the familiar, 'who needs a piece of paper to be happy?' So there was no piece of paper, and the relationship went giddily ahead – lovin' and fuedin' to the cry of the sea birds and the crash of broken glasses.

It was now the British director, John Boorman's turn to explore Marvin territory. *Point Blank* was to be his first Holly-wood film. At thirty-four, with only television work and one other film then to his credit, he viewed the prospect with a cheer-fully doomed smile. He and Marvin had met and talked over the script while Lee was shooting *Dirty Dozen* in England. Boorman, formerly a newspaperman, slid like a hand in a glove into Marvin's spectacular eccentricities. The story goes that it was Boorman, or more specifically his car, which figured in a fascinating interlude one night in Beverly Hills. It seems the actor and the director had been celebrating with real Anglo-American gusto. When the carousels ended, Lee crawled on to

155

the roof of the director's station wagon and refused to come down. The director, feeling that the cool night air might induce a change of attitude, began slowly driving down the street. A police car pulled alongside. 'Do you realise you have Lee Marvin on the roof of your car?' the officer asked. 'Of course I do,' the director frowned. 'That's all right then,' the officer replied, 'but drive carefully.'

The movie they made was a shade less neighbourly. An implausible tale tricked out with flashbacks and contorted camera angles, *Point Blank* even by current standards approached the ultimate in screen violence. Marvin, a long-termer at Alcatraz, escapes and is determined to track down the syndicate man who chiselled him out of his $94,000 split from a robbery. Driven by revenge and a murderous suspicion that his cheating wife was part of the conspiracy, he knocks out the front men with a viciousness that makes the punk-hoodlum of *The Big Heat* seem a beginner. The effect of the sledge-hammer violence such as tossing a naked adversary off a penthouse roof, close-up on a bloody, spreadeagled heap on the pavement below, is scary, but fleeting. Battering others to a crimson pulp has the same horrific, but momentary impact. Far more chilling because of the sustained violence, is the scene where Marvin uses a car as a weapon to thump information out of the terrified gangster beside him. With the victim pinned by his seat belt Marvin ruthlessly sends the vehicle through a frenzy of accelerated collisions – forward, reverse, lurching against concrete pillars, his passenger jack-knifing into shattered glass and metal.

So much for the histrionics of brutality. Suspicion and jealousy induce similar overkill as he bursts into his wife's bedroom and with nothing more to shoot at than her empty bed, rakes it with his sub-machine gun as though it was a Jap gun position in Saipan. With another actor, less skilful at orchestrating the slow, dangerous build-up of revenge, the violence might have blown the film apart. In fact Marvin, allying patience to his animal nature, ingenuity to his purpose, achieves a degree of credibility the film itself scarcely matches. (There was an interesting sequel to the shooting-up-of-the-bed scene. Michelle Triola's reaction to it at a private screening of the film was one of total horror. She remembered she was shaking all through the rest of the film. Subconsciously she wondered how much of

DONALD ZEC

Marvin's own low-flashpoint psyche simmered beneath the surface of that jealous outburst. Back home they went into the
kitchen for some ice. Michelle teased him with, 'Well, what
would *you* do if I took a lover?' Marvin looked at her with what
she said was 'a sort of smile'. 'Why don't you do it baby, and
find out?' he said. The subject was not raised again, not even
after, at Michelle's persistence, Marvin handed all his guns over
to Sam Peckinpah.)

Point Blank proved to be a dangerous venture in Marvin's
career. Critical reaction was mixed. Most reviewers praised
Marvin's performance and the ingenious direction by John
Boorman, but the sick treatment repelled most observers, notably the then doyen of film critics, Bosley Crowther who wrote,
under the heading 'The Marvel of Lee Marvin':

> By all standards of acceptence Mr Marvin should not be any
> more of a moviegoer's favourite than a dozen or so others
> I could name. He is granite-faced, white-haired, unloving
> and downright supercilious towards dames, whom he treats
> as mere creatures of convenience – and low ones at that –
> in his current films. Yet I heard a middle-aged woman
> awesomely and rapturously exclaim to her equally galvanised
> companion at a showing of *Point Blank* last week – right at a
> spot of hideous violence – 'What a gorgeous man!'

Crowther goes on to compare Marvin with the archetypal
'anti-hero' Humphrey Bogart with this difference:

> The films of Mr Marvin are much more violent and extreme.
> I don't recall a single film of Bogart's in which the incidents
> of violence were displayed with as much luridness and savour
> as they are in *The Dirty Dozen* and *Point Blank*. To be
> sure Mr Marvin is not responsible for these idiosyncracies.
> The current accretions of graphic violence, often without pur-
> pose except to rouse audiences into horror, are not his fault.
> He is a working actor who takes what he can get in the way
> of roles. But the very excessiveness of them . . . may prove
> the eventual undoing of Mr Marvin as a star. The peril of
> his usefulness to film-makers and his popularity with the
> crowd is that he will be too committed to sadism. This could
> be the death of him.

This sharp, but not unflattering (two full columns) dis-

157

sertation by a leading critic had a more salutory effect on Marvin's thinking than he cared to reveal. He conceded that *Point Blank* was the most violent film he'd made to date but argued that 'it is violence correctly used'. This didn't prevent Marvin and Violence being adversely linked in the minds of critics and the general public. Lee resented this misreading of his own attitude and persona.

Sure having killed in a war for impersonal reasons I would be quite capable of killing someone now for reasons of my own. But that has nothing to do with my feelings about violence on the screen which more often than not is fake – and therefore dangerous. Look; all life is a violent thing. You can see those old grandmothers dying peacefully in their beds with their thin rings on beautifully frail hands but peer through the pages of their lives and what do you find? The lynch mobs and the violent acts they tried to stop to save themselves or their families. Violence is ingrained in every drop of blood that I have because I came from the caveman, baby, like everybody else. There has always been violence on the personal level – who hasn't put kerosene on the cat's ass and put a light to it? – and on the general level, guys pouring boiling oil over the walls on other guys, or dropping a bomb to kill everybody at one go. Now I don't glorify violence. I try to get to the understanding of it. If you want to sell the revulsion of violence you just have to show it as it really is. Much of the violence on the screen isn't violence at all, it's sadism. The worst thing you can do is make it look easy so that the audience says, 'we could do that.' That's dangerous. I say make the violence so brutal, show the blow, the broken teeth and all so that the punch-up characters in the audience think twice before going the same route.

A plausible argument, one would suppose, to those coming fresh to Marvin territory. But on that day in his house in Malibu, the decor dominated by his guns and vicious-looking fish gaffs; his axe, combat knives and sundry relics of war, Lee Marvin hardly seemed the best guy to dilate on the subject.

As he developed the theme through a haze of cigarette smoke and favourite obscenities, it was hard to forget that this was the same fellow who got his youthful kicks chasing wild pigs with a knife stuck on the end of a javelin; the same character who wrapped a banjo round the head of a bar-room bore; the

man from a home where arguments were settled with fist-fights
in an atmosphere, said the first Mrs Lee Marvin 'straight out of
Eugene O'Neil'. As Marvin himself admits, 'I don't know why
it gives me pleasure to hit something in the distance with a
weapon.' Preferably something that moves. A pig, a deer, or a
Japanese soldier. No doubt about the vicarious thrills Marvin
derives from the hunt, and the kill. He gets no less fun out of
verbal stalking, culminating in a bitchy demolition of his prey.
It is a kind of social brinkmanship exquisitely perfected in a
profession where one star's eclipse is another's rising sun.
Nobody could do it better than Marvin, whose malevolent screen
image puts him leers ahead of his rivals. He has a boyish charm
with it, which he exploits as an antidote – though admittedly
long after the soufflé has hit the fan.

So though one might take his defence of the violence in *Point
Blank* with a raised eyebrow there was no denying the film's
popularity. It took big money throughout the world with
Marvin again being listed in America's Top Ten Box Office
draws of the year. The film did exceptionally well in Japan
where smashed limbs and a cascade of blood causes fewer
audience tremors than in the west. Toshiro Mifune noted his
friend's success in the movie with a new interest. A western he
had planned to make for Paramount called *The Red Sun* had
fallen through. Now making films for his own organisation, he
was hunting for a major international subject. Marvin had a
story, *Hell In The Pacific*, which seemed tailor-made for these
two actors, both veterans, on opposite sides in the Pacific war.
Its allegorical centre – the idiocy of war expressed in the antics
of an American pilot and Japanese officer thrown together on a
Pacific island – touched an identical nerve inside both of them.

Marvin flew to Tokyo to discuss the script, and to a stirring
reunion with his charismatic buddy. It was now Mifune's turn
to show Marvin Japanese hospitality, superstar style. Lee was
knocked out by the mesmeric effect the actor had in the streets
and restaurants of Tokyo. Not even Clark Gable at his peak
could match Mifune's spellbinding entry into a crowd, his dark
eyes glinting proudly across a landscape of bowing heads.
Flanked by his entourage, above which Marvin rose like a
lighthouse, Mifune commanded a table or some exotic delicacy
in the manner of an old-style Japanese Emperor. He gave
Marvin the whole Japanese routine from the first saki to the

final Sayonara. Marvin is understandably hazy about the whole affair but specifically recalls the liquor jars spread around them both like spice pots in a bazaar. There were the ritual, pre-banquet baths. And much musical tee-heeing, as Japanese maidens giggled gracefully behind fans at the sight of the long-limbed Marvin, scarecrowing out of a shortie kimono.

'We had a ball!' said Marvin staring nostalgically into his glass and seeing therein a night in Tokyo with Toshiro.

He aped me and I aped him and we had to communicate with a kind of sign language and a look in the eye. I mean all the English he could speak at the time was 'very good', 'c . . . sucker' and 'sonofabitch'. Don't know where he got it from. But the guy didn't need words. He could hypnotise you with his genius alone. Those eyes! The samurai warrior standing alone. He had this great honour thing; personally he's iust like me, a dummy, except he happens to be good. You force me to make a list of favourite actors and I might just kinda stop at one.

They flew to the island of Palau in the West Pacific, with plenty of booze but no script. It was a month before the story began to take shape. The slow progress worried the money men who at one time threatened to pull them out before the film's ending had been worked out. Marvin sent them the kind of messages that only stars with muscle dare concoct. 'We must have convinced them because we stayed as long as we needed to get it right – but not before we scared the shit out of them.'

But the film had to stand on more than the courage of Marvin's convictions. It missed, largely because there was too much meaning, too little plot. After a while Mifune's darting, hunted-animal eyes and Samurai ranting begin to pall. Likewise the close-ups on Marvin's face as he measures his cunning against Mifune's amid the growing awareness that each man's survival depends upon the other. Beautifully photographed and resonant with good intent, the film sags to a limp conclusion. Marvin was unimpressed by the bad notices. The film is high on his list of all-time favourites. But it was bound to have a deeper feeling for him, and also for Mifune. Both had fought, and seen men die in the Pacific. Both knew what survival was all about. If the mob couldn't get the message, bad luck for the mob. A friendship of some substance had been established out there in the Western Carolines. A few lousy reviews weren't going to hurt any.

The production had an additional spin-off. Marvin couldn't wait to get back to the islands, and take Michelle with him. To the island of Koror in particular. To the sultry 'chanteuse' of Las Vegas, the ocean breaking creamily on the coral reef; the sun slanting down across the mountain ridges to the palm trees below, 'was the most beautiful and treasured experience of my life. We built a boat there,' she said, 'it was wonderful to see it taking shape. Lee named it *Ngerengchol* which means "where the heart lies".' But Marvin's desert-island euphoria, chewing on a root, or laying odds on the fastest turtle on the beach, had a limited time-span. Though neither said as much, he began to miss the old stag-party routines while Michelle's ears picked up a tinkling intro from a piano across the sea. And the trouble with having a lovers' tiff on a desert island is, where d'you run to without a snorkel?

In the event it was work that took Marvin off the island and back to Hollywood. The film, *Paint Your Wagon*. A $20 million musical play by Alan Jay Lerner and Frederick Loewe. Director, Joshua Logan. Cast, Lee Marvin, Clint Eastwood, Jean Seberg and others. Production company, Paramount Picture Corporation. It is necessary to identify the main contenders for they were all about to figure in a behind-the-scenes drama of clashing personalities which might have made a better movie than the scenario on hand. But Marvin was, of course, blithely unaware of the traumas shaping up for him, and the other leading characters. Given just a hint of it Lee Marvin might well have taken to his boat the *Ngerengchol* heading westward to the South China Seas.

Chapter Twelve

'Not since Attila The Hun . . . '

Joshua Logan

More than a quarter of a century ago Lillian Ross, a distinguished contributor to the *New Yorker*, was commissioned by that magazine to write a series of articles on the making of a movie. She chose John Huston's film *Red Badge of Courage* 'in order to learn whatever I might learn about the American motion-picture industry.' The result – a brilliant dissection of the anatomy of Hollywood ruthlessness – was a best-selling book called *Picture*. In it she exposed the tear-stained megalomania of that monster behind the rimless spectacles, Louis B. Mayer, and his battles with Huston and producer Dore Schary. The book created a sensation largely because of its revelations of ego-warfare and malice behind the white-stuccoed façades of Culver City. *Paint Your Wagon* could have provided Lillian Ross with a worthy sequel. Just how nerve-grinding the whole experience was to Josh Logan can be imagined by this comment he made to me long after, 'It just seems to be that I was there for an entire century.' A further clue to Mr Logan's trauma was this mordant comment on the movie's wandering star, 'Not since Attila the Hun swept across Europe leaving five hundred years of total blackness has there been a man like Lee Marvin.' So what really happened out there at Paramount studios, or more particularly on that splurging extravagance of a location on the old Oregon trail?

It has not been contested that there were some early disagreements between the studio chiefs and Josh Logan in the pre-

162

paration stage of the picture. Nor is there any doubt that in the first days on the location there were some clandestine moves aimed at replacing Logan by the director Richard Brooks. No argument either that when the heat was on the dispute became sharply polarised into two factions – the one manoeuvring to dislodge Logan, the other closing ranks around him. Whether or not Lee Marvin actually urinated on Josh Logan's highly-polished boots in a disgruntled moment is a question that recedes somewhat in the face of later evidence. Rex Reed, New York's sardonic critic-about-town declares the incident occurred as an act of irreverence, before the entire cast and crew. Josh Logan, speaking to me in his New York apartment high above the East River, denies the whole affair. And he should know. They were his boots. In any event, measured against the whole brooding scenario, it is, as they say, pretty small beer.

All began sweetly at the start as befitted a major motion picture involving talent in the world class. Joshua Logan, tall, large and urbane, was treated with the respect due to the maker of *Picnic*, *Bus Stop*, *Sayonara*, *South Pacific*, and winner of the Pullitzer Prize. He had made *Camelot* with Alan Jay Lerner, the tense, strongly-motivated composer and writer who alternated those talents in such epics as *An American in Paris*, *Gigi* and *My Fair Lady*. They met, Lerner and Logan, in Charles Bluhdorn's Chief Executive offices at Paramount Studios where nobody seemed to blink at the projected cost then of around eight to ten million dollars. (It was the era of the Big Budget picture. The fiscal recklessness of *Paint Your Wagon* was destined to change all that. After that, heads rolled in Hollywood's major studios like a busy day at the Bastille.)

Casting of the film was crucial, in particular the role of the drunken prospector who teams up with another rough character in the mad gold rush days and shares the same woman. With Kid Shelleen drunkenly hiccupping in subconscious thoughts, Marvin was favourite. 'If we can get him would you like that?' Bluhdorn asked. Logan and Lerner reacted with simultaneous enthusiasm. Logan had long admired Marvin as an actor noticing facets which may have escaped others. 'He's *bold*!' Logan said. 'He doesn't consider effects – I love the way he just goes out and does it.' Logan said he also admired Lee 'as a type. He's really a typical Southern gentleman. He tips his hat, says "Sir," and does all those other things we were told to do in the South.'

So the approach was made. Lerner, Meyer Mishkin, and Marvin met in an office to discuss the deal. Lerner did not merely press Lee to agree to star in the picture. He sang some of the songs from the film. To have a man of Lerner's stature say, 'Look Lee, if you don't play this part I can't make the film,' was persuasive enough. To have that same genius actually wooing him with song proved irresistible. 'I mean it was like having Noel Coward doing a play-reading with you in the hope that he could nail you for the lead,' Marvin laughed.

There was another facet to Marvin's eagerness. Here he was among the élite, the modish group he'd glimpsed in his mother's world of high-level publishing. Logan and Alan Jay Lerner were a classy extension of it. 'I'd been raised among them in New York,' Marvin said. 'I understand these men. I was intrigued at the notion of working with them.' So Lerner sent him forty pages of the script. Marvin read them, said, 'WOW, yes!' and was signed for a reputed $1 million, plus a percentage, and $20,000 a day or $100,000 a week overtime.

There were some immediate skirmishes over whether the entire film, goldrush city and all, should be made on Paramount's vast back lot. That was Logan's choice. But in the end the view of the designer, John Trustcott, that the movie needed the space and authenticity of the real Oregon trail, was the one that held the day. So millions were spent constructing the two Gold Rush towns, 'Tent City' and 'No Name City' – a complete town wired up and mechanically operated so that roofs could fly off, ceilings cave in, the whole finally blowing up and sinking into the river like a deMille version of Sodom and Gomorrah. (In the event of a dud scene, all the buildings were structured to snap back into position for retakes.) Though the location at East Eagle Creek, near the 9,000ft Boulder Peak in the Wallowa-Whitman National Forest has some of the greatest natural fir and pine forests in America, some of the trees on the set were imported from Hollywood. Camera-broken horses with a flair for taking direction were driven in from Nevada. Water oxen snorted in from New England. The bear who does a wrestling act in the film was persuaded to cancel engagements in Honolulu to hug for Paramount.

While all this exquisite lunacy was taking shape on location, Marvin drove to Paramount studios to be refashioned as the grizzled, dung-caked prospector. They gave him silver locks

164

down to his shoulders; a whiskers-moustache-sideburns combination and a gamey ensemble of nubbly trousers, a horse
blanket of yellow zig-zag stripes, a frayed winter coat and an old
top hat. Putting Marvin in that kind of rig was an invitation the
playful Lee couldn't resist.

Two examples show what a million dollar contract can do for
a guy's confidence. Brushing past a table where Barbra
Streisand sat he tossed a twenty-dollar bill by her plate. 'What's
that for?' the puzzled star asked. 'Oh I don't know . . . its probably more than you made last night,' replied the joker behind
the sprouting whiskers. At the send-off party which preceded
the move to the Oregon location Marvin was introduced to one
of the publicists on the film. He looked lasciviously at her un-
buttoned white linen suit with its sheer blue blouse beneath.
'Well now,' he drawled, 'what have we here?' He reached out,
took the lapels of her jacket between thumb and forefinger,
separated them carefully and stared appreciatively at the goodies
beneath the see-through blouse. The inspection was interrupted
by an eagle-eyed Michelle Triola. Sliding between them like a
Presidential bodyguard she said with silken menace, 'Lee
darling, we have to run.'

Baker, Oregon (Population: 10,000 plus) was a stagecoach
centre during the early days of the Gold Rush. The unit checked
in with the temperature searing near the hundred. Jean Seberg
brought her Spanish maid from Majorca. Josh Logan and his
wife Nedda took a house and also prudently brought their own
servants. Clint Eastwood brought his motor-bike and holed in
on a ranch. Marvin didn't care less where they put him, but the
crates of beer had to be on emergency stand-by. Everybody
started growing their beards, going easy on the deodorant, not
bothering to wash the cow-dung off their hands to savour the
first Martini of the evening. Jean Seberg (who breastfeeds a
baby on the screen) became an instant fan of Marvin's special
brand of juiced-up humour. There was this scene where she
bends down on the banks of East Eagle Creek, and puts her face
in the cool clear water bubbling over the rocks. The cameras
rolled. Suddenly there was a roar of 'Stop!' from behind the
trees. Jean pulled back. 'My God! What's wrong?' 'What's
wrong?' snorted the outraged and snockered Mr Marvin, 'Don't
you realise the fish are fucking in there!'

Josh Logan smiled wanly beneath the large-brimmed straw

hat he'd worn when directing Marilyn Monroe in *Bus Stop*. He
had always regarded it as a good luck talisman. He was beginning to have second thoughts. Not that he hadn't been warned
about Marvin. Ken Hyman had told him that, in spite of everything, having Lee was 'a lucky break for a director. He's charming, wonderful, warm, and a decent fellow,' Hyman said to
Logan. 'The fact that he gets drunk and stops the picture for a
day or two is not important because he'll make it up to you in so
many other ways.' Logan received similar reassurance from
Richard Brooks who had learned the hard way filming Marvin
in *The Professionals*. Logan met Brooks at Alan Lerner's house
before the production began. Brooks said, 'Lee will be marvellous, if you know what you are doing. He may go off one weekend, you may have a tough time with him, that's his nature. He
drinks you know that. But he's honest and he'll give you all he's
got.'

So Logan, straw-hatted and confident, blithely began putting
Marvin through his paces. Lee's disenchantment with the way
the production was going, set in early. And like cuckolded
husbands, Logan was the last to hear about it. Key figure in the
drama was Joyce Haber, columnist of the *Los Angeles Times*
who had learned a sting or two from that syndicated scorpion,
the late Hedda Hopper. Under the banner, '*Paint Your Wagon,
Director Change*', she wrote on 22 July 1968:

... Logan is in so much trouble on Lerner's and Paramount's
big budget musical that they're saying from Hollywood to
Baker, Ore. that he's about to be replaced. Likeliest candidate
for Logan's job, Richard Brooks who directed last year's *In
Cold Blood*. Apart from his top reputation, Brooks is a good
friend of producer Lerner who has been consulted all along
on matters of script, cameraman and so forth. Brooks's
former assistant director, Tom Shaw, is Lerner's associate
producer on *Wagon*. As of Wednesday, Logan was still on the
set directing Marvin ...

The story exploded over Hollywood, and Paramount, with a
dark, ominous ferocity. Logan read it and was stunned. Marvin
mumbled obscenities and wandered off to douse his anger with
cool beer. The Paramount executive shuttle service (the Lear
Jet and helicopter) zoomed ceaselessly between Hollywood and
the Eagle Creek location. A nervous studio spokesman bleated

something about 'an interlocking of emotions'. Pressed for a more specific explanation, he declared with the ambivalence of the born alibi-maker, 'the cauldron will either die down or boil over'.

The two factions taking up opposed positions in the fracas resolved themselves into Alan Jay Lerner and Tom Shaw on the one side; most of the crew, the ace cameraman William A. Fraker on the other. Marvin, ill-at-ease and scared of his reputation bombing out, felt himself caught between the two. The money, the millions, didn't matter a damn. He was comfortably stacked for life. Apart from the giant haul he'd get from *Wagon* Mishkin had seen to it that earlier loot had gone into lucrative enterprise like oil, natural gas, and real estate. What bothered Marvin was not so much the movie but how he, Marvin, would shape in it. His apprehension (and its alcoholic antidote) got to Alan Jay Lerner who could now see an ultimate price tag on the film looming between sixteen and twenty million dollars. A lot of money to invest in possible disaster. He and Tom Shaw regarded Richard Brooks as being one of the few directors Marvin trusted totally. Lean, hard, with a shorn, military haircut, Brooks had the total recall of the trained writer. He remembered vividly the initial secret approaches made to him.

The first I heard about the problems was when Tom Shaw called me on the phone and said:

'We're in a helluva fucking mess up here – that's to put it mildly – and nobody's talking to anybody. If you're not doing anything except preparing maybe you could come up and finish the picture.'

I said, 'You asking me to finish the picture? This is crazy, Tom.'

He said, 'No, no. They asked me to ask you because they're afraid to call you.'

I said, 'What's the matter, what's happening up there?'

He said, 'Well, Lee's in trouble again and nobody can handle him. It's deeper even than that. Guys are running around with other people's wives or girl-friends . . . a lot of things are going on. Clint Eastwood is not talking to Lee or Lee is not talking to Clint Eastwood. Whatever it is, it's not working. There's a lot of money up here. The film's got a chance. It's a good show.'

167

Richard Brooks's response was quick and unequivocal. 'Well, Tom, in the first place I'm not suited to this kind of picture. In the second place, I'm busy. Forget it.'

Shaw's role dutifully but unsuccessfully performed, it fell to Alan Jay Lerner to bring up the main artillery. He flew from Baker, Ore. to Los Angeles in the Lear Jet to see Brooks.

'We talked and talked about it,' Brooks said, 'and he repeated the offer, "Why don't you come up and do it? Lee Marvin, when he shows up, is causing problems." '

I said, 'You mean he's been drinking?'

'Yeah, I guess that's what it is. And even when he's not we've got problems. I mean when he's sober too.'

Brooks was puzzled. 'That doesn't sound like Lee,' he told Lerner. 'There must be something wrong with what you're doing . . . because he's movie-wise. He knows what's right and what's wrong. Anyway, why come to me? Does Josh Logan know you've come to me? If he doesn't it's wrong and it's un-ethical.'

Lerner pressed on. 'Well we can't let Lee go until we've got someone else,' he said. Brooks replied tersely, 'That's the trouble with the whole goddam company. You chose Logan. You've worked with him before. You know the score.'

His mission failing, Lerner flew back to Oregon. Then Lee called Brooks himself. The director reprised Marvin's urgent pleas with a fair imitation of the actor's gentle, basso-profundo tones:

'Hey, baby, why don't you come up here and get this thing on the road?' Marvin said, a heartbreak in every word.

Brooks: 'You sound pretty good Lee.'

'I'm fine, Richard. But there's a lot of crap goin' on up here. Shit – they don't know what they're doin'. They don't know which end is where. They got some big tough guy playin' gee-tar (Eastwood presumably) – and they don't know what the hell he's doin'. There's this guy who's got this little broad up here and she's, Christ – it's a mess. Ain't nothin' wrong with the director, he's okay. But, you know, he's scared. He doesn't know quite what-the-hell. There's a lot of buildings fallin' down and there's gold-dust-time in the Yukon period and he doesn't quite understand the humour of the thing. He's not on the stage now. He's out there with real people and a real goddam wagon. Shit! – he hears a pistol goin' off and he shits himself.' (Lee was to backtrack sharply not long after.) 'I dunno – come up here and *do* something.'

Brooks: 'Lee, I can't do that. First of all playing God is not my cup of tea. Second, my coming up there isn't going to straighten anything out. Third, I don't know how to make a musical.'

'Well, hell Richard, the music is all done, everybody's singin' their piece, it's the rest of it.'

Brooks: 'Okay, well why don't you set an example for them? Stick it out. They're all looking at you anyway. The other parts will work out if you give them a hand.'

'So you won't come up?'

'It's not that I won't. I just think it's wrong. Could you direct it?'

Marvin was puzzled. 'Sure I could direct it. But what do you do?'

'Okay, direct it and at the same time don't direct it,' Brooks said. 'You know what I mean. Help them.'

Marvin wavered. 'Look, you know what I think of you. I'd like it if you came up. Why don't you just come up and say "hello" or something?'

'No, it won't work. It's shameful for the other man. You'd be cutting the legs off him. If anybody did that to you . . . '

'I'd step in and bust him one!'

'Then why do it to this fella?'

'Okay,' Lee conceded with an audible sigh, 'Maybe you're right.'

'Richard Brooks did not take over from Josh Logan. Four days after her 'Director Change?' story had squalled through Hollywood, Joyce Haber declared, under the bland heading of 'Plenty of Wheels Turn over "Wagon" . . . 'Logan is very much the gentleman in his willingness to step down . . . ' but . . . 'Lerner announced that Brooks was out and Logan would stay on as a director.' In fact it was Paramount, infuriated by the premature disclosures in the *LA Times*, who were to put things right with Logan. They wired him, 'You are going to stay, no matter what.'

During the shooting Marvin had a visit from an old friend and admirer. Don Siegel, who had directed him in *The Killers*. Siegel had come up to run a film for Clint Eastwood.

169

When I got there I found everything had closed down because Lee was, you know, incapacitated. I was running around like Tiny Tim telling everybody that I had worked many times with Lee, that he's a professional and will pull himself together. Nobody believed it, but it did turn out that way. I had breakfast with Lee. Breakfast with me is a kind of sacred rite. But there was no food in his house, just this one wrinkled avocado. When Clint came over to pick me up Lee gets to talking and it was gibberish. I finally said to Clint, 'Do you understand anything he's saying?' Clint couldn't figure him out either, then I said, 'Look, I came here for breakfast.' I'd already had four beers and I needed to eat. Marvin just sat there grinning, so I picked up the avocado and squashed it on his head. We both laughed. Clint thought we'd gone crazy. But there are moments when one act can be more expressive than dialogue with Lee Marvin.

Siegel returned to Hollywood grateful that when *Paint Your Wagon* was, in the initial stages, offered to him, he turned it down. It was one of the few movies he rejected that didn't turn out to be a winner. He felt a director's sympathy for the cross Logan had to bear.

What Joyce Haber had got right was Logan's 'gentlemanly' behaviour, in an atmosphere whose bitchiness, malice, and fork-tongued sweet talk offended a man of Logan's Southern dignity and sensitivity. He had had enough problems with Marvin. Lee did sometimes 'get lost', wandering away to get canned or go fishing. This wasn't Marvin playing the 'up yours' superstar. It was the actor perilously uncertain about a major scene. As he put it, 'With the studio heads it was a question of keeping to a tight schedule in a highly expensive picture. With them "bringing it in on time" is the big priority. But I don't work that way anymore. With me the scene comes first. An artist has the right to take forever to get something perfect.' So there would be a whole day lost here or there as Marvin took off to consult with the Muse or a can or six of Schlitz.

At one point on the set he announced casually, 'I don't see any point in wasting money here, shooting footage. I'm going fishing.' There were reports of a tall, wild-looking character who resembled Kid Shelleen's father, staggering down the main street of Baker, telling the startled inhabitants exactly what he thought of the production. ('These cocksuckers don't know their asses from their . . . KAVOOM!' is a fair summary of his boozy haranguing of the local populace.)

There were other peripheral problems. Hundreds of hippies who had streamed into Oregon from all over America to work as extras were going sour on the arrangements. They arrived beaded and long-haired proclaiming peace unto all and pinning flowers on everyone to prove it. But soon they started gorging Paramount into the red and further, demanding doggie bags.full of food for all their unemployed friends. They requested their daily stipend be upped from twenty to twenty-five dollars, chorusing 'Hallelujah' when Paramount grimly conceded the claim. A group of their followers who also wanted to be extras were told to get their hair cut. This so enraged them they started handing out poison ivy instead of flowers to the cast and crew. Logan took it all with Southern stoicism. When a couple of the hippies decided to get married (barefoot under a waterfall to the music of the Nitty Gritty Dirt Band) Logan was first on the guest list, with Marvin, Eastwood and Seberg all active in the ceremony. The Logan/Brooks controversy now over, a kind of peace reigned amid the pines, the snow-capped peaks, and along the precipitous 46-mile dirt road to Baker called 'Deadman's Curve'. (Now and again the road had to be made good at around $10,000 a mile. Paramount will not journey that way again.)

Though the telegram from the studio chiefs had ended speculation about the film's director, it hardly made Logan a hero overnight. Studio gossip, unlike any other kind of scandal-talk has a malevolence all of its own. One night, purely by chance, they ran a print of Logan's *Bus Stop* for the crew. At the end of it the entire audience applauded. From then on there was no doubt who cracked the whip and steered the *Wagon*.

Joshua Logan talks about it now, some ten years after, more sad than angry. 'Sure I felt bitter about it at the time. It discouraged me a little about the human race.' After all, he has had, he threw off casually, 'a few big ones'. Aside of *Annie Get Your Gun, Mister Roberts* and *South Pacific* on Broadway – he received the Pullitzer Prize for the last in 1950 – he won Academy nominations for *Picnic* in 1955 and *Sayonara* in 1957. He also wrote and directed the film of *South Pacific* which will go on coining money into eternity. But even if we had not known that, Logan's stature as a major talent is evident to the uninitiated in the signed portraits, trophies, assorted accolades

171

and letters from the great which make his apartment in New York reverberate with success. Everything in view bespoke a man who enjoyed – and returned – the affection of those who worked for him. When he said, 'I really love Lee Marvin' you know that Josh Logan is not promoting a useful 'quote'. He means it. Getting to know Marvin, as with any other performer, was crucial to getting the best performance out of him.

Maybe the fact that I was, in some senses, a stage director made him nervous. But I didn't know he was nervous. I thought he was just plain drunk. I don't know what the drinking thing is with him . . . it's not like somebody going off on a binge and not being able to pull themselves off it. Lee would go on it, then come right out of it the next day. So we wouldn't lose all that amount of time. And when it happened we just went on to something else. Lee was my pal. And Clint Eastwood stood by me too. Clint said he sent his agent to Paramount to tell them if they wanted to change the director they'd better see him, Clint, first or they 'might be in trouble'. It was a strong thing to do and I admired it. Sure when Lee got a little on the beer-can early on, that day was finished. It happened maybe six or seven times. But one night he asked me to give him a lift back to Baker in my car, a two-hour drive. We got talking about the theatre, acting, early New York, everything – and struck chords in each other. From that moment I had his confidence to the degree where I think he would have lain down and rolled over if I'd asked him.

Not the style of a man who would also urinate on the self-same hero's boots. Logan laughed at the tale.

It was my own son who came to me with the story. He said to me, 'Dad, what's this about you fighting with Lee Marvin? I didn't think you ever did.'

'I didn't,' I said.

'But didn't he argue with you so much that finally he came over and peed on your boots?'

'No, it didn't happen,' I said. But to convince him I sat down and wrote a denial to the paper.

Dear Sir, your allegation in one of your columns that Lee Marvin got so angry at me that he used my boots as dogs use a fire hydrant is false on two counts. Number one, when Lee Marvin is sober he is the most gentle of gentle-men. He is also the most punctilious, respectful and charming of men. He is also a good friend. Therefore, when he is sober it should be impossible for him ever to do such a thing. Number two, and when he is drunk it is equally impossible because with alcohol he gets so in-ebriated that he staggers about, slips off balance, careens desperately, trying to get his equilibrium. He is a burlesque comic drunk and in that condition he would have frantic and pitiful difficulty taking aim.

The Marvin-Josh Logan friendship was reinforced rather than strained by such controversies. Richard Brooks's long-distance counselling had touched a basic element to Marvin's nature. His loyalty. Canned or cantankerous – the one inva-riably induced the other – he nevertheless always supported his leader. 'There was never any real doubt that Logan could do the job if they (meaning the studio) would take other pressures off him,' Lee said after the storm had blown over. 'A director has to have artistic freedom. Logan has style. Like chasing a butterfly, you dart and spin in all directions, but finally, when you get close, it's beautiful!' But he admitted with a wry grin, that 'any director has his hands full with me!'

Marvin thought *Wagon* was a good film. Few critics agreed with him. 'The film is certainly spectacular, but why paint your wagon if you have to get out and push?' observed one disen-chanted reviewer. Philip French (*Financial Times*) found the film 'generally embarrassing' adding this bleak comment: 'Nothing is quite as sad as Lee Marvin's undisciplined hamming as a drunken prospector, a grotesque distortion of his beautifully judged performance as the alcoholic gunslinger in *Cat Ballou*.' To redress that, the London *Daily Express* said: 'One thing Lee Marvin exudes from the marrow of his bones is that indefinable theatrical quality known as "presence" . . . It is only Marvin, gesticulating furiously from his ankles to his eyebrows, swig-ging booze . . . his eyeballs darting about in their sockets like excited goldfish in their bowls, who sustained my interest.'

Yet the film clearly hadn't come off. It is a matter of fine argument whether it should ever have been started. It is an over-long, over-acted but undersized version of a much better stage musical. That Marvin should have topped the hit parade with his gruesomely unmusical rendering of the song 'Wand'rin'

173

Star' somehow reflected the absurdity of it all. The final price tag placed on this embarrassing escapade by Paramount has been put at anything between fifteen and twenty million dollars. Logan observed with a wry smile, 'I've never known any subject that's as full of holes as how much a picture made or cost. Whatever they tell you is not true.' Lee Marvin was more specific. '$16.5 million,' he said. $22 million is the figure they like to settle on but I saw Alan (Lerner) sign off the production costs.' When the other major studios saw the extent of Paramount's inordinate extravagance – the studio had been similarly spendthrift on other productions – alarm bells rang in accountants' offices. It revived that acidulous gem unearthed on the even more costly *Cleopatra* – 'The inmates are taking over the asylum'. Dozens of big budget projects were cancelled. Lavish contracts were slashed. The pocket calculators took over the studios.

Only one man seemed unconcerned. Lee Marvin. He had broken through the million-dollar barrier. Had picked up some additional loot in 'overages' and expenses. 'Wand'rin' Star' was selling in Britain at the rate of 21,000 records a day. He wasn't worried for Paramount. He knew that eventually, when the movie had been hyped everywhere from Tooting to Taiwan, it would eventually stagger out of the red. He and Michelle, despite the familiar convulsions, were having a ball. The fact that she had now taken to calling herself 'Mrs Marvin' was a detail Lee shrugged at. Michelle's decision, she explained, arose after a policeman stopped her for speeding on a road in Baker. 'He asked for my driving licence, read the name "Michelle Triola" and politely corrected me. He said he knew I was Lee Marvin's wife.' She told her friend, writer Ronnie Cowan, 'There was a bit of a to-do about my name when I went to pay my summons. It embarrassed me and it embarrassed Lee. We figured that as long as everybody called me Mrs Marvin, and as long as I signed my name Michelle Marvin, why not make that my legal name?'

That question was to look a shade less blithe-spirited when a year later posses of lawyers were galloping head-on towards each other in what may well become the suit of the century. At the time of her decision Michelle was helping Lee pack for a return trip to their paradise island of Palau in Micronesia. It was there he learned that his old college at St Leo, Dade City,

Florida, was awarding him an Honorary Degree of Doctor of Fine Arts. Marvin was clearly stunned by the gesture. He had flunked out of St Leo as a bad-mouthed youth, was going back there as a distinguished recipient of a degree. He wrote to the college on 25 March 1969:

My present plans are to leave Koror, Palau on or about April 4, which will put me back in Los Angeles on that same date through the 185th parallel. I will phone you directly . . . and confirm all arrangements, what I have to do, my arrival date etc . . . at the convenience of St Leo. It is foolish of me to express my feelings of honour, gratitude and humility at St Leo's desire, but in essence to be with you will be a most happy moment. Sincerely yours, Lee Marvin.

Happy moment it certainly was. Highway Patrolmen in riot gear, keeping two hundred and fifty protestors at bay, made absolutely certain of that.

Chapter Thirteen

'I gave Lee the best years of my life.'

Michelle Triola

'*Yeah? Well I also gave her the best years of* her *life.*'

Lee Marvin

The citation read:

> The Trustees, Administration and Faculty of Saint Leo
> College are privileged to confer this Citation and accom-
> panying Honorary Degree of Doctor of Fine Arts upon
>
> Lee Marvin
>
> For his determination and persistence in the pursuit of a
> career in the Performing Arts, prefaced by academic pre-
> paration at Saint Leo College and interrupted by World War
> II service with the United States Marines which resulted in
> severe wounds during the Battles of the Marshall and
> Mariana Islands. For his continued dedication to the excel-
> lence of portrayal of roles in the cinema, the theatre and the
> medium of television, which excellence commands the high
> respect and admiration of colleagues and public alike, cul-
> minating in recognition as one of the world's foremost motion
> picture stars, and additionally: for his prowess in athletics and
> interest in the drama during his student days at Saint Leo
> College together with subsequent honours and attainments
> for which he is noteworthily honoured here today.
> Accomplished at Saint Leo, in the State of Florida, on this

twenty-sixth day of April in the Year of Our Lord, nineteen hundred and sixty nine at the Third Commencement of Saint Leo College.

Anthony W. Zaitz, PhD,
President.

The tone, if not the substance of the soaring panegyrics, sounded as portentous as a Nobel Prize ceremony. Marvin, his mortarboard tassle rustling in the breeze, reacted with the mischievous, slack-mouthed grin of any one of his favourite hoodlums. It was a scene to savour. He was savouring it. Alongside him on the dais, mildly upstaged by the actor, was the then American Secretary of Defence, Melvin R. Laird, receiving the Degree of Doctor of Humane Letters. The Band of the US Strike Command from the MacDill Air Force Base played fanfare music; army and airforce brass glinted importantly in the Florida sunshine. Monks murmured, abbots rustled, Marvin tried to figure out how the hell a bad student who'd been bounced from more schools than most problem kids, had gotten himself up on a university dais, the band playing and all. He glanced around, felt himself wrapped in an ambience of scholarship, religion and strategic fire power.

The oddity of it was not lost on him. It went well with the whimsical images now careening through his mind of a Marvin in less illustrious guises. He had a vision of a well-stewed Kid Shelleen, pants down, crotch bulging, being installed as a Doctor of Philosophy . . . the image faded to a mad-eyed youth running like a Masai warrior, transfixing a squealing pig with one throw of a man-made spear . . . he saw the same Marvin PhD declaiming like a Roman orator to the startled populace of Baker, Oregon . . . 'these cocksuckers can't tell a movie camera from their asses!' He was nudged out of his reverie by the bursts of applause which punctuated the citation. As it wafted into 'prefaced by academic preparation' Marvin and Father Marion, his old tutor, exchanged winks. Both knew what almost everyone else did not, that not only had Marvin L. dropped out after scarcely more than eighteen surly months at Saint Leo. He had given the monks plenty to meditate upon while he was there.

Another thought brought Marvin perilously close to whooping out a mighty 'JEE . . . SUS!' or something a little less reverential. He knew, as Melvin R. Laird knew only too bitterly, that down the road a couple of hundred student protestors were being kept at bay by riot police with shields, batons, and spotter helicopters overhead. They had nothing against Marvin. Their banners, taunts, and slogans were directed against Laird's support for the Anti-Ballistic Missile, the Viet Nam War, and 'the industrial military complex'. While Lee's triumphs on stage screen and field of battle were getting the full oratorical treatment, the 'peacenicks' were being instructed by their leader, 'if knocked down by a cop, spreadeagle, and hope you don't get kicked more than twice.' A girl tried to pin a flower on a state trooper but removed it when the officer explained he was allergic.

In the event, the protestors never got within shouting distance. The ceremony was a total success. Lee Marvin opened the $580,000 dormitory built in his honour. Then he cracked a few jokes at a microphone, his ham-sized hands thrust in his pockets, narrow-bottomed trousers rising two inches above his shoes. The show was over. For all his surface clowning, Marvin did feel 'vibes' of achievement. That he had carved something worthwhile out of his life. He would have liked Betty to have been there. But more particularly his mother. It would have turned the circle nicely, the boy failure who was now the celebrated PhD smiling triumphantly down on Courtenay, the cultured, sophisticated New Yorker, who probably never thought he'd make it. But she had died some years earlier. His father had married again. He loved Marvin senior, was fond of his stepmother. But the aces he would like to have pulled out were with Betty and Courtenay.

Michelle Triola did not enter into these calculations. Lee had left her back in New York. Josh Logan and his wife were shepherding her around the city, wining and dining her, showing her the sights; further proof there were no hard feelings between the unpredictable actor and Logan of the unsullied boots. The director had given Lee and Michelle a lavish welcome-home party when they arrived back from their island in the Pacific.

But the tropical euphoria did not linger long with the couple. Marvin, apprehensive over the eventual outcome of *Paint Your Wagon*, wanted to get back to the security of the Hollywood womb. He was scheduled to start work on *Monte Walsh*, an uncertain, obscure Western which his buddy, William A. Fraker (who photographed *Wagon*) was to direct. Lee's relationship with Michelle was hitting bumps like a bad jet landing. The music they made together, harmonious in the overtures of their affair, was hitting a discordant finale. There were king-size fights, maudlin Martini-fuelled reconciliations. It was the sort of turbulence which could throw Lee into any kind of situation, fair or fraught. *Monte Walsh*, specifically the arrival on the scene of the elegant, sophisticated French star, Jeanne Moreau, did not help. That is to say it was not to help Michelle Triola.

Marvin's new film, a downbeat tale of two ageing cowboys pitched against the drudgery and despair of the 'real' West, brought him and Jack Palance back together again. Moreau was cast as the beautiful but doomed whore. The 'tart with the heart', as someone wrote. Fraker, who had observed Josh Logan's rough ride with Lee Marvin from behind the cameras on *Wagon* knew that directing Marvin would be a hairy experience. He and the two producers, Hal Landis and Bobby Roberts, wanted Moreau from the outset, convinced that the chemistry between her (the beauty) and Marvin (the beast) – as with Vivien Leigh in *Ship of Fools* – would reap lush harvets. They had two major worries: one, that Moreau might not want to make the picture; and two, that Marvin would oaf it up to the point where she'd storm out on the first plane back to Paris. The three of them, the two producers and Fraker, flew to France with the script and took the actress out for the finest meal Cinema Center money could buy.

Meeting her for the first time, like Ponti's first glimpse of the nubile Sophia Loren, had the three film men devastated, and hand-kissing with a vengeance. She gave them the full treatment with those large, dark, unfathomable eyes; swept ahead of them in the restaurant, imperious yet chic. Intelligent, amusing, and flirtatious, the French star could have demanded a million dollars and seventy-five per cent of the gross and Messrs Fraker, Landis and Roberts would have signed without a murmur.

Born in Paris in 1928, Jeanne was the daughter of a Lancashire chorus girl who had been a dancer at the Casino de Paris, before she met and married a French barman. From that unspectacular beginning Moreau was to become the first lady of the French screen. *Time* Magazine's unusually lyrical cover story declared, 'Film directors all over the world have to

struggle to praise her hard enough. There is no actress in Hollywood who can match the depth and breadth of her art . . . '
David Shipman in his *The Great Movie Stars* dubbed her 'the
art house love goddess'. That is how she looked at the restaurant
on the night of their arrival, holding court at the prime table
like a queen. Fraker observed her elegance, the delicate features
and the fragile manner, juxtaposing it all in his mind with the
lurching, bad-mouthing hero of *Cat Ballou* then back home in
Hollywood. It did not sharpen his appetite for the banquet
which Moreau had ordered with exquisite care.

'I will give you gentlemen my decision tomorrow,' she
announced with an encouraging smile. 'You will all come to
my apartment for lunch and we will discuss the business then.'

She received them at her stylish home in an exclusive corner
of Paris. With her was her close friend, François Truffaut, the
critic-turned-'new-wave'-director. She gestured the producers
and two agents to their seats at the table. She smiled at Fraker.
'You, Willie, I want to sit on my right because you are now my
director, and François, who will *always* be my director, will
sit on my left.' The American contingent knew it was all over
bar the fine print.

Meanwhile Fraker, Marvin's grinning image hovering in the
forefront of his mind, was determined to keep Moreau away
from Lee for as long as the schedule permitted it. His reasoning was this:

> I felt there was the risk that Lee might just destroy what we
> were trying to do. That Jeanne, who's so independent, might
> get offended at something he said or did, and announce, 'What
> do I need this for?' then just get on a plane back to France.
> I was so paranoid about the good of the movie I didn't want
> anything to spoil it. So I prevented their meeting until almost
> the end of the picture.

The danger, as Fraker saw it, was that if Lee did not feel
comfortable with her, or felt he could not work with her, 'he'd
just go off and get drunk and say something devastating, as
he does when he drinks – he's a killer – and she would say
"Well fuck you, Monsieur Marvin!" and walk off.' So Jeanne
Moreau was brought direct from Paris to Los Angeles, installed
in a Beverly Hills mansion with her own driver and secretary.
Fraker, with the adroitness of a juggler, kept them both in

separate orbits, to Marvin's growing irritation and Jeanne
Moreau's lively curiosity – feelings highly conducive to mutual
attraction. The more they were kept apart the more Fraker was
convinced that they would burn up the screen in their ultimate
confrontation. He was proved right, and some. But the ploy did
not come cheaply. There was one shot with Moreau when it
would have been easier for her to fly to Tucson, Arizona –
where Marvin was working – for one day. Fraker vetoed it.
'We'll shoot the scene when we get back to the studio.'

'That'll mean we'll have to build a special set,' the production
team replied.

'So build a set,' Fraker snapped.

Meanwhile, like the directors who had tottered along the
rocky route before him, Fraker was having the usual trouble
that went with the Marvin package. Fraker had made up his
mind not to shoot one frame of film if Lee had been drinking.
Particularly where it showed that Lee had been drinking. 'We
had only gone two days into the shooting when I wrapped the
company at nine o'clock in the morning and sent everybody
home. I just said, 'That's it!' and clearly Lee resented it.'

'What is this?' Marvin growled, 'I'm coherent.'

Fraker stood his ground. 'No – you're upsetting the other
actors. You've changed your whole characterisation. It's all
completely different.'

'I know my lines,' Marvin persisted.

'I know you know all your lines, but I can't help that. I don't
think it's good for the picture and I'm shutting down.' (Fraker
figured that he might just get fired off the picture for his action.
But he wasn't. The 'Marvin Syndrome' was now familiar to one
and all in Hollywood.) Don Siegel, Eliot Silverstein, Richard
Brooks, Josh Logan . . . Fraker was merely joining the list of
battle-scarred heroes. So Lee got drunk, sobered up; went to
parties, called everybody 'cocksuckers' then turned on the little
boy charm; he hung out with the stunt men, raised his usual hell
in Tucson; it was the mixture as before. Until he met Jeanne
Moreau.

The effect was like a sudden commotion in Heaven. A hint of
angels singing, violins playing. The two stars stood face to face,
measured each other to their evident mutual satisfaction. If
Fraker had been a religious man he might just have ascribed
Marvin's astonishing metamorphoris to divine intervention.

Since he wasn't, he didn't. Instead, he concluded that Marvin was hit amidships by his delectable co-star. And getting more than a superficial reverberation from the French goddess in question. One eye-witness on the closed set rhapsodied: 'I have never seen two stars sparking off each other the way those two are. You could light your cigar on the afterglow!'

The first valuable spin-off from the encounter was that Marvin went off the booze. Recalled Fraker:

> In that last three weeks of shooting, Marvin did not touch a drop. And the chemistry between those two was just tremendous. For the first time as an actor, Lee really opened up in his relationship with a woman. There was a softness, a tenderness that began to work in Lee that I'd never seen before. And Jeanne Moreau was the only one, it seemed, who could trigger it.

What else she was triggering depended largely on how one read the signs. In a blithe display of Gallic candour, Moreau was soon telling an interviewer, 'Lee Marvin is more male than anyone I have ever acted with. He is the greatest man's man I have ever met and that includes all the European stars I have worked with.' To someone else: 'An extraordinary man. He says more in less words, sometimes in no words at all, than any other American I have met.' (How, where, and at what particular high spot in their relationship Jeanne Moreau arrived at those ecstatic conclusions doesn't appear in any records. Happily married to the film-maker Bud Friedkin, Madame is content to leave the episode where it ended, in Los Angeles.) Hollywood's passion-spotters at the time, however, were quick to note that Jeanne Moreau's tremulous prose followed hard upon her long-rehearsed love scenes with Marvin. The *Hollywood Reporter*'s reviewer clearly caught in the slip-stream, declared afterwards:

> It is the love affair between Monte Walsh (Marvin) and the saloon hostess-prostitute, Martine Bernard (Jeanne Moreau) which constitutes the film's most literal romantic relationship. An almost silently profound understanding links the couple ... Miss Moreau ... takes thirty lines of dialogue and transforms them into a character, an aura of femininity, a magic. And Marvin, his face saying more about age,

182

masculinity and non-verbal emotion than any amount of
dialogue could possibly communicate, is more persuasive
than he has ever been before ...

The London *Spectator*'s critic also noted that 'Marvin and
Moreau have a presence, a palpable magnetism . . . together
they are fascinating to watch'.

And watching them, a shade less fascinated than that
observer, was Michelle Triola. Her eyes, and Sicilian-French
intuition, told her that the 'palpable magnetism' did not hum
back to zero when Fraker said 'CUT' and the lights were killed.
Gossiping eye-witnesses confirmed it. And the irony of it, as
expressed by Michelle, was that it was she, she said, who had
suggested Jeanne Moreau for the film. 'My feeling was that no
woman had ever really gotten to him on the screen. I thought
they would be terrific together. I thought she would draw
something out in him.' Whether in fact anything more than
mutual admiration was astir between Marvin and Moreau, it
is clear Michelle believed this to be so:

Jeanne was absolutely mad about Lee. When she went back
to France she frequently telephoned him. Sometimes he gave
me the phone saying, 'Here, you handle it.' Finally I challenged him. 'Are you having a thing with Jeanne Moreau or
are you not?' Lee just smiled. 'I wanna ask you something –
when do you think I have the time?'

The ambiguity of the denial raised the temperature of their
arguments. To be fair to Michelle, her guess that Jeanne
Moreau had a shade more than a co-star's interest in Marvin
was shared by many including a producer friend of both stars.

I know that Jeanne was immensely attracted to Lee, and oh
God, it wasn't difficult to fall in love with her. When the film
was over, I understood she asked Lee to come over to join her
in St Tropez from where they would launch a whole new
world together. But Lee can't deal with that. All somebod/
has to say is, 'Okay Lee, put on your tux we're going to
Prince Rainier's Ball,' and he'll disappear for ever. No question he found Jeanne Moreau as intoxicating as anything
he'd ever drunk in his life, but sipping cognac on the Left
Bank or queuing to get on to Sam Spiegel's yacht at Cannes
was not for Lee Marvin.

One can also safely assume that being called out late at night by a Malibu bartender to haul a stupefied Marvin back to base may just not have gone down well with the delicate Parisienne.

But though the image of Jeanne Moreau had receded from the picture, the Marvin-Triola partnership was now approaching disaster stations. *Monte Walsh*, for all Lee's belief in it, hadn't come out the way he and Fraker had hoped. The director admitted to me that:

> in all honesty the film was too slow. I wanted my first directorial effort to reflect as much truth as I could get into the film. Today I would do it entirely differently. The honesty would be there but it would have much more bezaz. In the reviews there were things like ' ... very auspicious debut for a director ... ' so the only people who sold me short on the picture were the audience. The film didn't make money. It was primarily my fault.

One would have to search a lot of territory to find a director as refreshingly self-critical as that. But the fatal flaws in the film, it seemed to me, were not his. They're more likely to be found in the casting. Palance – as one of the superannuated cowboys mourning the death of the West they knew – gives by far the more engaging performance. His is an appealing low-key characterisation. Whereas a quality of 'big I am-ness' seems to bleed into Marvin's role as Monte Walsh. There is a sequence at the end of a cattle-drive when, stinking after months without a wash, he baths, shaves, pomades his hair, dresses in his best clothes (a scene owing much to the bullfighter's suit-of-lights episode in *Cat Ballou*). He goes to the whore-house where Moreau, his old flame, would never think of charging him. He then, we understand, makes love to her as only an old master can. Marvin brings a narcissistic air to his self-grooming – a sense of the under-acted and superstarred. A hint of unease too which may stem from Marvin tackling a part not only sympathetic but in the final analysis, downright sentimental. Palance, not worried by the superstar gloss, settles back into a real, in-depth performance. It is his film. Jeanne Moreau's considerable talents just about conceals her miscasting.

The uncertainty of the movie, and his own drink problems gnawed at Lee Marvin. There were moments when he felt a yearning for the cool, rock-firm support of his divorced wife

Betty, or someone like her. His arguments with Michelle merely emphasised the hopelessness of their reconciliations. The atmosphere became heavily charged. It exploded in one blazing row with Lee storming from the house and staying out all night. The following morning Michelle received a phone call from an embarrassed colonel of the US Marines base at Camp Pendleton along the coast. Lee Marvin, it seems, was trying to rejoin the Marines. It was a revealing excursion by Lee Marvin, admittedly tanked-up at the time. He would never have run from a bullet, a brawl, or a broken bottle. But a broken love affair was something else. He hadn't the stomach, or the dialogue for that. From where he sat, the Marine Corps looked as tantalising as the Promised Land. No clinging broads, no tears, no arguments, no lawyers.

No chance. The Colonel at the camp said to Michelle:

'Excuse me Ma'am, do you think you could please come down here and get Lee Marvin. He's had a drink or two and he's trying to re-enlist. He's got some honorary rank but I don't see how we can take him back. I'd be obliged if you could arrange for him to get home.' (The Marine Corps may have been down on volunteers but it was not yet driven to re-enlisting brave, pensioned-off veterans.) Michelle replaced the phone with a giggle. How like Lee to search for a little peace and quiet with the US Marines. Her second phone conversation, a few moments later, left her somewhat deflated. It was with Lee's agent, Meyer Mishkin. It was from him that she learned that Lee had decided it was all over between them. She felt shattered. 'What do you mean?' she asked him. 'That was Lee's message,' Mishkin said, 'I'm just passing it on to you.'

Alarmed, but unwilling to believe that their close-to-seven years together were over, Michelle set out to find her maverick lover. She rang their friends. From one of them she learned that Lee, respectfully rejected by the Marines, had gone on to La Jolla, the tourist trap of a town across the border into Mexico. She traced him to a hotel there. Her version of their soul-searching discussions had them finally driving back together to their beach house to 'talk things over'. She said, 'We talked a long time and realised that the chemistry was still there. I don't mean just physically. We were communicating as we had always done. But midway between the said communications the phone rang. It was Lee's agent. Lee talked to him for a few minutes then hung up. He told Michelle he had to drive into Hollywood immediately. She didn't hear from him the rest of the day. Or on the following day.

On the third day she received a letter from Lee's attorney. In essence, it asked her to list everything in the beach house that she considered belonged to her. Michelle said she found that impossible. 'How could I? I'd always looked upon everything as *ours*.' Then she received a further call enquiring how soon she might be able to leave the house. The request struck a nerve. 'Me – leave the house? I can't, I won't' declared the now-scorned mistress. Then she cried. 'I was stunned for days,' she said, her dark eyes brimming with the memory of it all. Meanwhile lawyers came and went. The beach-house at Malibu resounded with the noise of axes grinding. It was Hollywood's familiar Ritual Dance of Disconnection. With one significant novelty. The two parties were not married. They'd merely been behaving that way. It was a fine distinction which Marvin Mitchelson, one of California's most relentlessly successful attorneys was to make much of in the Supreme Courts not long after.

Understandably, Michelle was reluctant to vacate the beach on Malibu. But finally she agreed. No point in trying to hold on to the nest from which the bird had flown. She still wanted to live on the beach though and rented a small house along the coast highway. She had now received her first cheque under an arrangement providing her with regular monthly payments. She left most of her belongings at the old house, with the lingering hope that they would provide a possible lever towards a reconciliation. One afternoon she went back to the house to collect some books. Uncannily the phone rang. It was Lee calling from New York. Why he was calling, whether in the back of his mind too there hovered ideas of returning to the old relationship, was not explored. Michelle's attempt to sound casual dissolved into a burst of high emotion.

Marvin was likewise disturbed. In a display of tender loving concern by both parties it was agreed that the situation could only be resolved by a face-to-face meeting when Marvin returned from New York. He flew to California and after their first meeting it was almost 'business as usual', though cautiously, both keeping to their separate establishments. (Marvin had asked for, and was instantly given, 'visiting rights' to their dog La Boo, a black, amiable beast of indeterminate breed who had

186

learned to walk carefully through broken bottles, and never flinched at a gun fired at close quarters. You don't desert dogs like that in a hurry.)

Friends of both parties were now betting on a reconciliation. Michelle declined to confirm or deny it. Lee Marvin smiled his inscrutable smile, whistled, pointed a finger, and went 'POP!' – his all-purpose response to questions he can't or won't answer. The reason for his reticence was to become only too clear within the next few days. He again had to fly back to New York. Michelle kissed him goodbye, told him she'd be waiting. While in the city, Marvin learned that his father, Lamont, had been taken ill at his home in Woodstock. This delayed Lee's return to the coast. But he and Michelle talked frequently on the phone. But it was the final phone call Michelle received from Marvin that was the clincher. It was late at night. Lee didn't fool around with preliminaries.

'I've just gotten married,' he said briefly.

'You what . . . ?' Michelle's tone said, 'you've got to be kidding!' Fear forced out a joke. 'If it's Jeanne Moreau I'll kill you.'

'No. It's true baby. I've just married Pamela. You know, Pamela Feeley' (the childhood friend he met twenty-five years earlier on a river bridge at Woodstock).

Michelle's reaction as she slowly replaced the phone can fairly be imagined. 'I couldn't breathe,' she said, 'I don't even remember putting the phone down.' She called a couple of friends and they came over and took her to their home. It was 18 October 1970.

Lee Marvin, it transpired, had been somewhat energetic in the preceding week. He had been joined in New York by Jeanne Moreau to promote the opening of *Monte Walsh*. This inevitably restirred the juicy gossip which gurgled into the headlines during the making of the picture. The speculation diminished somewhat when after the première he put Jeanne back on a plane to Paris. It evaporated entirely when, at a press conference after a screening of his film, Marvin told reporters he would never marry again. An odd line for a man to shoot who, while that underwhelming quote was spinning on the news presses of America, was on the phone to his press agent, Paul Wasserman in Beverly Hills;

'Wasso, this is Lee. Just want you to know I'm getting married.'

'To whom,' his friend Wasserman asked mildly, 'Michelle or Moreau?'

'Pamela Feeley,' Marvin said.

'Who is *she*?' Wasserman asked, concerned now with how he was going to break the news of a bride nobody had heard of. Marvin asked to speak to Jim Mahoney, the head man of the PRO outfit who at the time 'handled' Frank Sinatra the most sought-after client in the entertainment world. Mahoney had all the essential qualifications for master-minding the public images of such turbulent, unpredictable characters as Sinatra and Marvin. A tough, taciturn, unshockable lieutenant, he took Marvin's announcement on his office phone in Beverly Hills casually, between suppressed yawns.

'Congratulations, Lee,' he said.

'Yeah, well this is the score, Jim,' growled Marvin from New York. 'I want to get this done, I want to do it fast, and I don't want anybody to know about it because I don't want to have any monkey wrenches in before it's finished, okay?'

'All right, if you're determined,' Mahoney replied. 'If that's the way you want it that's the way it'll be. Where you getting married?'

'Las Vegas,' Marvin said with the half-amused tone of the man who'd been that route before.

Lee and Pamela Feeley (an attractive, brown-haired woman, three-times married – with four children) flew from New York to Los Angeles going swiftly to ground at his home on Malibu. Meanwhile Mahoney had been talking to Frank Sinatra. Typically, Sinatra acted with style. 'They can have my plane,' he told Mahoney. The lavish Lear Jet in which the singer may enjoy the same intimately exotic lifestyle he commands thirty thousand feet below. His appreciation of Frank Sinatra's handsome gesture figures largely in Marvin's recollections of that wedding day.

The plan was that at 4.30pm we'd leave the house, all dressed, and go to Cloverfield Airport nearby. We got there and Jim Mahoney and his wife met us. Then WHOOAHOO' [roared Marvin in a fair imitation of a jet landing], this big DeHavilland sneaks in. We climb aboard, then, 'SHOOEEE OW . .

OO! [Marvin was coming in to land at full throttle] we hit the deck at Las Vegas. There's this Mormon priest waiting for us upstairs. He meets us, ties the knot, we cut the cake, pour the champagne, back in the car to the airport, in the plane, 'VROOM . . . VROOM . . . KER . . . WOWOOOO!'. land, drive home, and we're back in bed watching the tube at 8.30 that night. Waiting for the phone to explode. How's that for a good day's work?

Pamela, the second Mrs Marvin, frowned at Marvin's virtuoso performance on their entry into holy matrimony.

'It was far more beautiful than you can realise from Lee's description,' she said with a studied glance at her informative spouse.

'It took all of five, maybe seven minutes,' declared a grinning Marvin, 'though I admit this priest did give us a little sermon afterwards. He said, "Before you go to sleep at night make sure you both resolve any differences." ' Marvin acknowledged that this was a marginally better service than the one he received from the reverend pastor at his first wedding. (Remember Rev. Lovable's yawning, 'Do you take this er . . . so on and so forth . . . ')

While Lee and the new Mrs Marvin set up home, not far along the coast, the rejected mistress, Michelle Triola, took stock of her life. She had no illusions about her singing career. That had, in effect, faded out when she took on the more demanding role of being Lee's woman. She got a job as a secretary, but she looked a whole lot better than she could type. Almost exactly one year later she received a call from Lee's business manager that no further cheques would be arriving.

It just stopped. I remember the date only too well, November 12. I just didn't know what I was going to do. I knew I had to talk to Lee about it. So I phoned him. I couldn't believe it. But before he had a chance to say anything, Pam took over the phone. She talked about the whole money arrangement, saying she thought it was ridiculous, that I wasn't entitled to anything. She ended up by saying, 'Why don't you find yourself another boy friend?'

At that precise moment, Shakespeare's 'Hell hath no greater fury . . . ' allusion was a thousand degrees cooler than Michelle Triola's anger. 'It absolutely destroyed me,' she said.

It was then she called her friend, the Beverly Hills attorney Marvin Mitchelson. Michelle issued a suit claiming that though she lived with, but did not marry Marvin she was still entitled to all the rights of a legally divorced wife. The effect upon America, Hollywood in particular, was predictably startling. Marvin, from whom Michelle was asking half his assets – allowed a hard grin to set into his corrugated features. 'These things happen. It doesn't disturb me one bit. The whole thing is ludicrous. About one dollar would settle it for me.' To the argument that Michelle gave him the best years of her life Marvin rasped back: 'Yeah? Well I also gave her the best years of *her* life, but that's all right.' The stage was set. Marvin Mitchelson, attorney-at-law, prepared his tear-stained but resolute client for the opening scenes.

Chapter Fourteen

'What a can of peas you've opened!'

Rock Hudson

Michelle Triola-named-Marvin went to the Los Angeles Court wearing her best 'woman-scorned' outfit, a sober-coloured suit discreetly necklined. She also wore the mandatory tinted glasses which sympathetic judges are supposed to imagine hide tears, or at least brave but dark-ringed eyes. The attorney Marvin Mitchelson, whose famous divorce clients have included Zsa Zsa Gabor and the ex-Mrs Groucho Marx, carried bulky documents, nodded at the respectful smiles from admiring smaller fry in the court. Everybody there sensed that history was about to be rewritten. Somewhere among the exhibits were the seven rings which the open-handed Marvin gave Michelle over the years, all wedding rings according to his litigious love-companion. Her suit which, if eventually successful, could make Michelle the most expensive mistress in the world, claims in effect, that she was Marvin's wife in every respect apart from the clincher of a three-dollar marriage licence. Further, that she and Lee had an oral agreement to combine 'their efforts and earnings and would share equally any and all property accumu-lated'. The brief also states that 'during the time the parties lived together, Michelle and Lee would "hold themselves out to the general public as husband and wife" with Michelle rendering her services as "a companion, a homemaker, housekeeper and cook".'

To reinforce the argument it was noted that Michelle had changed her name to Marvin, had Marvin on her apartment bell,

191

Marvin on her passport, and Marvin on her pay slip from a show-business agency. She was certainly following through. (The property Michelle seeks a share of includes motion picture and recording properties, and real estate acquired from 1964–70. If she is denied rights to half of the actor's property her suit seeks in excess of $100,000 for her lost career.)

Meanwhile in interviews, Mitchelson enlarged on the theme:

> A woman should have the right to a good divorce and community property even if she is not licensed to marry the man she loved and lived with . . . It costs three dollars to get a marriage licence. I say that for this money one should not have different rights than one who has the same relationship but doesn't pay the three dollars. I consider this unequal protection under the law.

Immediately the case was brought, other couples who hadn't 'paid the three dollars' in the free-wheeling movie city, hastily reappraised their situation. The dialogue can be inprovised.

The Man: 'Honey, we don't . . . er . . . have any kind of you know, oral agreement, I mean about, well, my property, earnings, and silly things like that . . . '

The Woman, thoughtfully studying her outstretched fingernails: 'Funny you should mention that, darling, but wasn't it always kind of understood that our relationship was, well, you know, more meaningful than just a couple of people having fun . . . ?'

Not as fanciful as it sounds. One significant result of Michelle Triola's mind-boggling suit was that celebrities are now asking their live-in lovers, no matter how casual the liaison, to sign wavers of any claim to potential property rights. These tender, loving arrangements are being described as 'pre-nuptial agreements'. A further indication of Hollywood's nervous tremors was a remark made by a laughing Rock Hudson to Michelle Triola at a party: 'What a can of peas you've opened!'

But for a time, it seemed the now famous mistress would have to put the lid back on the can. The Los Angeles court ruled against her. Round one to Lee Marvin who was declaring, along with his lawyer, that Michelle hadn't had any money nor was she going to get any. One of the defence arguments seemed to be that, if any 'oral agreement to share property' was entered into in 1964, it was invalid because Lee was still married to Betty Marvin at the time and would be bound by law to share his earnings with her. But Michelle's claim and Marvin's vigorous rebuttal were to be tossed on oceans of legal argument before eventually a Supreme Court was to give the mistress her right to sue as a wife.

Lee Marvin's other preoccupations kept him from concerning himself unduly with the then favourite talking-point at Hollywood dinner parties. He had a new wife, and a film to make with Paul Newman. The turmoil of his relationship with Michelle; the aftermath of his fling with Jeanne Moreau; the illness of his father – all combined to make Lee feel the need for a comforting maternal shoulder. His first wife, Betty, had fulfilled the role admirably. But that was over. The run of indifferent pictures was beginning to take some of the gloss off the superstar image, sour his relations with the media. His needling and bad-mouthed insults in interviews and press conferences no longer had the bad-boy charm to sweeten their effect.

At one New York press lunch his performance was described as 'surly and incoherent'. Correspondents who'd come, eager to record Marvin's lively throwaways, put their ball-points away when the largely unprintable four-letter words far outnumbered the rest of the monologue. Discussing *Monte Walsh*, Marvin said, 'I hate Westerns. I hate horses. I hate guns and I hate being around all those men. I put on the rags, made the picture, rode off into the sunset and collected the money. End of sequence.' When the lunch ended he dismissed the news men and women with: 'You've had a free ride, and a free flick, and that's about it.' One of the writers present, trying to account for Marvin's outburst decided, 'He seems to be reaching a turning point in his career and it shows.'

Which, of course, was only part of it. He had been drinking, for sure. No other reason why he should knock Westerns, men, guns and horses, which he'd sooner have around him than almost any other diversion on offer. The irascibility reflected his uncertainty about himself, about his career, and his personal life. He fell victim to the familiar ambivalence – a craving for the kind of life he'd jeered at with a passion. Married life. Not a movie-star marriage. Nor the liberated kind of wedlock as practised, say, by Shirley MacLaine and her long-distance spouse in Tokyo. Marvin yearned for the good old-fashioned-hearth-and-home marriage. Where the new Mrs Marvin would glance proudly at him of an evening and then contentedly return to her sewing.

Pamela Feeley seemed just this kind of Earth Mother. When they dined secretly in New York, he learned she was divorced, already had four children, was a grandmother courtesy of the eldest, a daughter then aged 22. Suddenly Lee saw this warm, quiet, round-cheeked matron with soft brown hair, blue eyes, as the woman he most needed. She had no interest in the film business. Disliked it, in fact. She loved children, needed to with their combined offspring totalling eight. Seeing them together in Lee's Malibu beach-house, it was obvious that Pam had clearly cast herself in a subordinate role. While he talked, swore, bird-watched, or vilified the 'shit-heels of the front office' she freshened our drinks then quietly backed off with the delicacy of a Geisha girl. Lee looked at her, toyed with a joke, then decided he didn't really want to be smart at all. 'God, what an amazing woman,' he said, loudly enough for her to hear. 'To think I had it on offer when she was fifteen and I was twenty-one. All that love going begging all those years, it doesn't bear talking about . . . '

Filming the downbeat Western, *Pocket Money* with Paul Newman, gave Lee Marvin a salutory lesson in the classic, self-preserving rites of the superstar. The Number One superstar at that time, with Redford still having several smiles to go. The film company flew to the Santa Fe location. Marvin watched, fascinated, as the golden-haired idol, who likes to keep his body as lean and hard as an athlete's, unpacked his slant-board (for press-ups); regulation hospital scales; a snorkel; and a portable sauna. 'Jee . . . zus, that, pals, is style!' Marvin grinned, as crewmen assembled the sauna on the spot. There was Newman's own personal sweat cabin. At dawn each morning, before his co-star Marvin had coaxed open one bibulous eye, the young god had gulped lungfuls of the desert air, launched into a hundred sit-ups on the board, swum fifty laps in the pool with his snorkel, before finally squeezing hell out of his pores in the sauna. The ritual was partly to sweat off the prodigious intake of wine and beer the night before. But mainly it was Paul nurturing his multi-million-dollar asset – Newman.

The two men could have come from different planets. Newman, the boyish, almost-too-beautiful phenomenon of the movies, clean-limbed, open, almost shy. Marvin, the terrorist, the intimidator, the wrecker whose language permutates the genitalia to the point where he's running out of ideas. Candice Bergen, the stylish actress-turned-writer, joined the two actors for the wrap party at the end of the production. She noted perceptively in *Vogue*:

> Lee Marvin . . . was everything I hoped and feared he would be – as unpredictable, honest, intimidating and inflammable as I imagined. He is unusually interesting; in the way that war is more interesting than peace. I thought if I got out of there merely disfigured I'd be lucky.

Marvin took this as an oblique compliment. Playing the lovable brute was part of his act. He preferred that to Newman's magic which was constructed from college-style humour, tanned virility and undiluted charm. He witnessed, but declined to share in, a fascinating episode which underscored star-power, the star-power of Mr Paul Newman.

The last day of shooting was at a station outside Santa Fe where it just so happened Paul's wife, Joanne Woodward, was aboard the train due to pass through on its way to New York. Informed of this train, officials arranged, actually arranged, to have the express slow down. Shooting stopped. The crew, cast, and others stood in line as the train snorted into view. And there was Joanne Woodward at the carriage window, in dark glasses, waving like royalty to her husband Paul Newman. Everybody shouted and waved in return. Everybody, that is, except Mr Lee Marvin. He lay back in his canvas chair, his eyes closing on private thoughts which his wife Pam beside him read down to the last exclamation mark.

Politically the two actors are not so far adrift from each other as their public personas might convey. Newman is a serious, highly-motivated character whose stand on Civil Rights, political chicanery, and environmental pollution, is well known. Marvin's own concerns and convictions figure in few records because he rarely gives voice to them. Ten years earlier he had gone to the Democratic Convention in Los Angeles to root for Kennedy as President, because he believed the senator would make Civil Rights a major policy issue. Later, when actors became too heavily involved, he pulled out of that scene. But though he doesn't care for actors overtly 'latching on to good causes' Marvin contributes generously but quietly to several civil rights organisations.

It was Paul Newman who asked Marvin to star with him in *Pocket Money*, an odd, modern Western about two slow-off-the-mark cowboys in Arizona. Cowboys who are never going to make it. Written by Terry Malick, directed by Stuart Rosenberg (*Cool Hand Luke*), the idea of he and Newman, playing losers in a Western appealed to Marvin's keen sense of disaster. The last scene in the movie has the two of them having lost everything, standing on a railroad station, talking over what they should have done, where it all went wrong. Fade out. End of picture. If Paul Newman, the Number One winner, was prepared to go out in a movie that way, Marvin figured 'Who am I to start worrying?' The dialogue was equally off-beat. Sample, Marvin to Newman; 'Look at those two cows, you notice they're always together?' Newman: 'Well they have friends too.' But both actors sailed into the production as though an Oscar awaited them over the horizon. The director, Stuart Rosenberg, had been around Hollywood long enough to have heard all the Marvin stories. But as he said to me afterwards, 'I never respond to gossip. I never respond to what other people's experiences are. I don't ever try to "handle" actors. I lay it on the line right from the beginning.'

So he too delivered the standard invocation which by now Marvin was almost beginning to cherish. Said the quiet-voiced Mr Rosenberg to Lee: 'I understand you have a drinking problem. That's your problem. I'm not a psychiatrist. Just keep it your problem and let's have an enjoyable time.' Marvin was so touched he nearly hauled himself to his six feet three, and saluted. But he arrived on the set slightly loaded a couple of days later.

'Go home. There'll be no more shooting for you today, Lee,' Rosenberg said.

'Why?' Lee muttered.

'Because it's not fair to you and it's not fair to me. So let's not do it again and everything'll be terrific.'

And everything was terrific, according to Mr Rosenberg.

196

In fact he said it was 'a marvellous experience' working with Lee.

He is one of the most inventive, creative, instinctive actors in the business. He's my kind of player. He brings just everything to you. Sometimes I would just let the camera run on and on and Lee would fill it with sounds, gestures, hilarious things with the gun, there's no one to touch him as a visual actor.

Trouble was everybody fell about laughing, except the audience. Maybe the film would have come off with a couple of unknowns in the lead. As Rosenberg conceded: 'To have Newman and Marvin fail in business, fail with each other, and even fail with girls – well you could just feel the audience leaving.' But with Paul Newman's company making the deal, Paul Newman starring in the film, Paul Newman approving the screenplay – who is going to tell Paul Newman, 'You and Marvin are wrong for this picture?' Certainly not Mr Rosenberg who was also chosen by Paul Newman. And not Marvin either. He'd been paid and that was that.

Somebody asked Lee Marvin at the time what the picture was called. 'Paul Newman,' he said innocently. The story goes that Lee had such faith in the script he took a smaller-than-usual salary, a paltry $500,000 against twenty per cent of the profits. After he saw the rough cut of the film Newman offered his co-superstar a flat $1 million for his twenty per cent. Lee refused. He should have grabbed it. Movie audiences do not like their heroes to bite the dust. Reaction to *Pocket Money* was generally lukewarm, the overall feeling was that it was a good idea that didn't work. Both actors were given points for trying hard, but the public failed to support the movie. Lee decided making films alongside a big star name had its dangers. 'It never works out,' he told reporter Jim Sirmans. 'It was Paul Newman's production company. By the time they cut the footage, Newman was the star. I dunno, I guess the old ego got the best of him. What can you do?' No doubt Paul Newman could have nailed that – and Marvin – to the deck.

But smart superstars don't chew over past flops. Newman knew he could recoup overnight. Marvin was less certain. His next venture, *Prime Cut*, directed by Michael Ritchie, seemed to offer the actor the chance to regain lost ground. It brought

Marvin back to familiar and fruitful territory, as gory as any of the evil gangster epics he'd played in before. Worse. This one has such niceties as a henchman being ground up in a meat factory and returned to his mob boss in Chicago as a string of sausages. Drugged, naked girls (from a local orphanage, where else?) lie around in cattle-stalls waiting for buyers.

This preposterous backdrop has Lee Marvin as the hit man sent to Kansas City to kill the rival mobster, Gene Hackman. But no performance could rescue the film from its sheer nastiness, though Jay Cocks commented in *Time*: 'Against all odds, Marvin summons up a measure of dignity. Hackman looks abashed.' No question now, Marvin's career was, on the basis of *Pocket Money* and *Prime Cut*, on the down slope from the peak of *Cat Ballou*. Maybe it was his realisation of this fact which prompted a highly contentious comment (in *Rolling Stone*) on *Prime Cut*'s director Michael Ritchie. Even without his successful track record, *Downhill Racer*, *The Candidate*, and later, *The Bad News Bears*, Ritchie deserved better than this broadside which suggests that Lee must have had a long lunch:

I've made some mistakes I wish I hadn't. One of them was working with Michael Ritchie on *Prime Cut*. Oh, I hate that sonofabitch. He likes to use amateurs because he can totally dominate them. Nothing worked with that guy, and the picture just fell apart before we even got started.

I rang Ritchie to enquire whether he'd care to comment on Marvin's remarks, as quoted in *Rolling Stone*. His response was courteous, but negative.

I am prepared to talk about, say, Burt Reynolds, Robert Redford, Walter Matthau or any other pleasureable subject. But not about Lee Marvin. He said some wicked things about me and I am not disposed to reply in kind. Nor, on the other hand, am I disposed to say anything favourable either.

Yet understanding the caprices of the motion picture business as well as anybody, Ritchie would know that the word 'never' is excluded from the Hollywood vocabulary. Given the chance, Lee Marvin would probably have been glad to eat his words the following morn. Besides it is curious how, in movies, personal feuds vanish at the sound of a good deal being made, with fat percentages.

But what Lee had to face at that time was that his recent movies were short on the kind of success which had produced an Oscar, and had twice put him with the top-ten money-earners in the country. It depressed him, not merely because, like any other star, staying at the top was crucial to the whole fragile process. He needed the money. He had a divorced wife, a new Mrs Marvin, several mouths and young careers to support. Moreover, hanging over him was Michelle Triola's precedent-setting lawsuit. Playing the role of America's legal guinea-pig didn't appeal to Lee Marvin who figured Michelle's claim came pretty close to being a joke. Discussing it once, he said to me that he had tried to end things with Michelle on several occasions over the years.

I asked her hundreds of times to leave, but it was difficult. I'm really not the kind of guy who could physically throw some-one out. I didn't enjoy having to tell her that I was marrying Pam, either. But it's a phase that's gone. It's like a guy who's been incarcerated for a certain crime – five years for so-and-so. You'll ask him what it was like and he'll say it's over, but at least I came out of it alive. That's the way I feel about that particular episode.

He was less stoic when, in 1972, he was phoned in California with the news of his father's death at Woodstock. He had anticipated it, but was shattered by it. Their relationship, deeper than either man cared to admit, was sustained by few words or outward emotion. Neither father nor son was constructed that way. Public expressions of affection – or worse, love – were okay for the soft-collared types, but not for the men of the Marvin dynasty. Not long before his death, Lamont Marvin was asked about his son, Lee. He smiled, and as quoted earlier, said, 'He was a wild, harmless, innocent, crazy kid. Between us though there never was a period of misunderstanding. I wouldn't say that he understood me, but I understood him.' All that ended with the phone call from New York. In his sadness, staring out at the ocean from his verandah at Malibu, Marvin remembered that it was Lamont who had taken him out to sea, taught him how to fish. Another thought induced a smile. He and his father were fishing off Mexico. They had got in among a great mass of saltfish. It was a broiling hot day. Lamont watched, disgusted, as the Mexican fishermen in the boat clubbed the fish to death. 'How can they kill a beautiful creature like that?' Lamont had asked him.

'Chief, these guys live off them,' Marvin had said. 'They sell the fish for money.'

'Well why don't you just give them the money yourself?'

'No there is a process they must go through. The mystique goes from the mind to the hand to the line to the hook to the strike of death.'

But Lamont remained unpersuaded. He had been equally disapproving when Lee took him along to a typical Hollywood film-deal negotiation. Lee had been offered $500,000 for a part. He refused it casually, saying he really didn't want to do the film. His father was appalled. 'Do you realise son, that this is twice as much as the President makes?'

'So what, Dad?' Lee had shrugged, 'He's got nothing to sell.' (Tactfully, Lee had not told Lamont that in that same week he had turned down half a million dollars to film a TV commercial for a hangover with the much-quoted comment, 'Goddamit is nothing sacred!')

Lee thought of the coming funeral, shuddering momentarily at the visions it swept into his mind. Of tears, the dark uniformity of mourning, the platitudes, and the mandatory expressions of grief, felt or assumed. Rituals he loathed. If he had to go through with it, he'd make damned sure the people there would be those who cared, or who had meant something to his father. He phoned his first wife, Betty, who had shared a rare affection with Lamont. 'Come to the funeral,' he said, 'and bring the kids.' It was one of the few talks they were to have together after Lee remarried. She was glad he had asked her to go to Woodstock. Glad of the chance to murmur a final goodbye to a difficult but scrupulous man, a man with a steely concern for integrity.

So she went with the children to Woodstock. The funeral of Lamont Marvin did not proceed in accordance with the solemn, silk-lined plans of the morticians. Tristram Coffin Colkett the Third, MD, Marvin's devoted drinking companion across several bar-shattering years, prefaced his unexpurgated version of the ceremony with, 'You have to remember that pathos is just not Lee's scene.' He went on:

Now, I wasn't in the room but as I understand it when our boy gets into the house everybody is standing around immobilised by their grief. There's some big problem as to what to do. There's a rope cordonning everybody off. Behind it is arrayed everything that belonged to the deceased. The way it was before he died. The hat, the guns, you name it. But Lee sees nobody is getting anything *done*. Like he's come a long way, man, and he's here to see his dad buried. Instead, everybody's hung up staring at the last living semblance of the loved one. Well as I understand it, Lee claps his hands, hauls himself over the fucking rope, and says, 'Okay, that's enough, right!' His respect for his father wouldn't tolerate all that shit. So he claps his hands and the show gets on the road. That's real respect brother!

Marvin and Pam returned to the Malibu beach-house – Lee to prepare for *Emperor of the North Pole*, the second Mrs Marvin to appraise Marvin's Californian lifestyle. One thing Pamela Feeley's Irish blood told her was that she was going to be a different kind of woman from the previous incumbents at 21404 Pacific Coast Highway, Malibu. She had no intention of becoming 'one of the guys' hauling empty bottles out on to the front stoop, elbowing Lee's hungover friends into their cars, the early sunlight hammering at their eyeballs. Adroitly, she put the news around that Mr and Mrs Lee Marvin were no longer at home' to unscheduled visitors like homeless tipplers, pie-eyed mavericks, rich but bored inhabitants of the Malibu Colony who found Marvin a great piece of free entertainment. She made Lee change his phone number. The old one was unfortunately offloaded on to a sensitive, middle-aged soul who stopped him one day on the road. 'Did you ever have this phone number?' she asked, reciting the figures she'd inherited.

'Yeah, I had that number.'

'Well I have to tell you, Mr Marvin, I really am sick and tired of being telephoned by your friends at all hours of the day and night, saying they're on their way.'

'You have a point, Ma'am,' Lee said gravely. 'I'll see they get the message.'

Marvin was also getting the 'message' from Pamela. He did

not immediately give up drinking. Getting nailed when the need for it overpowered him, was clearly vital to Marvin at the time. But he certainly eased off. He could now distinguish between drinking out of need and taking it on as fuel for his hell-raising image. That image had given him a good ride, but no longer made sense for a star whose status was confirmed by his million-plus price tag; who half a dozen of Hollywood's finest directors had declared to be one of the best performers around. If Marvin began showing all the signs of a sudden attack of maturity, it's clear that Pamela had a discreet hand in the proceedings.

She helped the slow metamorphosis by sharing Marvin's passion for deep-sea fishing. No hardship for her as it turned out. (On one trip she set up a record for a woman, hauling in a 607lb Blue Marlin. They went together to Cairns, in Northern Australia, fishing for even bigger stuff off the Great Barrier Reef. For a forty-plus grandmother to be strapped to a seat on a heaving deck, fighting it out with a thousand pound monster at the other end of the line, it was no easy ride. She took that, the bloody mayhem of the killing, the needle-sharp salt-spray on her sun-flared skin, with the same good cheer she displayed in the face of Marvin's roaring insults. They were as wild, zesty, and uninhibited as a honeymoon couple – albeit with eight children to support.

They returned from Australia with a sizeable haul of trophies, the huge fins of the big black marlin, and a considerable respect for Australians. The beer-sudded machismo of the Australian male appealed to Marvin's male-chauvinist soul. He believed in the 'dominant male' syndrome. Pamela sweetly sustained his self-delusion. Lee was now purring to one and all, 'This woman makes me feel so goddamned comfortable. Marrying an old sweetheart sure cuts through the years. You don't have to go through this "shall we dine?" stuff. She knows who I am, what I'm full of, and who's kidding whom.' He was also back in business, filming *Emperor of the North Pole* with Ernest Borgnine.

The film, set in the years of the American Depression, centres on the hobos who hauled themselves on to the freight trains, battling it out with the guards ordered to club them out on to the track. Marvin is cast as the cunning, viciously resourceful hobo 'king' who measures his wits against the malevolent train conductor, Borgnine. Written more incisively, directed without Aldrich's familiar overkill, the film might have had more to say, and said it to a much wider audience. But the emphasis on blood, brutality, and hate, plus the cliché-ridden dialogue which clogs the action, shreds credibility. It is hardly as bad as New York's Judith Crist implied: 'It's hard, contrived, pointless in its thesis, repulsive in its people, singularly joyless and contemptible in its glorification of the bum and the freeloader.' But it sure is a nasty way to hop a train. Borgnine reprises his *From Here To Eternity* thick-skulled sadism. Lee Marvin plays it entirely from the gut. The total effect was sickening. Some kind of artistic rehabilitation was long overdue if Marvin was not to be thrown back to being your favourite neighbourhood thug.

Offered *The Iceman Cometh*, John Frankenheimer's film version of the Eugene O'Neill classic, Marvin jumped at it, though as he told Roderick Mann at the time, 'O'Neill drives people away in droves.' But Twentieth Century Fox obviously dissented from this view, relying on Frankenheimer, together with Marvin's versatility as an actor to prove them right. Critics were evenly divided on the outcome, though even those against it excluded Marvin from their censures. It was left to Stanley Kaufman in *The New Republic* to make Lee Marvin feel that at last, at almost fifty, he'd 'shown the bastards how'.

To crown the work there is Lee Marvin. To put it simply, Marvin was born to play Hickey. He had a perfect understanding of the man and the perfect equipment to deal with it. Marvin is wonderful. I have seen James Barton, the first Hickey, and Jason Robards (along with others) and Marvin goes past them – so powerfully that he makes the crux of the play clearer than I have ever found it before, on stage or on page.

With praise as unequivocal as that, Marvin felt he could safely write off to experience his recent pratfalls. What he could not do with equal certainty, was to co-star in a new movie with a famous actor whose encounters with hard liquor were no less spectacular than his own. With Richard Burton. In *The Klansman.*

This ill-fated production which ran riot through a sedate little Californian town; upset the menfolk, teased the girls and made them cry; was to become the apogee, the last gulp, in both Lee Marvin's and Richard Burton's long years of grog. My friend, director Terence Young, who didn't flinch or falter on the battlefields of World War II, visibly winces at the memory of it all.

Chapter Fifteen

'Richard Burton would be a corpse today . . . '

Terence Young

The calculating characters who put up the millions to make movies, recognised that both Lee Marvin and Richard Burton were 'bankable' properties. Together, their accountants' logic proceeded, the controversial stars would be riotously profitable. Burton's own brooding charisma had the powerful stimulus of the long-running spectacular which passed for his ill-starred life with Elizabeth Taylor. They were then (December 1974) engaged in one of their highly-audible reconciliations following some lively hostilities in Europe, America, and down at their Mexican retreat at Puerto Vallarta. Marvin's own cohabital confusions were also fresh in the public's mind, highlighted by Michelle Triola's still-simmering lawsuit.

Casting them in *The Klansman*, the film based on William Bradford Huie's inflammatory best-seller on the Ku Klux Klan, seemed to bear the touch of genius. The flavour of money. Just a question of whether to buy a Cadillac or Rolls after the première. If they had any apprehensions of how the two Goliaths of hard liquor might behave, talent against talent, thirst against thirst, it scarcely bothered them. Acting on the old delusion 'there's no such thing as bad publicity', the company invited one and all to come and witness the event. Like 'papering the house' at the Bastille The story goes that one eager press agent in Los Angeles told press callers, 'If you want to come up here okay. If you want to interview one drinker and watch another drinker fall in the camellia bushes, come ahead.'

At that stage the two actors had never met. But an executive, sounding as though he was trying to convince himself more than the assembled press, declared breathlessly: 'This is potentially the most explosive combination I have seen in thirty years. We've got thunder and lightning meeting under the same roof.' So the anticipation was pretty well stoked when the principals and the hundred-odd crew checked into the North Californian town of Oroville, scene of one of the first gold stampedes in the early 1800s. A neat place of ranches, modest homesteads set amid almond blossom. Oroville was selected as a look-alike alternative to a real Southern town. There was no way Georgia or Alabama were going to allow this time-bomb of a film (rape, riots, castration and lust) inside State borders. The film men were billeted on the Prospectors' Village motel, a happy place out on the Oro Dam Road.

Well it was happy on Day One. Lee Marvin arrived with Pamela. One of their marriage resolutions demanded that they never be separated. Quite apart from keeping the relationship aglow it had to be conceded that, away from home and with Burton cheering him on, Lee could bring a fair-sized roof down. So Pamela's soft, maternal influence was considered by all the interested parties to be the best antidote on offer. The Burtons were to be housed at a mansion at Paradise Valley nearby with four armed guards on round-the-clock surveillance.

Why they needed these heavies with the hardware was difficult to fathom. True there were minor fears that some crank of a KKK supporter might make a show of violence, or worse; a notion which received powerful stimulus after a rock smashed through the windscreen of actor Cameron Mitchell's car on the day before shooting began. Police said it had fallen accidentally from a bridge. This hardly squared with the Klan card found amid the broken glass on the seat. But a few days into shooting and the normally urbane director, Terence Young, might not have objected if a whole posse of Klansmen had descended on the production with white hoods and flaming torches. For trouble, in one egocentric form or another, flared almost from the start.

Lee Marvin had top billing but there was no doubt who the crowds had turned out to see on that crisp, sunny day in Oroville, California. Burton, his corrugated features sallow and red-blotched, smiled at the onlookers as he cushioned Elizabeth Taylor into the back of the limousine. Compared with the Marvins' low-key entry into town, this was Barnum and Bailey stuff. Twenty minutes later Burton unleashed his tongue on politics, Wales, love, life, and booze. Three tumblers of vodka martinis into his theme, he launched into, 'I do my most serious reading during my hours of insomnia, 2.30 to three o'clock in the morning. Gibbon, Milton, that sort of thing. Always I would wake up, reach over for that febrile body, then start to read . . . ' The said 'febrile body' transmitted signals of mordant disapproval which Burton's clouded, slate-grey eyes were swift to pick up.

The stage was now set for the two actors to meet. Bulbs flashed, movie cameras whirred as the two booze-battered old campaigners exchanged embarrassed grins and bad jokes for the media. 'I suppose you know I get top billing in this,' Marvin mock-sneered. 'Yes, but I'm getting more money,' said Burton. Neither wanted to hang around much after that. Lunch was being poured for them nearby. O. J. Simpson, the sports star making his acting debut in the film, joined them, then reeled away with, 'Holy Moses! – those characters had seventeen martinis apiece!' It was not the best time for Elizabeth Taylor to appear on the set to wish Marvin, with whom she'd worked on *Raintree County*, good luck on the film. In a gigantic mis-calculation of time, place, and Miss Taylor, he flung back, 'Why don't you just fuck off, sweetie!' Burton, who could be guilty of almost anything but bad taste, half-rose from his chair. But Elizabeth Taylor, no novice at recognising the crassness of a garrulous drinker, defused the moment with a smiling, 'Ah, I see you haven't changed a bit, Lee.' Then she vanished from the set. They did not speak to each other, I am told, for the rest of the production.

Terence Young (Bond films, *Mayerling*, *The Valacci Papers*, etc.) had no illusions about the dangerous problems ahead. He hoped his long experience handling high-priced egos would carry him through with Burton. His active war service was bound to win him points with Marvin. Burton was cast as Breck Stancill, the lame, debauched Southerner who confronts Marvin as Sheriff Big Track Bascomb, the crude, cunning roughneck who attempts to steer a middle course between the Ku Klux Klan and the influential bigots of the town.

Young needed a scene from Marvin on that day of the seventeen-martini lunch. But Lee's performance that day lost points on clarity. His voice was slurred. His movements clumsy. Young cut the cameras and the lights, later saying that the shot was 'a mess' and that Marvin was 'awful' in it. But hell, it's early days, he told himself. And after all, Burton and Marvin meeting for the first time was some kind of event. It was the only occasion on the film when a Marvin scene had to be cut. Both actors began to work seriously. Terence Young, and the film's two producers, Bill Shiffrin and William Alexander, believed they would get the performances they hoped for. Marvin, with some backstage help from his wife Pamela, restricted his drinking until the evening. Then he would suck at it like the old Chicago Super Chief taking on water for the last run to the coast.

After one such marathon – a St Valentine's Day party at the unit's hotel – he was invited to help cut the huge cake, fashioned into the shape of a heart. He rose unsteadily to his feet, did a 360-degree turn, then sat down, in the middle of the cake. With meringue, chocolate, cream and a ' . . . PPY VAL . . . ' embossed on his backside, he staggered out into the street to address the crowds. They expected a friendly speech. This did not feature in Marvin's immediate plans. Flinging wide his arms, Lee roared: 'Cocksuckers of Oroville, united we stand . . . !' The rhetoric from a half-drunk actor with creamy meringue stuck to his backside didn't carry the crowd. Marvin was quietly steered back inside. Oroville went to bed convinced that nothing as crazy as this had happened since the Gold Rush.

Attention now focused on Richard Burton. If clamping down on his liquor intake had been part of his reconciling 'deal' with Elizabeth Taylor, he showed no signs of it. Studio aides still remember the day when Burton sank an eight-ounce tumbler of vodka in one gulp before breakfast. Unlike Marvin who becomes (almost) everybody's favourite clown when oiled, Burton displayed the unpredictable behaviour of a wounded predator. Using words as lethally as an assassin's knife, that basilisk smile on his face, Burton was all attack. And perversely, all charm too. That charm, totally seductive when this Welsh arts graduate turns on the eloquence, produced devastating repercussions. The bar of the Prospectors' Village Motel, was where, everybody said, you find 'the action'. The dining-room too was open to the public so the local men came in with their wives or girl friends to gape at the apes from Hollywood. Sometimes the men wore straw hats with empty beer-cans glued to them. They jostled the stars pushing their wives at Marvin and Burton, delighted when either actor would make a pass in return. Saturday nights, a live combo played as crewmen danced with local girls, some of whom they had pre-empted for their long, lonely stint in Oroville.

In that heady atmosphere of fun, drink, and Hollywood glamour close enough to touch, anything could happen, and did. Two nubile streakers, every night on the hour, made a bouncy turn of the bar, over to the pool, then out into the night. Groupies, sexy out-of-towners, were more adventurous. One formidable veteran of the game, all of seventeen, waylaid Burton in a passage, 'Kiss me,' she demanded. He kissed her on the forehead with a 'How's that, dear child?' Not much. She pushed him against some packing-cases, kissed him hard on the lips. An assistant director was angry, but cautious. 'If she isn't *somebody* throw her off the set!' Indeed she might well have been somebody. Somebody like the waitress at Sambo's restaurant, a former Oroville 'Miss Pepsi', the 17-years-old Kim Dinucci whose encounter with Burton soon got to Marvin's ears.

Introduced to Burton in the bar, something more than the bland, surface smiles of the fan-and-film-star greeting flared between them. Burton, old enough to be her father, was flattered. The young beauty of Oroville, a friend now of *the* Richard Burton, walked around in a daze. Within a week she was invited on to the set, was photographed with Richard, the rumours spread, Elizabeth Taylor fumed. So insiders said. 'Humiliated' was the word that went around. They quarrelled and Burton drank. Heavily. Whether Burton bought Miss Dinucci the $450 ring – a notorious 'exhibit' at the time – before the final row with Elizabeth or after, became irrelevant. His wife abruptly left the location. Burton knew he had a divorce on his hands. While the girls left Lee Marvin mercifully alone, another girl, Ann di Angelo, a former switchboard operator at the motel, flitted across Burton's dimly-visible horizon.

Then came the unexpected bonus which the ecstatic publicity men decided could only have been engineered by that Great Press Agent In The Sky. The husband of one local girl who had allegedly been seen around with Burton, stomped into the motel bar one night, announcing that he was going to shoot the actor. Executives on the film declined to take the threat seriously. But delicious thoughts shivered in their minds. What publicity! 'JEALOUS HUSBAND SHOOTS AT FAMOUS MOVIE STAR'. Too flat. 'BURTON SLAIN ON KU KLUX KLAN SHOCKER!' Now that would be something. The fantasy faded but the farce continued.

The impact of all this on Lee Marvin was predictable. They were there to make a hard movie. His co-star's boozy hoop-la off the set had him grinning but without that old self-assurance. Not that Lee Marvin could have been accused of falling short on his reputation for good-natured belligerence. One observer saw a Filipino photographer catch Marvin unexpectedly in a candid camera shot. Lee swung round with World War II reflexes yelling, 'The little Jap got one!' To call a Filipino a 'Jap' even in fun, is no minor insult. That score settled, Marvin, that old demon in him looking for laughs, picked up a blank-loaded rifle being used in a scene, turned to the crowd of spectators and actors telling them to 'Clear off or I'll fire!' He then acted on his threat, the crowd fleeing, an assistant director moving in to end the fusillade. That caper, and Richard Burton's off-stage performances, augured badly for Terence Young's peace of mind. Having had battle experience both in World War II and Hollywood Young sensed that he was unlikely to emerge from this encounter with any medals.

Interest had now shifted from production problems and the serious issues which *The Klansman* sought to probe, to Burton's marital gear-crashing with Elizabeth Taylor and his antics with starstruck camp-followers. Marvin found himself in a three-legged race with a troubled superstar who, despite the surface confidence and corrugated Welsh humour, appeared to be on a fast ski-descent to only hell knew where. According to the *Sunday People*'s John Hiscock, Marvin was now calling the film 'The Clownsman' possibly with Mr Burton in mind. Few observers were fooled by the playful verbal interchanges between the two actors, in public. The tension between them was so taut, no one could ever be certain whether the insults, jeers, and jibes they traded were the familiar smart-ass talk, or danger signals. Private bets were laid among the crew and actors on which of the two would take the first swing at the other.

Small wonder the director, Terence Young, was to say at the end of it all, 'There were moments in this film when really I was tempted to throw myself out of the window. In one week we had Elizabeth Taylor deciding to divorce Burton; he was running around with a waitress; the husband of another woman was threatening him with a gun; and Lee Marvin was contributing to the general entertainment.'

Burton's reaction to it at the time was his well-tried expression of pained, rueful disbelief. He had always come through as the brilliant professional he is, on all his movies. No doubt he felt he could steer a successful course through the reefs on this one. He railed at the newspapers one day for the way they had 'kicked us around savagely' meaning him and 'this sweet lovely child', Kim Dinucci. The young girl's boyfriend, ranch-hand Daniel Daniels, saw it differently. 'Kim's relationship with Richard Burton has been a nightmare,' he said. 'I just wish it had never happened.' So might have Marvin and the rest of the company. As Burton appeared to be drifting closer to the edge, it was interesting to see its effect on Marvin. As Burton teased, japed and drank, Lee recognised the symptoms. Hell, if Marvin couldn't detect that old snare, pulling corks to ease the pain, then nobody could. He saw, perhaps even more clearly than the celebrated victim, that Burton was going to need a lot of help to pull out of this dive. Lee now came on as one of Burton's leading rescuers. He didn't just help Burton, he 'handled' him, the way Marvin himself had been 'handled' in the splintering years before.

The analogy of 'the blind leading the blind' is tempting but inappropriate. Burton was drinking excessively, recklessly – out of need. Passionately devoted to Elizabeth Taylor, their relationship like a fusion of hot metals, he was devastated by the certain knowledge that it was all over. Burton's own statements years later confirm, that wilfully or not, he was steering himself dangerously close to oblivion. So the more Burton tended to lubricate the troubled areas of his mind with massive gulps on the vodka bottle, the less inclined was Marvin to follow him along the same route. Nothing concentrates one drinker's mind more wonderfully than the sight of another's hitting it rough. On one shot, scheduled for a Saturday noon, all was ready, except that Burton hadn't emerged from his trailer. Discreet taps on the door evoked no response from the Welshman within.

Whether Burton was being playfully perverse, or just pie-eyed, is largely a matter of how you read the assembled evidence. The consensus seems to favour Robert Kerwin's version in the *Chicago Tribune*'s magazine section. 'There are no broads with him,' a crew member said. 'He's alone.' They tried in a quiet way to rouse him and were considering kicking in the door when along stumbled Marvin, on his day off. Marvin knocked quietly. 'Richard . . . !' For the first time there was a reaction from inside.

'Yes . . . ?'

'Richard, it's Lee.'

The door opened. Marvin slipped inside, the door closed. And for the rest of the day the Burton trailer was the liveliest spot in town; laughs and stories, great raucous recitations of Shakespeare and singing of Welsh and American songs.

But there was still a movie to complete. $4\frac{1}{2}$ million had already been staked on it, and fortunately ninety-five per cent of it was in the can. A few final scenes with Burton over the next two or three nights and it would be over. Marvin, Terence Young the director, Bill Shiffrin the executive producer, the whole crew got close to praying that Burton, drunk, ill, or despairing, would be able to draw on his masterly reserves, and come through. Not that Richard shared in the pervading apprehension. Welsh miners' sons, as sturdy as the pit props which keep the mountains from falling in on them, smiled at Marvin and all, like an errant schoolboy. The spirit was willing. But as for the flesh – one observer, John Austin, reported from Oroville that one evening Burton had arrived on the set supported by an aide and guided by another who held his left arm. After the Welshman had tried three times to find his chair, Terence Young asked him to stand in the foreground of the shot. There were, however, difficulties in lining up Burton, and Terence Young was heard to exclaim, 'This is impossible!' Burton's double was called in to complete the shot. Whatever Lee Marvin's emotions were at the time, compassion must have been the strongest. He was seeing a consummate actor with formidable world-class successes behind him (and ahead of him too as it turned out), caught in a one-off catastrophe. One scene took fifteen takes. As Terence Young remembered it, 'Towards the end of it we were breaking it up into one-liners. I'd read the lines to him and he'd repeat them like a parrot.'

The scene required Marvin as the sheriff to feed Burton the line, 'You gonna let 'em use your mountain?' – to which Burton's response as the debauched but liberal Southerner, Breck Stancill, was, 'I don't mean to be *contrarying* the country people's feelings . . . ' Not the easiest words to roll round an uncertain tongue, even one that had given us one of the best Othellos, Iagos, Hamlets and Henry the Fifths on record. Burton changed 'contrarying' to 'feuding'.

'Cut!' ordered Terence Young. The script girl gave Burton his line, and Marvin came in on cue. Burton now substituted 'offending'. 'Cut!' Terence Young's eyes beseeched the Gods, and Mr Burton peered innocently at the script. For the next five takes, says writer Robert Kerwin, 'Burton plays with synonyms, a perverseness creeping into his eyes. 'Don't mean to be quarrelling with . . . getting on the wrong side of . . . rubbing the country people's feelings the wrong way . . . ' It's a game. After each of Young's cuts, Burton grins and points a finger at Young. 'Got you, Terence old man!'

Finally Burton made it. Flashing Marvin a guilty smile he walked off the set. The actor in him constructed an impressive exit. But Marvin and Terence Young observed that he was coughing badly. And trembling. His eyes were bloodshot. He glanced back at the crew, a glimmer of an apology on his face. Marvin heard him murmur, 'I'm sorry Terry. I'm terribly sorry everybody . . . ' But it was Burton's last scene in the movie that Terence Young remembers – could hardly forget. Talking to me about it in his penthouse apartment in Beverly Hills not long ago, Young stressed that

Richard was a terribly sick man. When I saw how bad it was I told everybody that we'd just better wind up the shooting. He was making a great effort, having to force his whole body just to get the words out. His face was shaking like a man with the ague. He was white, he was blue, and he was yellow. His colour was changing all the time. It was a terrifying physical experience. I got a doctor down and the man said, 'This man is dying. He'll be dead in three weeks.'

I said, 'You must be kidding, what do you mean?'

And he said, 'No. I must change his blood. I don't think he's quite got cirrhosis of the liver yet, but he's practically in the last stages of getting it. His kidneys are diseased and he's in terrible condition.'

213

We were working on the scene in the film where Burton
is supposed to lie there dying. I said to Ronnie, the make-up
man, 'You've done a great job.'

He said, 'I haven't touched him.'

At that moment I was really scared and said, 'Come on,
we'll shoot that scene as fast as we can.'

I finished with him around ten o'clock that night, earlier
than anybody else. I decided to get Burton's death scene in
and then finish the rest of the picture afterwards. I had
arranged for a car to take him to the airport and a private
plane to fly him to Los Angeles. They got him to hospital
there and went to work on him literally within five minutes
of his arrival. They took his clothes off, put him on the
trolley, ran him up to surgery and started to give him blood
tests, then transfusions. [A quick check showed he had a
temperature of 104. He had influenza, tracheobronchitis and,
to add a touch of colour, a lacerated hand from a bad fall
behind a tree.] He was desperately ill for about a week, but
they saved him. Looking back I think I probably helped save
his life. I believe if we hadn't moved that fast with the car and
the plane, alerting the hospital, Richard Burton would be a
corpse today.

Burton, with his customary brute frankness, does not dissent
from that view. In fact, like any reformed character, he relishes
the exercise in coming clean. Rejuvenated by a happy marriage
(to the former Suzy Hunt), and by an impressive upsurge in his
career, Burton is handsomely penitent. Remorse comes easier
when you're back on a winning streak. Burton has now stoutly
squared his account. His talents are again at full throttle. His
Equus on Broadway was a triumph. And to prove he wasn't
fooling he repolished the gem in the film version. He is right
back in the superstar business – not bad for a man who almost
killed himself.

A fair summary of his published reflections on that long,
unhappy night in Oroville, goes something like this:

I was on the edge of self-destruction. I am very lucky to have
deliberately, brutally destroyed my career with my own hands
– and then been given the chance to come back. If I am not an
alcoholic, I'd say I am one drink or one outburst away from
it. That was an interesting week (in the hospital in California) waiting to find out if I had cirrhosis of the liver. I

didn't. Now I can go anywhere and enjoy the drunks falling down and even take them home without turning a hair.

With Burton having his liver and blood stream checked in Santa Monica, Terence Young, with a fair amount of extra-curricular support from Lee Marvin, wound up the rest of the picture.

Marvin's ideas on the script were always intelligent, imaginative and not line-grabbing the way you get with some actors who are usually only interested in their part in the picture. He contributed a great deal. He is very responsive and terribly quick. At times he would go into the whistle-fart-kavoom routine, banging his arms like a chicken, but it was a useful respite from the strain we were under.

Young felt he owed it to Richard Burton to recall that when he came back to the unit after being hospitalised,

he had changed completely. He was controlled, intelligent, and determined. He came for lunch and we all drank Frescas and Pepsis. He said, 'God man! I know you want a bottle of wine. I know the moment my back is turned you'll go and have one. So go ahead – drink.' We did. Often. Burton watched the vodka and wine being poured, but never touched a drop. It was all rather sad. He had a nurse with him. He had obviously been through hell. The divorce from Elizabeth Taylor had hit him harder than anyone realised. It's all over now. Burton proved he can bounce back. He's as expensive and as hard to get for movies as ever. Lee Marvin demonstrated that he's a generous human being as well as being a damn fine actor. But it is not an episode I am likely to forget.

The same goes for the people of Oroville. I suspect they would not feel deprived if Marvin and Burton never came their way again.

At the beach house on Malibu, Lee Marvin studied the trade reviews of *The Klansman*, threw them across to Pamela with some appropriate obscenities. Six months had passed since the fiasco on the location. He had been glad to write it off to experience. The reviews by the important *Hollywood Reporter* and *Daily Variety* – both vital graphs to an actor's market value

– jerked the episode back into his mind. They were not just bad notices. Rarely had an American film featuring world-class actors been mauled with such savagery. The *Reporter* was marginally less lethal. To its critic, John H. Dorr, 'Everything falls flat, reducing highly ironic situations and bizarre, colourful dialogue to false-ringing Hollywood artifice.' The action scenes were 'gratuitously violent', the music 'vapid', the editing 'disjointed', the production design 'rehashed Hollywood cliché of the deep South . . . ' Almost a rave compared with the vitriol from a character signed 'Murf' in *Daily Variety*.

The Klansman is a perfect example of screen trash that almost invites derision,' he began. 'This miserable film stars Lee Marvin as a Dixie Sheriff with lots of unoriginal, cliché racial trouble on his hands and Richard Burton as an unpopular landowner in a performance as phoney as his Southern accent. There is not a shred of quality, dignity, relevance or impact in this yahoo-oriented bunk. Paramount hasn't had its name on a fetid carcass like this in well over a year.

Marvin didn't bother to read any of the other notices. He didn't need to. What really hurt was the fact that it was rare for him not to win points for *something* in a film, even if it was the dog of the year. Another kind of actor might have tried to shovel this truckload of critical sludge on to his fellow stars, the producers, director, or any other fall-guy to hand. Marvin did not. The opposite. He telephoned the screenwriter Millard Kaufman (who shared writing credits on the film with Samuel Fuller) and told him, 'I know what the script was like and I know what happened to it. What we have on the screen is not what was in the script and I want you to know that I think you behaved extremely well and you're a hell of a guy.'

Kaufman, who had been unnerved by the whole painful experience, was moved by Marvin's gesture.

'Lee, you're a hell of a guy yourself,' he said.

'Bullshit!' growled the caller from Malibu. And rang off.

One test of an actor's pulling power is whether, after his latest film has bombed out, he can still command major roles and half a million dollars plus. Marvin proved that he could, surviving both *The Klansman* and *The Spikes Gang*, a brooding, brutal Western he had made earlier. (I asked the man who directed it, Richard Fleischer, one of Hollywood's top talents, how the film came out. 'A disaster,' he said with cheerful candour.) Scores of scripts were delivered to his home at Malibu. Several of them were rehashes of *Cat Ballou*, and bad ones at that. He had to be discerning now. The national box-office returns indicated he was still one of America's top money-spinners. In recognition of it, the magazine *Cosmopolitan* invited him to pose in the nude for their centrefold, the horizontal status symbol for the full-frontally inclined. He told the then-editor Helen Gurney Brown, 'I'll do it if you'll do it with me.' Invitation declined.

Marvin was offered the late Robert Shaw's role in *Jaws*. He turned it down for an unexpected reason. In no way, he said, was he going to act with a mechanical fish. (Part of the predatorial underwater action was shot, necessarily, using mock-ups.) Marvin's respect for the monsters of the deep wouldn't allow him to engage in that kind of hokum. 'Sure it would have made me a lot of money,' he agreed. 'But in the first place I can't spend all that I make now. And, second, what would I tell my fishing friends who'd see me come off a hero against a dummy shark?' In a more philosophical mood he reprised an old theme – that fishing meant more to him than just a life-and-death combat between him and the prey. 'Next to acting, fishing is about the only way I get any feeling of real existence. Fishing is thinking time. Peace time. God's time. I love it.'

It was during one of these bouts of contemplation that Malibu's most raucous resident decided he was going to pick up his booze and saddles, sell out, and go. He had, he declared to Pamela one night, had enough of the whole 'frigging circus'. He was tired of his drunken mates using his house as a hotel, hauling themselves over every hour on the hour, disturbing the peace, wielding his Oscar to crush the ice. He detested the new tycoons of the movie business with their 'coke' parties, their kaftans, and the herd instinct that stampeded them from one 'in' place to another. He wouldn't concede it, but if you hadn't served in the Marines, or at least heard a gun fired in World War II, you weren't his kind of man. Unless you had pulled in a 1,000lb marlin. That might just win you diplomatic immunity. To him, Malibu had lost its style. The beach, on to which Michelle Triola-turned-Marvin used to toss entire dinners after a blazing row, now featured nothing more startling than a nubile semi-nude surfer hoping to froth her way into a screen test.

Lee Marvin, for all his macho posturing and party-shattering sex talk, possesses a strong puritan streak stretching right back to the earliest Marvins. The Hollywood of that time with its sex obsessions and borderline attitudes disgusted him. He felt as far removed from that as, say, Julie Andrews would feel from Roman Polanski. His wife, Pamela, had had enough of Malibu too. Playing mother hen to Marvin's brood of boozers was not her idea of marital bliss. They wanted to get away from that, the hustlers, and the gossip queens who had driven Paul Newman to Connecticut, Robert Redford to Utah, and a couple of legendary stars to a despairing, melancholy end. When the day came Lee and Pamela left Malibu as elated as lifers out on parole. Malibu police, several drinking joints and certain neighbours were just as blissful. End of an era. One Marvin era.

His friend, writer Edna McHugh, on whose porch Marvin had cracked his skull and become uproariously hospitalised, felt a pang of sadness. 'Nobody could wreck a dinner party quite like Lee,' she sighed. 'No blood will ever flow here again.'

The new Marvin homestead is a twenty-acre ranch five miles out of Tucson, Arizona. To get there you drive through scrub and undulating desert towards the purple mountain ranges where the US Cavalry once fought the Apaches. Along the route, giant cacti, as tall as eight John Waynes, trigger memories of a score of favourite Westerns. It is cold at night, bleachingly hot by day. The sky is picture-postcard blue. A factor, no doubt, in the selection of the area for military flying. Somewhere over a hill, they trained U-2 pilots. Arab and Israeli officers practise on the planes which the US sells to both parties. Marvin bought an old gold mine close by. It was going cheap, and anyway what else is there to buy when you already have real estate, oil wells, investments, and you name it? Marvin started working the mine immediately his claim was notarised. He produces a small bottle of gold dust on demand. Not many actors have their own private gold mine to fall back on when the energy flags, the reviews are bad, or the public has turned to other idols. The bottle of yellow gold dust was the only kind of bottle he was likely to produce at the time: January, 1975.

For the day he decided to leave Malibu and the Hollywood colony, he made another, infinitely more sacrificial, resolution. He would stop drinking. A small step for mankind, but a gigantic decision for the longest-serving tippler in the trade. Who, or what, induced it offers a string of possibilities. Burton's catastrophic drinking on *The Klansman* gave Marvin plenty to brood about. He knew his own liver had only an even-Steven's chance of surviving the battering he was giving it. Having weighed the situation judiciously, Marvin ruled that the pleasure wasn't worth the pain. And then there was his wife Pamela. No shrinking violet in drinking company, she nevertheless backed off from Lee's wilder marathons. The odd friend who now comes to the ranch is offered cordial, and a meaningful glance from the resolute Mrs Marvin. So Lee drinks fruit juices, spits disgustedly, and talks fast about anything but booze. Thirsty friends, though, have been known to search dark corners for the odd bottle that might have been mislaid.

But taking the pledge and keeping to it, in the serenity of a soft, silent Arizona night, is one thing. When you're back on the treadmill, when the intensity demanded of a performance is strung tight enough to snap, you turn to the only painkiller you know. With movies to make, a lawsuit to fight, a marriage to protect – that was only part of Marvin's dilemma. The hardest bit of all was sustaining the image. He had built a triumphant reputation as one of the most belligerent characters in – and out – of motion pictures. But it couldn't be done without the juice. How do you present yourself as being a gulp ahead of Robert Mitchum if you're now having to hide in a closet to get away from the stuff? Anyway, a hell-raiser has to be seen to raise hell. Even if it kills him. And some, just a few, were saying that it was beginning to kill Lee Marvin. So the definitive battler of the screen now had a more serious fight on his hands. Lee Marvin versus himself.

Chapter Sixteen

'I've had the luck to be present when the sun was shining . . . '

Lee Marvin

Fifteen weeks. 105 days for anyone disposed to count them. As Lee Marvin was, filming *Shout at the Devil* in South Africa. It was probably the longest he had been without a drink in more than a quarter of a century. Maybe the most valiant fifteen weeks of his life too, and that includes the time he and the Marines went in at Saipan. Lee had everything against him. Not least was the role he had to play. He was cast as an Irish-American ivory poacher who also happened to be a tearaway alcoholic. To be called upon to play a drunk when you're fighting to forget the stuff is turning temptation into a bad joke. The fact that the character's name was Flynn clinched it. It was hot out there, too, in the Transkei.

Heat, thirst, and drink fall naturally together. The equation was hardly to work in Marvin's favour. And then there was that old craving at night when the actor needed to uncoil the tension – and to do so his way. Satan at his most malevolent could not have devised a more enticing array of bait to trap the dry-throated Mr Marvin. He resisted it all, bringing added significance to the film's title *Shout at the Devil*. He had some help. When the going was rough, Pamela put her hand over his, transmitting the kind of signals that tell a patient he's loved, and doing fine. There must have been much of Pamela's own resourcefulness behind Marvin's pledge, made just before they

220

left London for Africa: 'I'm finished with drink, the aggressive sonofabitch image, the hard living. I've been burning myself out. It's been getting too harrowing, too shattering, too frightening . . . ' If his co-star on the film had been, say, Keenan Wynn, or the director Sam Peckinpah, Lee Marvin may not have survived the sound of liquid gurgling into a glass. In fact, his fellow actor, Roger Moore, after the fashion of James Bond, reserved his vodka-martini for the cocktail hour. By Marvin standards this was total abstinence.

But there were a couple of minor lapses towards the end of Lee's long dry-run. The film was nearly over. He had heard from Hollywood that Michelle Triola-Marvin's lawsuit was crescendoeing towards the California Supreme Court. The need for a snorter, and fighting it, made him agitated, and depressed. He decided one little drink might just dispel the gloom. It was the last few days shooting on the island of Malta. He got smashed. He turned up that way on to the set. True it had happened many times before. But then the remorse faded at the first belter of the day. Now it was different. Maybe because of Pam, or a sudden flash of insight – but Marvin saw what was happening to him. And to those others who had to carry him. The cast and crew. It dawned on him at last that while it might be okay to screw up his own work, he had no special dispensation to do it to the actors and the rest of the unit.

He strolled over to the director, Peter Hunt, and apologised. He did the same to Roger Moore and Barbara Parkins. Typically, he decided the gesture was not complete. He went over to the rest of the stage men and made his peace with them too. It was a handsome display of repentance. The production shimmered in the after-glow for hours. The producers forgave him instantly when the day's rushes revealed what a fine performance he was giving. A fair adventure movie came out of it too, though it was not one of Lee Marvin's best efforts. But most critics agreed that Roger Moore had rarely done anything better. He thought so too, and gave the credit to Marvin.

Moore returned to England with a respect for the American star perilously close to hero-worship. At a press reception in London to launch the première, the likeable British actor said and evidently meant, 'I love this gentleman.' (Pamela, within earshot, beamed agreement at that description.) 'Thanks to him I have given my best performance ever. I can only be as good

221

as the other guy. Working with Lee Marvin hauls you up,
forces you to try to reach his level. Thank you, Mr Marvin.'
Lee shifted with embarrassment, lifted his eyes, emitted a choice
obscenity to the Adam ceiling: 'I can't take any more of *that*!'
he muttered. 'It could make me break the habit of a lifetime
and turn to drink!' He gave the same old grin. But it broke on
to a face now gaunt beneath the fading African tan. He was
asked his age, gave it as fifty-two and nobody responded with
the double-take of astonished disbelief.

There were all the familiar Marvin routines; the needling, the
whistle and the pop. The ritual image-bolstering. But Lee's
heart wasn't in it. It was as though he was hearing the words
for the first time. Like a puppet catching a sudden glimpse of
the man who holds the strings. If his publicity man, Paul Wasserman, had been there; and his agent, Meyer Mishkin, both would
have picked up the message in the tired eyes: 'How long can I
go on shovelling this stuff? I mean do I really have to? When
can the real Marvin stand up?' He was glad when Pamela
hauled him back to their hotel. That was one thing he'd stage-
managed. He'd kept his wife, with her formula for keeping their
marriage afloat and sailing well, out of the headlines and the
gossip columns. He was prepared to go along with the act as a
solo performer. Jump through the hoops. Put his fists up once in
a while. Raise a little hell. Deliver the sexy one-liners to give
the women writers their vicarious thrills. But when it came to his
relationship with Pamela, that, he declared, was private. 'We've
got a damn fine thing going. But it belongs to us. I've got an
audience as an actor. I don't need one in my parlour, or my
bedroom.'

They were enjoying a life of boisterous tranquility. The only
kind of life Marvin could take. He was becoming totally dependent on her. More involved with Pamela, needing her in a way
that he had not needed Betty Ebeling or Michelle. He was a
different character then. Now, behind the riotous façade, Marvin
was a man under siege. Vulnerable as hell and, as he said,
scared. Perversely that dependence on Pamela brought out the
old threat-to-his-manhood panic. But now he was admitting
grudgingly, there was no way he could beat the system. 'Guys
think they can do without women but they can't.' Whenever
'the whole marriage bit' drove him to howl 'Who the hell
NEEDS this!' an inside voice responded, 'You do, you

schmuck!' Short of a sudden spectactular dive back into drink, he believed he was home,'and dry. But he knew he would have to fight all the way. And now and again he lost a couple of rounds.

A memorable occasion was in Durango, Mexico, filming *Great Scout and Cathouse Thursday*, a tedious horse-opera about gold mines and whorehouses. Thrown opposite Britain's decidedly economy-class hellraiser, Oliver Reed, Lee must have had misgivings the night before filming began. Or perhaps it was nothing more original than a contest between two reputations, the one long established, the other striving. In any event, the ambitious Mr Reed, Britain's young pretender, coming face to face with the real McCoy, vowed he would drink Lee Marvin under the table. A table in a small Mexican cantina, salt-lick for such famous thirsts named Wayne, Mitchum, and Glenn Ford and more.

Oliver Reed pointed to the tequila bottle on the table. 'I am going to have a drink,' he said. Marvin's iron resolution wilted at what, in reflex, he took as a challenge to his fifty-years-odd masculinity. They belted away for ten hours. (It was easy to be precise. Onlookers too mesmerised to leave the action, checked their watches on the final gulp.) It must be fairly stated that Oliver Reed was the one who walked away, his pale-blue eyes fixed glassily upon some indeterminate horizon. Lee Marvin lay unconscious. Now and again he stirred, opened one unseeing eye, closed it, and slumbered on. Someone tried to rouse him, and failed. A cowboy fired a six-gun into the air. But Marvin who claimed he snoozed during the first salvoes at Guadacanal, barely moved.

The morning after, director Don Taylor expected a hungover actor to stagger guiltily on to the set. He hadn't reckoned with Marvin's capacity to recoup. Marvin knew his marks, his lines, and his moves. He was back on the wagon after that. And needed to be. He flew back home to find Michelle's 'Rights for Mistresses' lawsuit had won a significant victory in the California Supreme Court. Overruling the lower courts which had twice thrown out her claim, the Supreme Court declared: 'The fact that a man and woman live together without marriage and engage in a sexual relationship does not in itself invalidate agreements between them relating to their earnings.'

In essence this gave Michelle the right to be treated as a wife for the purpose of deciding her legal rights in any property settlement. She always claimed she was called 'Mrs' and felt a Mrs. 'I washed dishes and Lee put out the garbage.' She also alleges that she and Lee agreed to share earnings during their six years together on Malibu. The implications for Marvin, and his money, were as plain as a daylight bank heist. He and Pamela first heard the Court ruling on television. Then it hit the news-stands. 'PAY YOUR LOVER! ACTOR TOLD' was a sample of the headlines which scowled at Lee over his breakfast cereal. 'LEE'S GIRL CLAIMS A FORTUNE' made him smile. Let it ride. She was entitled to her day in court.

Across the town, his now-famous mistress was holding court like a movie queen. True she was a long way from the hands-in-the-wet-cement treatment outside Grauman's Chinese Theatre. But there was no denying that on this crisp December morning, 1976, in Los Angeles, Michelle Triola-Marvin was the woman of the hour. 'There are millions of women like me,' she told reporters, 'women who simply could not hold back on loving someone until they got a piece of paper with signatures on. Now this trial will show them exactly where they stand.'

Or fall. There was still a case to be fought on the question of whether an agreement had in fact existed between her and Lee Marvin to share earnings and property. But the Supreme Court's ruling had to weigh heavily in her favour. Her lawyer, Hollywood's resourceful Marvin Mitchelson, shared Michelle's elation.

In his plush suite in Beverly Hills' prestigious Century Plaza he said: This is what we have been fighting for. She was a wife to the man for years and deserves to be treated as such. What this means is that Michelle's courage is standing up for her rights could result in legal protection for the growing number of unlicensed wives who find themselves in her situation.

Mr Mitchelson's soaring phrases reverberated through California, right across America, particularly the bit about 'unlicensed wives who find themselves in her situation . . . ' – the rush to lawyers' offices across the states, by 'unlicensed' playmates and their nervous sponsors, was, according to one awe-struck attorney, 'getting close to a stampede.' It was a laugh to everyone except those who had something to lose. Like money.

Lee Marvin, and his lawyers, were determined this was a case they had to fight. The 'other side' would have to wait for their money until 'hell freezes over'. Until this point in the legal fracas Lee Marvin had watched Michelle make all the running. Now, on the advice of his lawyers, he suddenly came up with a claim of his own.

Marvin sued Michelle. It was a plot-change which bore the imaginative touch of the best Hollwood scenario. He sued her for a million dollars. He claimed compensation for the 'companionship, counselling and entertaining' he gave her during their life together. And he asked for damages on the grounds that she failed to live up to her agreement to devote her full-time attention to him. That is how it stood with the two contestants at that time. Michelle, cast as the Joan of Arc of America's kept, but not legalised, womenfolk was convinced she could not lose. Lee Marvin, riled at being the chosen patsy for the nation's uncertificated lovers, believed he had an 'open and shut case'.

So the battle 'Marvin v Marvin' was neatly poised when Michelle Triola-Marvin, on 9 January 1979, went before Judge Arthur Marshall at the Los Angeles County Court demanding one and a half million dollars, supposedly half of Lee's earnings between 1964 and 1970. Michelle, then forty-six, arrived for the hearing in a black crêpe suit, prominently displaying a heavy gold chain bearing the large letter 'M'. If the crowd of curious onlookers wondered whether it stood for Michelle, Mitchelson, or even Money, the lady quickly spelled it out. Turning to the newsmen and TV interviewers, she said, 'Once in love, always in love as far as I am concerned. I had made up my mind I was not going to cry today, but my mouth has gone dry and this is a very emotional experience for me, watching the man I lived with for so long, ignoring me.'

Lee had marched into court with Pamela on his arm, without a glance in Michelle's direction. Though she sat less than fifteen feet from him, her sprucely turned-out ex-lover looked at the ceiling, the floor, everywhere else but at her. At any rate during the opening skirmishes. Once she began to unveil her version of their six-year relationship all the intimacies raked out into the open, Lee surveyed her with that old basilisk grin.

He sensed the going would be rough. As anticipated, Mitchelson led his tearful client through the early traumas of the ill-fated love affair. And on to that most tender and volatile of all subjects, in America, Motherhood, and Michelle's alleged termination of it.

Close to tears, her voice faltering into a half-whisper, Michelle claimed that two abortions which Lee had allegedly encouraged her into, had left her sterile. 'He just wasn't interested in having children,' she said. At this point Marvin, who hadn't uttered a word so far, shouted 'I can't hear her!' Invited by the kindly judge to speak up, Michelle obliged – in spades. Marvin may have asked himself whether he hadn't been a shade hasty. Mitchelson, eager to show how much Lee relied on Michelle's love and devotion, asked his client to describe Lee's drinking bouts. Looking towards the judge through enormous spectacles, the round-cheeked plaintiff recalled how in 1965, when he was filming *The Professionals* in Las Vegas, she heard screaming in an hotel room. She burst in to find Marvin holding a woman out of the window by her legs. 'I nearly fainted,' she said. That chilling caprice (true or false) had a similar impact on the crowded courtroom. It evoked visions of Lee's more brutal film characterisations dominated by, say, *The Killers* or *Point Blank*. That bomb deftly planted, Mitchelson took Ms Marvin on to liquor. Heaving a sigh, she described how she once threw alcohol into the Pacific to try and stop Lee drinking. She even boiled the stuff in an attempt to get rid of its alcoholic content though Marvin never knew this. Marvin's jaw sagged momentarily. It seemed a hell of a way to treat booze. A smile spread around the courtroom. Reporters phoned their city editors with the joyful news that the case was 'getting down to the nitty gritty'.

Precisely why Mitchelson had introduced the abortion testimony was not clear. Maybe he considered that it was all grist to the mill in establishing the depth of their relationship. Legally, the burden of proving that she and Marvin had an 'implied contract' to share their property, rested squarely with her. The California Supreme Court decision of 1976, which allowed that she should be treated as a wife in alimony cases, had created the precedent. It was now up to Mitchelson to go in to bat for all he could get. So Michelle told the judge how she had believed that Marvin had planned to support her indefinitely. 'I was

226

stunned,' she said, 'when his lawyer told me, "You have no legal rights . . . you'd better take what you can get and don't make him mad or you'll get nothing." ' She said the lawyer offered her 800 dollars a month if she was a 'good girl, and did not tell her story to newspapers.' (Not much of an offer since a month or two later publishers were reportedly offering her a great chunk of money for her updated version of her life with Lee.) Marvin later sent her $1,050 a month which gave her $800 after taxes, but the payments were stopped in less than a year, she said.

Set against Lee's big earnings, the sums did not seem excessive. Veterans of alimony suits in the crowded Room 509 of the court expressed private views that at that stage sympathy was probably veering slightly in Michelle's favour. The maxim, 'a man must pay for his fun' is nowhere more vigorously defended than in Hollywood. The manner in which Lee apparently ended the relationship, therefore became crucial. Crucial to Michelle. She retold the story she had once told me, of her phone conversation with Lee's new wife Pamela. Her eyes brimming with tears, the court hushed, she explained that she had simply phoned Lee to find out why he had stopped payment on her cheques. But it was his new wife Pamela who took the call. According to Michelle, 'Get lost – why don't you get yourself a new boy-friend,' was Pamela's decidedly short and frosty response.

There were more tears from Ms Marvin when she claimed that the actor had made her pregnant three times because she did not like birth control devices. She said all the pregnancies were subsequently terminated. More intimate details followed and Lee's face on which a wry grin hovered, now abandoned all expression. He was fighting this case – at least from where he stood – as a matter of principle. Now he was hearing the woman he'd loved – he deliciously defined the word later – and lived with, telling Los Angeles, and the world, how she used contraceptives at the start of their affair, but, 'later Lee said that contraceptives kind of bothered him physically and also psychologically. I quit using them.'

Contraceptives discontinued . . . pregnancies . . . abortions . . . 'Get lost . . . why don't you find yourself another boy-friend . . . ' given that the facts were true, the portrait they painted of Lee Marvin made the porcine male chauvinism of the average American, seem positively saintly. Mitchelson's case, though understandably lingering over emotive issues, looked formidable. His heart-swelling scenario seemed to be this:

> *Beautiful young singer with promising career falls hopelessly in love with big, tough, famous actor. She gives up glittering future to be his long-suffering mistress, nursing his hangovers, hiding his liquor, enduring his wild eccentricities, aborting her pregnancies, all out of selfless devotion to the man whose name she had proudly adopted. And now, discarded like an old glove, she was merely asking for fair and decent recompense . . .*

Marvin took the witness stand knowing that Michelle's case would take some demolishing. Yes, he agreed he had given Michelle £300 for one of her abortions. Sure he had never used contraceptives. But hadn't he loved her? Mitchelson asked him. Hadn't Lee in a letter to her in Hawaii written (from London) 'Things are about the same – dull. Not that I ain't looking. But there's nothing here that compares with you, you, you.' The letter referred to Michelle as 'love'. Mitchelson challenged Marvin with 'was she your love?'

'No, that's an English figure of speech,' said Marvin. Sure on occasions he'd told her that he loved her but he did not really mean it, thus adding a new word to his list of bad characters – cad. But wait. What is this thing called love, according to the precepts of Mr Lee Marvin? Like a tank of gasoline apparently. Quietly and deliberately, playing the young professor, Marvin delivered himself of the following:

'It's like looking at the petrol gauge in your car. You can be empty, half-full or full.' (If Michelle baulked at the notion of their love being measured by the gallon, it didn't immediately show on her face.)

'Love is a matter of scale,' Marvin told the judge. 'There's young, frivolous love, the child-like love with a Teddy-bear. Then when you go up the scale the ultimate love would be one between people where the deep regard for another person, truthfulness, loyalty, fidelity, and a tremendous sense of selflessness would be the other extreme. So on which area of the scale did his love for Michelle fall? Lee Marvin switched the metaphor from the gasoline gauge to cuddly toys. His love for

Michelle, declared the Number One Sadist of the Screen, was that of a child towards a Teddy-bear.

But Teddy-bears are not sued for a million and a half dollars. A whole gallery of witnesses were called, with his friend and agent Meyer Mishkin painting a roseate picture of his valued client. He asserted that Michelle was at one time responsible for Lee's heavy drinking. 'She definitely made the problem worse,' he said. He recalled a visit he made to the island of Palau where Lee was filming *Hell in the Pacific*. Marvin became so drunk he lost control of himself. 'There was so much bickering and quarrelling I couldn't cope with it. My wife and I would have stayed much longer but we couldn't wait to get away.' According to Mishkin, 'Lee and Michelle were involved in an argument which went on for hours. That night they slept in separate bedrooms. The next day Lee was drunk. I suggested to Michelle that she left Lee alone and stopped nagging him all the time.'

Responses by the two main contenders were predictable. A grin from Marvin, steely glance from the plaintiff. A brief appearance by a fisherman from Hawaii produced the first sensation in court. His name was Rope Nelson, flown in from Kona, Hawaii, to testify for Michelle. The fact that Nelson had lost a court action to Marvin over the ownership of Lee's boat *Blue Hawaii* would not be lost on the judge or on Lee's attorney David Kagon. But they did not anticipate Nelson's emotional outburst in the crowded courtroom. At the end of his hour-long testimony, he was asked why he had flown all the way from Kona to testify. Nelson stared darkly at Marvin. 'Because of him!' he said angrily. 'He and I were buddies, pals. We fished together. We were like brothers. And look at us today. I really ... he was my buddy and I was his. And through his stupidity and lies, here we are. She used to be my sister. Now he's doing it to her.' He then turned directly towards Marvin. 'You have to grow up Lee. Stand up and be counted for. You're not the Lee Marvin I knew.'

Judge Arthur K. Marshall waved a hand deciding that this Nelson had had his Trafalgar. He ordered an immediate recess for temperatures to cool. But Mr Nelson continued his attack outside the courtroom. 'I feel sorry for him,' he said of Marvin, 'he was a man before, but not now. Just lies, lies, lies.' Back in the courtroom he recalled happier days, on the sparkling Hawaiian waters taking Lee and Michelle fishing on the *Pua*

Kai (Flower of the Sea). Had he observed their conduct aboard the boat? asked Mitchelson. Nelson shrugged. 'You can't miss them. It's not that big.' He took it for granted that they were married because they had a suite together and because Marvin often introduced her as 'Michelle Marvin'. Later, he said Marvin told him they were not married but 'they went to the judge' to have her name changed 'to save embarrassment when they travelled abroad'. A bland statement, and understandable, given the 'raised-eyebrow' reactions still prevalent among some European and Far Eastern hotels.

But the missile boomeranged dreadfully, when one of Lee's business associates, publicist Jim Mahoney, gave his own explanation as to why Michelle changed her name to Marvin. According to this chunky veteran of the Hollywood press agents (he ran a long stint with Frank Sinatra) Ms Marvin consulted him about the name change in 1968, before she and Lee flew to Japan for the première there of *Hell in the Pacific*. Mahoney claimed, to some old-fashioned grins in the court, she told him she wanted to be called 'Marvin' because she didn't want the Emperor of Japan 'to think I'm a hooker'. (The assumption, presumably, was that she and Lee would be presented to the Emperor during the shindigs for his film). Michelle's immediate reaction in the courtroom was to laugh loudly. Mahoney paused, then persisted, 'I distinctly remember that.' This did it for Michelle. She suddenly slumped into moaning sobs. Penny Mercurio, her attorney's assistant, put an arm around her and led her from the courtroom. At the break she recovered sufficiently to offer a pallid smile. 'I just didn't understand what Mr Mahoney was talking about. My feelings got hurt. I would never have said such a thing even in jest.'

But from that moment it was clear that Marvin's lawyer, David Kagon was massing sizeable legal artillery against Lee's hapless former mistress. Pamela, the second Mrs Marvin was now to have her day in court. As she took the stand she came under the full scrutiny of a courtroom fascinated to see the woman who apparently, to use the current label, 'had tamed Marvin'. The seventeenth witness in the case she testified in a quiet, measured voice that Michelle Triola Marvin told her after the wedding to Lee, 'You may be married to Mr Marvin but don't forget he's still keeping me.' How did she feel about that? 'The phraseology, the terminology disturbed me but not that he was giving her the money, it had nothing to do with me.' But she denied sharply that she had influenced Lee to stop the monthly $833 payments to his former live-in lover. (It was Marvin Mitchelson's argument that the payments were stopped at her behest but the new Mrs Marvin insisted just as trenchantly that she did not.) According to her, she was bothered by frequent phone calls from Michelle which 'started the night we were married and continued for a year and a half'. True she made some calls, conceded Michelle casually, one to wish Lee a 'merry Christmas' and at other times because she was concerned about the payments.

She then added a comment which triggered understanding nods from a couple of women nearby. 'I wanted my bed back,' she said. 'It bothered me that they were sleeping in my bed.'

If Jim Mahoney's testimony ('I didn't want the Emperor of Japan to think I was a hooker') took Ms Marvin by surprise, the unexpected testimony of a thirty-four-year-old former Peace Corps member, Richard Doughty, threw her, and the court, into some turmoil. A mystery witness, Doughty's evidence was kept under wraps while Judge Arthur K. Marshall deliberated on whether it could be ruled admissible or not. It gave a somewhat steamy account of a love affair he alleged he had with Michelle during the 'relevant' years of the Marvin-v-Marvin case, and it was clear Mitchelson would fight to have the testimony ruled inadmissible.

But after two days the judge overruled Mitchelson's objections.

Doughty was not called upon to deliver his tale to the court. Instead, his nine hours of testimony was read to reporters by the judge's clerk. It was quite a number, first the clerk Gwen Healey reciting the opening sequences of the romantic interludes, then after the lunch recess, a court reporter Pat Richker, reading the closing acts. It added up to this; Doughty said he began his affair with Ms Marvin in 1969 when she and Lee Marvin were visiting the island (Palau) where the actor was filming. His affair with Michelle began, he said, after he had been introduced to her by Marvin. A former research biologist and diver for the Peace Corps, Doughty claimed that Ms Marvin showed up at his office one day and asked his boss, 'If I (Doughty) could have the afternoon off to take her out for a picnic on the beach where they shot *Hell in the Pacific*. He said that on the picnic they became intimate for the first of about twenty-five times in Palau. Later, when he left the Peace Corps and decided to try to become an actor, he returned to the United States and lived briefly with Marvin and Michelle. On several occasions after that, including, in Tucson on the set of *Monte Walsh*, the affair continued. Finally, the candid testimony went on, Doughty insisted on ending the affair, feeling as he did, that he was being a 'false friend' to Marvin.

Mitchelson's reaction to this sensational intervention was predictably fierce. He knew the reverberations would extend far beyond the court into the next day's headlines. While Marvin and Pamela chatted contentedly in a corridor, Mitchelson railed to reporters, accusing Doughty of manufacturing a 'cock-and-bull story' shrewdly hedging his bets with, 'Even if it were true it doesn't wipe out a six-year relationship.' And he warned, 'I'm going to argue that the weight (being given to the evidence) be less than one ounce.' Michelle supported him with this haughty dismissal of the 'intimate revelations'; 'the man is obviously lying. I'm upset that he (Marvin) would grab at straws like this. I think it's tacky.'

It became decidedly tackier when Mitchelson, panther-like, went for the jugular in Doughty's testimony. He accused Michelle's alleged lover of lying. He went further. He said he believed he was a homosexual for whom such an affair would have been unlikely. Since Doughty had at first told Lee's attorney that he had not had sexual relations with Michelle Marvin but changed his story just before the trial, Mitchelson asked the judge to allow him to subpoena the notes taken by the lawyers at the first interview. The request was denied. Anyway, argued one of Lee's attorneys Berndt Lohr-Schmidt, even if Doughty were homosexual, it would not preclude him from having sexual relations with a woman. 'Homosexuals, often known as bisexuals, do have relations with heterosexuals,' he said.

Listening to it all, the tale of abortions, drunken rows, secret affairs, Marvin may well have wondered whether it was all worth it. The dirt was being shovelled with a vengeance. Bill Stout, the influential commentator of CBS, in a personal taunt at the tawdry disclosures in the case, spoke on peak-time television of 'the smut oozing out beneath the court-room door'. Maybe Marvin's legal rebuttal of Michelle's case required this dredging exercise. But as he listened to it all, Lee Marvin must have reflected how benign his divorce action with Betty Ebeling had been by comparison. The old American maxim 'pay the two dollars' – meaning it's often more prudent to settle than risk the roof falling in – must have occurred to him once in a while. Whatever he may have done in war or on film, it was not his nature to put the boot in where a woman was concerned. He could not have enjoyed Michelle's discomfort as his lawyers bored into her, demolishing as best they could, the notion of a woman who had sacrificed a big career as a singer out of devotion to her lover.

Bringing Hollywood's much-loved Gene Kelly into the act as an expert surprise witness was powerful artillery. He was subpoenaed to refute Ms Marvin's testimony that in 1964 she had been 'offered something in *Flower Drum Song*' which she felt 'was an escalation in my work, but I gave it up to be with Marvin'. A nimble sixty-six-year-old, the famous singer-dancer-actor gave cold comfort to Michelle. He said he had not offered her a part in the Broadway production of the show, did not even remember talking to her about one. True he knew both of these people (Lee and Michelle) well, 'and liked them'. But he did not recall talking to the singer about the musical, which he directed, and in any case could not have offered her a job as a singer or dancer in 1964 because he had left the production after it opened on 1 December 1958.

This formidable disclaimer was reinforced by the testimony of Sam Distefano, entertainment director of the Playboy Clubs. Flown in from Chicago he said the club records showed that Ms Marvin had worked only one two-week engagement in Phoenix. (She had testified she sang on the Playboy circuit.) Over strong objections from Mitchelson, he was allowed to produce a performer's rating card which said 'she was rated poorly during the engagement'. Later in the hearing Michelle's lawyer produced equally persuasive testimony to her voice being 'as good as or better than several singing stars'.

Michelle's allegation that she once ran into a hotel room to discover Marvin holding a woman out of the window by her legs was also rebutted by Lee's lawyers. According to stuntman Tony Epper, it wasn't a woman but two 6ft 2in men with their shirts off. And they weren't dangling, they were out on the ledge – on the fifteenth floor of the Mint Hotel, Las Vegas. Moreover, neither Lee Marvin nor Michelle were even in the room – at least not that he could remember, he said. He suggested that Ms Marvin 'must have gotten the incident mixed up' with what later became known as the 'Robin Hood' event, when he and another stuntman-actor, Woody Strode, decided to silence the talking 'Howdy Doody' sign outside their window by shooting arrows at it. This prank has been persistently accredited to Mr Marvin, who with equal persistence had never denied it.

When he read the reports of the previous day's proceedings, Marvin, at the centre of it all, would not have missed this advert in the morning paper:

LIVING TOGETHER??
Breaking up is hard to do . . . What's happening today
could happen to you!

Attorney-prepared
COHABITATION AGREEMENT
Sample property and earning agreements for unmarried
couples – $10.00 per set. Send check to:
"Living Together"
1666 The Almeda, San Jose, Calif. 95126.

Just how many affairs could tolerate the lover craftily sliding the said document in between the sheets, is something to conjure with.

On 28 March both sides rested their cases. In terms of emotional impact, Michelle Triola-Marvin might well have been seen to have made the better final appearance. Clutching a cracked heart of stone – devastating symbolism by any standards – she told the court there had been no man in her life since Lee Marvin left her nine years before. In a low, husky voice, she said, 'I always had the greatest amount of respect for him (Marvin). I loved him very much.' The stone she wore, green-coloured with a sizeable crack in it, had been a birthday present from Lee. By contrast, Lee's closing testimony, was a throwaway. He denied that he had given Michelle the 'broken heart' gift. Whether he was responsible for her broken heart – and would pay heavily for it – was now for Judge Arthur K. Marshall to decide.

He did so on the morning of 18 April 1979. His decision was a triumph of judicial whimsy leaving everybody wondering who had won. He decided that Michelle Triola Marvin had not established that a contract existed between her and the actor during the time they lived together. So she would not get the million and a half dollars plus she had demanded. Instead he awarded her $104,000 for 'rehabilitation purposes so that she may . . . re-educate herself and return from her status as a companion of a motion-picture star to a separate . . . but perhaps more prosaic existence'. The award, more avuncular than legal suggested that the good judge may have felt that six years of Lee Marvin required more than standard severance pay. The half-smiles on the faces of the contesting lawyers and the crooked grin on Marvin's, recorded satisfaction that neither party was being sent home without a bag of sweets. There was a bonus for Marvin. Dealing with Michelle's complaints about the actor's drinking habits, the judge observed; 'Her testimony would indicate that he (Marvin) was virtually awash with alcohol. Yet during this same period he starred in several major films all demanding of him physical stamina, a high degree of alertness and verbal as well as physical concentration . . . ' The two contenders, man and ex-mistress, reacted to the court decision according to their style. Marvin cracked jokes to the TV cameras. Michelle, smiling through tears in that old familiar manner, declared magnanimously, 'Lee is a good guy. I say Gung Ho to him just as he says Gung Ho to me.' The court emptied, the two legal battalions streaming back to base to debate the formidable implications of the judge's precedent-setting ruling. Mitchelson, with similar cases pending, was certain that the judgement gave the green light to several celebrated claims breathing hotly in his chambers. Whatever else the case had achieved, the result had certainly raised the status of the live-in mistress in the eyes of American law. As for Marvin's own status, the consensus was that he had come out slightly ahead, his public image, if anything, enhanced by the affair. The Marvin v Marvin case, the longest-running spectacular in public linen-laundering, was over.

But the lawsuit had been preceded by that old recurring problem. Marvin was back drinking again. And it showed, not in his work, but in his face, now painfully drawn, the old smile barely able to haul itself across the furrows. He came to

Europe with Pamela to film *Avalanche Express* in Germany and
The Big Red One in Israel and Ireland. True his liquor intake
did not match those royal juice-ups in Mexico, Arizona, Las
Vegas and other befuddled locations. But he was hitting the
beer with a vengeance. As an actor he did everything required of
a veteran performer carrying superstar status and a major invest-
ment on his back. The discipline and professionalism took care
of that. Significant, and sad, was to see the old warrior no
longer fighting-trim – thin rather than lean, his spirit soured by
doubt and disillusion. He was still Marvin, 'The Old Fox' spoil-
ing for a fight, and loving it if some Joe gave him one. But it was
sub-standard stuff from the once Great Needler of the profession. Yet out there on an Israeli beach, where they restaged the
First US Infantry Division's assault on Normandy, Marvin
regained some of his old spit and fury.

It was the feel of the uniform that did it. Its effect was almost
tactile. Wearing the gear and the hardware triggered a score of
memories, damned happy ones. As he slid into his combat
jacket, took the butt of a sub-machine gun almost affectionately
into his hand. Lee Marvin looked out across the Mediterranean
–but saw the Pacific. When the director, Samuel Fuller (whose
own war experiences form the basis of the film), barked orders,
Marvin heard only a sergeant . . . at Eniwetok . . . Kwajalein . . .
Garrapin. Though nobody would believe it. Except his father,
maybe. He would have understood. Lee brooded over it at night.
And unable to explain it in words others could understand, he
drank. He knew his lines, was dead on cue, gave his best. But he
drank.

And so it came to the final week's shooting on the film. At a
castle in Dublin. Lee arrived there to find some understanding
character had installed an ice-box in his dressing-room jammed
every which way with bottles of beer. Throughout the day
Marvin drank as relentlessly as some people chain-smoke. Wiping the neck of the bottles with his sleeve, he gulped the stuff
down a throat upon which the skin flapped like a frog's. If he
was aware of the extent of his intake it scarcely mattered. He
was working damned well, wasn't he? He was still the master,
performing with the intuitive skill that not all the hard liquor
in the world could drown. Strangely, he was deriving strength
from the uniform he wore. He felt comfortable in the soldier's
rig. More the real war veteran, less a star acting a role.

When an assistant director moved across to help him with his lacings, Marvin slammed him up against a wall. 'Never touch a soldier's leggings,' he snarled. 'And leave my helmet ALONE!' he shouted at his chauffeur who'd made a move to hand it to him. It was a combat soldier's reflexes, not those of a bar-room drunk. A rare display of personality-reversion was taking place in that Irish castle. It was not Marvin sitting sprawled there, knocking back the Carlsberg specials. But ex-soldier, Marvin L. (Purple Heart) formerly of the US Marines. The man who had tried – but failed – to re-enlist. Where he'd be now if events had turned out differently.

Lawrence of Arabia, at odds with his own legend and identity, changed his name twice in a bid to bury himself away in the RAF. Marvin was driven by the same compulsion. He had lived for years on such confected images as 'The Screen's Number One Sadist', 'The Lovable Brute', 'The Gorgeous Killer', and he loathed it all. There was only one safe, secure haven away from all that horse manure. The Marines. The nostalgia shaped into uneasy thoughts. He uncapped another bottle. Drank the lot. He looked down at his boots. Reflective now. 'You know my father had been a regular soldier in the First World War and then went in again in 1939.' This we knew. 'But when he came out again, the second time, he just couldn't face up to things. Had a massive nervous breakdown.' We knew that too. 'Tried to commit suicide twice.' Marvin said it without emotion. A throwaway. An episode which had never been told before. In the infinity of words recording the life and squally times of Lee Marvin, no mention of that stark moment in his life.

The revelation had been a long time coming. An exorcism. It could only have emerged from a character bent on total self-revelation. Truth time. He'd played it *their* way all his working life. He'd gone along with the barefaced hokum and the horseplay that grabbed headlines, rocketed his asking price. He had learned a trick or two from Robert Mitchum. When that actor had been busted on a marijuana charge he was convinced he was finished. His career soared. In the age of the anti-hero, inspired by Bogart, the soft-centred villain with the homely features was in with a big chance.

So Marvin boozed, battered, cuffed and smart-assed his way to the coveted $1,000,000 mark. Big deal. By the time divorce lawyers and a mistress had got to that, the noughts began to fall like rotten apples. The hell-raising banner which had passed from Flynn to Mitchum, and from Mitch to him, was available any time Steve McQueen cared to take it on. What did it all amount to anyway? It did nothing to soften the guilt that still gnaws at him; for having had the gall to come out of the Marines, alive. A different throw of the dice, and the guy who got it between the eyes, sighed 'Oh', then fell lifeless on Lee's chest, could just have easily been born with the name Marvin. The thought still hovers. And puts the superstar image into a clearer perspective. When you've had that kind of luck, says Marvin, the Oscar, the cover stories and the million bucks don't add up to a row of beans. 'Anything over forty's gravy,' was how he said it fourteen years ago.

He underscored the theme that day in Dublin. He was now fifty-four. And as he himself admitted, looked ten years older. But it didn't bother him. The movie companies were still chasing him. The roles were big, and so was the money. Sure, his face looked as craggy and creased as cart-tracks on an unmade road. Well it may worry a star whose charisma requires him to look as flawless as Redford. Or the kind of guy who takes off once in a while for the short reprieve of plastic surgery. Only the actor with that kind of hang-up would be tormented by what Marvin was now seeing in his mirror each morning.

I look there and I see some strange guy staring back at me and I think, 'Who the hell is that?' I can't believe it's me. I look awful. Goddamn terrible. And it shakes me up. I've lost 15lbs this last few weeks and I can't afford it. I'm tired, dead beat, and I need a rest.

There was more of that to come. Marvin switched from self-immolation to a scathing appraisal of his long career. It was the sort of don't-give-a-damn honesty that makes press-agents sweat. A shaft of light from the castle window slanted across his face throwing everything else into shadow. 'You know what hurts, I mean what really hurts deep down? I'm no good. In seventy-five films I've been a failure.' He sighed deeply, moved towards another beer, then changed his mind. 'I mean, how many of my films can anybody remember? You,' he growled, pointing a finger at reporter Ted Macauley of the London *Daily Mirror*. 'How many do you remember?' Macauley remembered plenty. Marvin spat. 'They've all been lousy. And so have I.'

Well we could have rebutted his argument citing *Cat Ballou*, *The Killers*, *The Dirty Dozen*, *Point Blank*; reminded him of those 117 episodes of *M-Squad* which sired *Columbo*, *Kojak*, and all the rest. We could have told him he had achieved a body of work that, when all the dust has settled, will testify to his considerable stature as an actor. An actor as unique in his particular territory as the more impeccable superstars are in theirs. There are signs too that he's mastered his particular problem of how to perform on all cylinders without the aid of hard liquor. Without any liquor. He is coasting happily now on the longest 'dry run' of his career. When he appeared for the court hearing in Los Angeles he looked as sharp, clear-eyed and sober as the Judge. Now and again, as he told Roderick Mann, he comes off the wagon, 'just to see if I'm missing anything. But the rattles and whips and chains next morning convince me I'm not. Anyway, there comes a time when you've got to ask yourself "what for?" ' The fact that he asks that question underscores Marvin's new determination. It will take a mighty upheaval in his personal or professional life, to send him careening back to the bottle. Given a healthy prognosis and a fair run on the wagon, and there are still some big movie roles, maybe even another Oscar ahead for Lee Marvin. Well that's okay by him. As long as nobody tries to sell him the notion that having his name above the title in a $20-million movie, puts him close to God's right hand. 'They put your name on a star in the sidewalk on Hollywood Boulevard. You walk down afterwards and find a pile of dog manure on it. That tells the whole story baby.'

Marvin talk. The flip put-down, reminiscent of freak-out time on Malibu beach. It goes with the image. Not with the substance of the man. That craggy decency, admired and respected as much by the trade as by his two wives and the eight children, four fathered, four acquired. Marvin is content to settle for that. 'Honestly, I'm not asking for one damn thing more than is coming to me. I've had the luck to be present when the sun was shining, the rain falling, and the fish biting. As long as I can look out at the ocean, or lie warm in bed at night and hear the wind howling, not one darned thing can hurt me.'

List of Films

The earliest films, mostly cameo parts for Marvin, are not listed in full here. But for curio-collectors they included programmers like You're In The Navy Now *and* Diplomatic Courier (*both directed by Henry Hathaway which opened the door to Hollywood*); Down Among the Sheltering Pines, We're Not Married, Seminole, Gun Fury, Hangman's Knot, Duel at Silver Creek, The Stranger Wore a Gun *and* Glory Brigade.

Year of Release	Title	Director	Co-stars
1952	Eight Iron Men	Edward Dmytryk	Bonar Colleano Arthur Franz Richard Kiley
1953	The Big Heat	Fritz Lang	Glenn Ford Gloria Grahame
1954	The Wild One	Laslo Benedek	Marlon Brando Mary Murphy
..	Gorilla at Large	Harmon Jones	Anne Bancroft Lee J. Cobb Cameron Mitchell
..	The Caine Mutiny	Edward Dmytryk	Humphrey Bogart Jose Ferrer Van Johnson
..	The Raid	Hugo Fregonese	Van Heflin Anne Bancroft Richard Boone
..	Bad Day At Black Rock	John Sturges	Spencer Tracy Robert Ryan

240

Year of Release	Title	Director	Co-stars
1954	A Life in the Balance	Harry Horner	Ricardo Montalban Anne Bancroft
1955	Violent Saturday	Richard Fleischer	Richard Egan Victor Mature
..	Not As A Stranger	Stanley Kramer	Robert Mitchum Olivia de Havilland Broderick Crawford Frank Sinatra Gloria Grahame
..	Pete Kelly's Blues	Jack Webb	Jack Webb Janet Leigh Ella Fitzgerald
..	I Died A Thousand Times	Stuart Heisler	Jack Palance Shelley Winters
..	Shack Out On 101	Ed Dein	Keenan Wynn Frank Lovejoy Terry Moore
1956	Attack!	Robert Aldrich	Jack Palance Eddie Albert
..	Pillars of the Sky	George Marshall	Jeff Chandler Dorothy Malone Ward Bond
..	The Rack	Arnold Laven	Paul Newman Walter Pidgeon Edmund O'Brien
1958	Raintree County	Edward Dmytryk	Elizabeth Taylor Montgomery Clift Eve Marie Saint

Here Lee Marvin broke off for three years to star as the police lieutenant in M-Squad, *interrupted by one film,* The Missouri Traveller (*1958*).

| 1961 | The Comancheros | Michael Curtiz | John Wayne
Stuart Whitman |
| 1962 | The Man Who Shot Liberty Valance | John Ford | James Stewart
John Wayne
Vera Miles |

Year of Release	Title	Director	Co-stars
1963	Donovan's Reef	John Ford	John Wayne Dorothy Lamour
1964	The Killers	Don Siegel	John Cassavetes Angie Dickinson
1965	Cat Ballou	Eliot Silverstein	Jane Fonda
..	Ship of Fools	Stanley Kramer	Vivien Leigh Jose Ferrer Simone Signoret Oskar Werner
1966	The Professionals	Richard Brooks	Burt Lancaster Claudia Cardinale Jack Palance
1967	The Dirty Dozen	Robert Aldrich	Ernest Borgnine John Cassavetes Robert Ryan Charles Bronson
..	Sergeant Ryker (A TV film, 1963)	Buzz Kulik	Bradford Dillman Vera Miles Lloyd Nolan
..	Point Blank	John Boorman	Angie Dickinson Keenan Wynn Carrol O'Connor
1969	Hell in the Pacific	John Boorman	Toshiro Mifune
..	Paint Your Wagon	Josh Logan	Clint Eastwood Jean Seberg
1970	Monte Walsh	William A. Fraker	Jeanne Moreau Jack Palance
1972	Pocket Money	Stuart Rosenberg	Paul Newman
..	Prime Cut	Michael Ritchie	Gene Hackman Sissy Spacek
1973	Emperor of the North Pole	Robert Aldrich	Ernest Borgnine
1974	The Spikes Gang	Richard Fleischer	Gary Grimes Noah Beery Jnr

Year of Release	Title	Director	Co-stars
1974	The Klansman	Terence Young	Richard Burton Cameron Mitchell
1976	Shout At The Devil	Peter Hunt	Roger Moore Barbara Parkins
..	The Great Scout and Cathouse Thursday	Don Taylor	Oliver Reed Kay Lenz Elizabeth Ashley
1978	Avalanche Express	Mark Robson	Robert Shaw Linda Evans Maximillian Schell Horst Bucholz
1979	The Big Red One	Samuel Fuller	Mark Hamill Robert Carradine Bobby Dicicco Kelly Johnson

Index

Albert, Eddie, 51, 81, 241
Aldrich, Robert, 81, 82, 146–8,
  151, 203, 241, 242
Alexander, William, 208
American in Paris, An, 163
American Weekly, 44
Andrews, Julie, 218
Angelo, Ann di, 209
Annie Get Your Gun, 171
Archer, Eugene, 102
Ashley, Elizabeth, 243
Attack!, 81, 82, 146, 241
Austin, John, 212
Avalanche Express, 236, 243

Bad Day at Black Rock, 12, 13,
  21, 69, 70, 79, 240
Bad News Bears, The, 14, 198
Ballantine, E. J., 47
Ballantine, Stella, 47
'Ballinger, Lt. Frank', 84, 85, 91
Bancroft, Anne, 67, 240, 241
Barrymore, Jack and Lionel, 47
Barton, James, 203
Beery, Noah, Jr, 242
Benchley, Robert, 46
Benedeck, Laslo, 65, 240
Bergen, Candice, 195
Betz, Jack, 26–8
Big Heat, The, 12, 21, 63, 64, 71,
  81, 156, 240
Big Knife, The, 82

Big Red One, The, 236, 237, 243
Billy Budd, 51
Blackboard Jungle, The, 139
Black Cloud, 74–6
Bluhdorn, Charles, 163
Blue Hawaii, 229
Boehm, Sidney, 63
Boetticher, Budd, 81
Bogart, Humphrey, 7, 11, 51, 53,
  67–9, 78, 116, 142, 143, 157,
  237, 240
Bond, James (films of), 207, 221
Bond, Ward, 241
Boomerang, 65
Boone, Richard, 240
Boorman, John, 155–7, 240
Borgnine, Ernest, 70, 78, 202, 203,
  242
Borzage, Danny, 93
Bowman, Father Marion, 9, 18,
  26, 28–31, 177
Brando, Marlon, 61, 65–7, 82, 84,
  134, 138, 240
Brill, Lt. Col. A. P., 33
Bronson, Charles, 148, 149, 242
Brooks, Richard, 12, 135–44, 163,
  166–9, 173, 181, 242
Brothers Karamazov, The, 139
Brown, Harry, 54
Brown, Jim, 146
Brynner, Yul, 139
Bucholz, Horst, 243

244

INDEX

Burr, Raymond, 67
Burton, Richard, 14, 67, 124, 135, 203–16, 243
Bus Stop, 163, 166, 171

Cahn, David, 91
Caine Mutiny, The, 67–9, 240
Callan, Mickey, 129
Camelot, 163
Camp Pendleton, 34
Candidate, The, 14, 198
Cannon, Dyan, 35
Cantor, Eddie, 171
Cardinale, Claudia, 137, 144, 242
Carradine, John, 94
Carradine, Robert, 243
Cassavetes, John, 101, 146, 242
Cat Ballou, 7, 67, 80, 114, 123–35, 137, 138, 173, 180, 184, 198, 217, 239, 242
Cat on a Hot Tin Roof, 139
Challantanoa, 35, 37
Chandler, Jeff, 81, 241
Chicago Tribune, 212
Choirboys, The, 82
Cleopatra, 174
Clift, Montgomery, 82–4, 241
Cobb, Lee J., 66, 67, 240
Cocks, Jay, 198
Cohn, Harry, 53, 54, 57, 63
Colket, Tristram Coffin, the Third, MD, 9, 71–7, 96, 200, 201
Colleano, Bonar, 240
Colliers, 70
Columbo, 84, 239
Comancheros, The, 91–3, 241
Confidential, 117
Connery, Sean, 148
Cool Hand Luke, 196
Cooper, Gary, 50, 51, 53
Cord, Alex, 114
Cosmopolitan, 217
Cowan, Ronnie, 174
Coward, Noel, 149, 164
Crawford, Broderick, 241

Crist, Judith, 79, 94, 203
Crossfire, 70
Crowther, Bosley, 157
Curtiz, Michael, 92, 93, 241

Daily Express, 173
Daily Mirror, 239
Daniels, Daniel, 211
Dein, Ed, 240
Desert Fox, The, 146
Desilu Playhouse, 90
Dicicco, Bobby, 243
Dickinson, Angie, 102, 242
Dick Powell Theatre, 90
Dillman, Bradford, 242
Dinucci, Kim, 209, 211
Diplomatic Courier, 53, 240
Dirty Dozen, The, 11, 82, 146–9, 151, 157, 239, 242
Distefano, Sam, 233
Dmytryk, Edward, 57, 67, 68, 240, 241
Donovan's Reef, 95, 100, 242
Dorr, John H., 216
Doughty, Richard, 231–2
Douglas, Kirk, 97, 125, 126
Down Among the Sheltering Pines, 13, 240
Downhill Racer, 14, 198
Duel of Silver Creek, 53, 100, 240
Dunn, Michael, 105, 106, 112, 113, 123

Eastwood, Clint, 161, 165, 167–172, 242
Edward, Father, 30
Egan, Richard, 241
Eight Iron Men, 54, 57, 61, 240
Elmer Gantry, 137
Emperor of the North, The, 82, 201–3, 242
Eniwetok, 35, 36, 236
Epper, Tony, 233
Equus, 214
Evans, Linda, 243

245

Ferrer, Jose, 67, 102, 103, 122, 128, 240, 242
Financial Times, 173
Finney, Albert, 67
Fire in the Sky, 91
Fitzgerald, Ella, 241
Fleischer, Richard, 217, 241, 242
Flight of the Phoenix, The, 82
Flower Drum Song, The, 233
Flynn, Errol, 7, 33, 238
Fonda, Jane, 129, 132, 134, 242
Ford, Glenn, 54, 63, 64, 139, 223, 240
John Ford, 15, 91, 93–5, 100, 241, 242
Fort Apache, 93
Fraker, William A., 12, 167, 178– 182, 184, 242
Frankenheimer, John, 152, 203
Frankovich, Mike, 128, 132, 133
Franz, Arthur, 240
Fregonese, Hugo, 240
French, Philip, 173
Friedkin, Bud, 182
From Here to Eternity, 54, 203
Fuller, Samuel, 216, 236, 243

Gable, Clark, 14, 52, 53, 78, 79, 159
Gabor, Zsa Zsa, 191
Garrapin, 35, 236
Garson, Greer, 53, 69
Gigi, 163
Glory Brigade, 63, 240
Gober, Cecile, 24
God's Little Acre, 70
Goldman Emma 47
Goldman Louis 122
Goldwyn Sam 53
Gone With the Wind 82
Goodbye Columbus, 120
Gorilla at Large, 67, 240
Grahame, Gloria, 63, 64, 240, 241
Grand Hotel, 102

Grand Prix, 152
Grant, Gary, 96
Grant, Jimmy, 92
Grapes of Wrath, 146
Great Movie Stars, The, 180
Great Scout and Cathouse Thursday, The, 223, 243
Greer, Germaine, 19
Grimes, Gary, 242
Gun Fury, 63, 240
Gurney Brown, Helen, 217

Haber, Joyce, 166, 169, 170
Hackman, Gene, 198, 242
Hamill, Mark, 243
Hangman's Knot, 240
Harrison, Mike, 37, 38
Hasty Heart, The, 51
Hathaway, Henry, 50–2, 240
Hathaway, Robert, 122
Havilland, Olivia de, 241
Hayes, Ira, 91
Healey, Gwen, 232
Heflin, Van, 240
Heisler, Stuart, 241
Hellinger, Mark, 100
Hell in the Pacific, 152, 159–61, 229, 230, 232, 242
Hemingway, Ernest, 8, 100
Her Twelve Men, 69
Heston, Charlton, 9
Hickman, Swayne, 129
Hill, The, 148
Hiscock, John, 210
Hitchcock, Alfred, 53
Hollywood Reporter, 182, 215, 216
Home of the Brave, 48
Hopper, Hedda, 53, 166
Horner, Harry, 241
Houston, Penelope, 64
Hudson, Rock, 191, 192
Huie, William Bradford, 205
Hunt, Peter, 243
Hunt, Suzy, 214

Hush Hush, Sweet Charlotte, 82
Huston, John, 162
Hyman, Kenneth, 146–9, 166

Iceman Cometh, The, 203
I Died a Thousand Times, 80, 241
In Cold Blood, 166
Ireland, Jill, 148
Is Paris Burning?, 111
Iwo Jima, 7, 46, 91

Jagger, Mick, 78
Jalinski, Andrew, 48
Jaws, 217
Johnson, Kelly, 243
Johnson, Nunnally, 146
Johnson, Van, 67, 240
Jones. Harmon, 240
Jong, Erica, 19

Kael, Pauline, 133, 144
Kagon, David, 230
Kaufman, Millard, 13, 82, 83, 216
Kaufman, Stanley, 203
Kelly, Gene, 233
Kennedy, John F., 67, 195
Kerwin, Robert, 212, 213
Kiley, Richard, 240
Killers, The, 12, 20, 100–2, 169, 239, 242
Killing of Sister George, The, 82
Klansman, The, 13, 14, 203–16, 219, 243
Klu Klux Klan, 205–7, 210
Kojak, 239
Kramer, Stanley, 7, 12, 54, 57, 67, 102–6, 241, 242
Kulik, Buzz, 242
Kurosawa, Akira, 151
Kwajalein, 35, 36, 236

Laird, Jack, 85
Laird, Hon. Melvin R., 18, 177, 178
Lakeland High School, 24, 25

Lamour, Dorothy, 242
Lancaster, Burt, 137–9, 141–4, 242
Landis, Hal, 179
Lang, Fritz, 12, 63, 64, 240
Laughton, Charles, 72
Laven, Arnold, 241
Leigh, Janet, 241
Leigh, Vivien, 16, 102–6, 112, 122, 149, 150, 179, 242
Lenz, Kay, 243
Lerner, Alan Jay, 161, 163, 164, 166–9, 174
Lewis, Richard Warren, 29, 50, 145
A Life in the Balance, 79, 241
Loewe, Frederick, 161
Logan, Josh, 8, 12, 25, 161–73, 178, 179, 181, 242
Lohr-Schmidt, Berndt, 232
Long Voyage Home, The, 93
Lord Jim, 139
Loren, Sophia, 137, 179
Los Angeles Times, 166, 169
Losers, The, 8, 98
Loveable, Rev & Mrs, 58, 189
Lovejoy, Frank, 241
Lunt, Alfred, 51

Macauley, Ted, 238
MacLaine, Shirley, 193
MacMurray, Fred, 67
Mahoney, Jim, 188, 231
Mahumit School (New York), 20
Malick, Terry, 196
Malone, Dorothy, 241
Manchester Guardian, 122
Mann, Roderick, 150, 203, 239
Man Who Shot Liberty Valance, The, 12, 91, 93–5, 241
Marshall, E. G., 67
Marshall, George, 241
Marshall Islands, 36, 176
Marshall, Judge Arthur, 225, 226, 229–231, 234, 235

Marvin, Betty (*née* Ebeling), 10, 16, 22, 54–63, 71, 72, 74–6, 79, 87–90, 92, 96, 99, 100, 106, 107, 112, 114–6, 118, 119, 121, 135, 154, 155, 178, 185, 193, 199, 200, 222

Marvin, Christopher, 63, 71, 89, 100, 155

Marvin, Claudia, 71, 89, 155

Marvin, Courtenay (Sr), 19–23, 31, 34, 43, 44, 46, 51, 61, 62, 71, 178

Marvin, Courtenay (Jr), 71, 89, 155

Marvin, Cynthia, 71, 89, 155

Marvin, General Seth, 19, 34

Marvin, Lamont W., 19–25, 30, 31, 34, 35, 43, 51, 61, 62, 71, 178, 187, 199–201

Marvin, Lee: background and descent, 8, 10, 19–21, 24, 34, 90; family, 19–25, 30, 31, 34, 35, 43, 44, 46, 51, 61, 62, 71, 178, 187, 187; early education, 20–25; St Leo College, 9, 18, 25–31, 174–8; Marines, 11, 13, 15, 30–44, 47, 71, 80, 97, 147, 185, 217, 237; apprenticeship in theatre, 45–9; drinking and hellraising, 7–10, 14, 15, 49, 50, 71–7, 89, 90, 96–100, 119, 121, 122, 141–50, 153–6, 165–8, 172, 181, 193, 194, 201, 205–12, 223, 227; early films, 50–4; and Meyer Mishkin, 52–4, 63, 80, 90, 116, 135, 144, 174, 167, 185, 222, 229; and Betty Marvin, 10, 16, 22, 54–63, 71, 72, 74–6, 79, 87–90, 92, 96, 99, 100, 106, 107, 112, 114–6, 118, 119, 121, 135, 154, 155, 178, 185, 193, 199, 200, 222; and Marvin children, 63, 71, 89, 100, 155, 231; and Fritz Lang, 12, 63, 64; and Marlon Brando, 61, 65–7, 82, 84, 134, 138; and Humphrey Bogart, 67–9; and Tristram Colket, 9, 71–7, 96, 200, 201; and Spencer Tracy, 52, 53, 70, 78, 138; and Gable, 14, 52, 63, 78, 79, 159; and Paul Newman, 9, 11, 80, 81, 105, 139, 193–7, 218; and Robert Aldrich, 81, 82, 146–8, 151, 203; and Montgomery Clift, 82–4; and *M-Squad*, 78, 83–7, 90–2, 126, 141; as Lt. Ballinger, 84, 85, 91; and John Ford, 15, 91, 93–5, 100; and John Wayne, 50, 51, 78, 91–4, 138, 218, 213; and Vivien Leigh, 16, 102–6, 112, 122, 149, 150, 179; and Michelle Triola, 10, 107–16, 118-21, 134, 135, 141, 142, 144, 145, 147, 149, 150, 153–7, 161, 165, 174, 176, 178, 179, 183, 185–93, 199, 205, 217, 218, 221, 225, 226; and his Oscar for *Cat Ballou*, 124, 133–5, 137; and *Cat Ballou*, 7, 67, 80, 114, 123–35, 137, 138, 173, 180, 184, 198, 217; as Kid Shelleen, 7, 67, 125–7, 129–33; 135, 141, 163, 170, 177; and Burt Lancaster, 137–9, 141–4; and Charles Bronson, 148, 149; and Toshiro Mifune, 151, 152, 159–61; and Josh Logan (*Paint Your Wagon*), 8, 12, 25, 161–73, 178, 179, 181; and Jeanne Moreau, 16, 179–84, 187, 188, 193; and Richard Burton in *The Klansman*, 14, 67, 124, 135, 203–16; and Elizabeth Taylor, 82, 139, 205–11, 215; and Pamela Marvin, 35, 48, 187–9, 193–5, 199, 201, 202, 206, 208, 215, 218–22, 227; Marvin *v.* Marvin, 10, 224–35, settling down, 193, 194, 201, 202, 206, 211, 217–22,

227, 230; fishing, 17, 29, 170, 199, 200, 202, 217, 239; political stance, 195, 196; professionalism as an actor, 12, 13, 126–32, 138–40, 143, 144, 151, 156, 157, 168–70, 176, 197, 203, 239; Marvin Matthew, 19

Marvin, Pamela (née Feeley), 35, 48, 187–9, 193–5, 199, 201, 202, 206, 208, 215, 218–22, 225, 230, 232, 236
Marvin, Robert, 20, 21, 34
Marvin, Ross G., 19, 24, 90
Marx, Mrs Groucho, 191
Mastroianni, Marcello, 47
Matthau, Walter, 14, 198
Mature, Victor, 79, 241
Mayer, Louis B., 53, 162
Mayerling, 207
McGivern, William P., 63
McGraw, Ali, 120
McHugh, Edna, 71, 218
McQueen, Steve, 65, 78, 105, 238
Mercurio, Penny, 230
Mifune, Toshiro, 151, 152, 159–61, 242
Miles, Vera, 241, 242
Mishkin, Meyer, 52–4, 63, 80, 90, 116, 135, 144, 174, 167, 185, 222, 229
Missouri Traveller, 91, 241
Mister Roberts, 171
Mitchell, Cameron, 67, 206, 240, 243
Mitchelson, Marvin, 186, 190–2, 224, 225–36
Mitchum, Robert, 53, 80, 105, 219, 223, 237, 241
Monroe, Marilyn, 166
Montalban, Ricardo, 241
Monte Walsh, 16, 179–84, 187, 193, 232, 242
Moore, Roger, 221, 222, 243

Moore, Terry, 241
Moorehead, Agnes, 82
Moreau, Jeanne, 16, 179–84, 187, 188, 193, 242
Morgan, Dennis, 143
Moscow Arts Theatre, 48
M-Squad, 78, 83–7, 90–2, 126, 141, 241
Mule for the Marquesa, A, 137
Murphy, Audie, 53, 100
Murphy, Mary, 240
My Fair Lady, 163

Nelson, Rope, 229
Newman, Walter, 125
Newman, Paul, 9, 11, 80, 81, 105, 139, 193–7, 218, 241, 242
New Republic, 203
New Yorker, 46, 162
New York Times, 102
Ngerengchol, 161
Nimitz, Admiral, 34
Nitty Gritty Dirt Band, 171
Nolan, Lloyd, 242
Not as a Stranger, 80, 241

Oakwood (NY), 22
O'Brien, Edmund, 241
O'Brien, Richard, 146
O'Connor, Carrol, 242
O'Hara, John, 70
Old Man and the Sea, The, 117
Olivier, Laurence, 15, 68, 124, 135, 150
O'Neil, Eugene, 16, 61, 62, 159, 203
O'Rourke, Frank, 137
Oroville (Arizona), 13, 206–12, 214, 215
O'Toole, Peter, 67, 139

Paint Your Wagon, 8, 161–74, 178, 179, 242
Palance, Jack, 64, 81, 82, 139, 179, 184, 241, 242

Parker, Dorothy, 46
Parkins, Barbara, 221, 243
Parris Island, 31
Parsons, Louella, 53
Pawnbroker, The, 134
Peary, Admiral Robert Edwin, 19
Peck, Gregory, 16, 53
Peckinpah, Sam, 8, 98, 99, 157, 221
People Need People, 91
Perelman, S. J., 46
Pete Kelly's Blues, 80, 241
Petrified Forest, The, 143
Phillips, Bob, 147
Picnic, 163, 171
Picture, 162
Pidgeon, Walter, 241
Pierson, Frank, 124, 125, 133
Pillars of the Sky, 241
Playboy, 146
Pocket Money, 194-8, 242
Point Blank, 12, 155-9, 226, 238, 242
Polanski, Roman, 218
Ponti, Carlo, 179
Powers, Allen J., 26
Preminger, Otto, 63
Prime Cut, 14, 197-9, 242
Professionals, The, 12, 70, 137-44, 146, 166, 226, 242

Quine, Richard, 114

Rack, The, 80, 241
Raft, George, 142
Raid, The, 69, 240
Raintree County, 13, 15, 82-4, 207, 241
Raphael, Father, 30
Rashomon, 151
Reagan, Ronald, 102
Red Badge of Courage, 162
Redford, Robert, 14, 24, 47, 78, 105, 194, 198, 218, 238
Red Sun, The, 159

Reed, Oliver, 223, 243
Reed, Rex, 163
Reynolds, Burt, 198
Richker, Pat, 232
Ritchie, Michael, 14, 15, 197-9, 242
Roadside (Emlyn Riggs), 48
Robards, Jason, 203
Roberts, Bobby, 179
Robson, Mark, 243
Rolling Stone, 14, 198
Rosenberg, Stuart, 12, 196, 197, 242
Ross, Lillian, 162
Roud, Richard, 122
Route 66, 90
Rubenstein, Helena, 19, 22
Ruhmann, Heinz, 102
Runyon, Damon, 147
Ryan, Robert, 69, 70, 78, 139, 143, 144, 240, 242

Saint, Eva Marie, 82, 241
Saipan, 32, 35, 36, 46, 80, 156
Santana, The, 53, 116

Sardi's, 49, 50
Savalas, Telly, 126, 146
Sayomara, 163, 171
Schary, Dore, 162
Schlitz Playhouse, 90
Schnell, Maximillian, 243
Scott, Geroge C., 134
Seberg, Jean, 161, 165, 171, 242
Segal, George, 102
Seminole, 63, 240
Sergeant Ryker, 97, 242
Seven Men From Now, 81
Seven Samurai, The, 151
Shack Out on 101, 80, 241
Shaw, Robert, 217, 243
Shaw, Tom, 142, 166-8
Sheridan, Ann, 143
She Wore a Yellow Ribbon, 93
Shiffrin, Bill, 208, 212

Shipman, David, 180
Ship of Fools, 102–9, 113, 116, 122, 150, 179, 242
Shout at the Devil, 220, 221, 243
Siegel, Don, 12, 100, 101, 105, 169, 170, 181, 242
Signoret, Simone, 102, 103, 122, 242
Silverstein, Elliot, 12, 67, 123–34, 181, 242
Simpson, O. J., 14, 207
Sinatra, Frank, 11, 54, 188, 230 241
Sirmans, Jim, 197
Sixty Ways to Kill a Man With Your Bare Hands, 147
Sound of Hunting, A, 54
South Pacific, 163, 171
Spaceck, Sissy, 242
Spectator, 183
Spikes Gang, The, 217, 242
Stagecoach, 93
Stanislavsky, Constantin, 45
Starsky & Hutch, 84
Steiger, Rod, 134
Stevens, Stella, 114
Stewart, James, 94, 138, 241
St Leo College, 9, 18, 25–31, 174–8
Stout, Bill, 232
Stranger Wore a Gun, The, 63, 240
Streetcar Named Desire, A, 51
Streisand, Barbra, 78, 165
Strode, Woody, 142, 144, 243
Sturges, John, 240
Sunday People, 210
Suspense Theatre, 90
Synanon, 114

Tapotchau, 35, 37
Taylor, Don, 223, 243
Taylor, Elizabeth, 82, 139, 205–11, 215, 241
Taylor, Robert, 102
Thompson, Howard, 102

Thunder Rock, 48
Thurber, James, 46
Time, 151, 179, 198
Tobacco Road, 146
Tracy Spencer, 52, 53, 70, 78, 138, 240
Travolta, John, 78
Triola, Michelle, 10, 107–16, 118–21, 134, 135, 141, 142, 144, 145, 147, 149, 150, 153–7, 161, 165, 174, 176, 178, 179, 183, 185–93, 199, 205, 217, 218, 221–235
Truffaut, François, 180
Trustcott, John, 164
Twilight Zone, 90

Vadim, Roger, 134
Valacci Papers, The, 207
Variety, 100, 215, 216
Violent Saturday, 79, 80, 241
Vogue, 195

Walker, Robert, 55
'Wand'rin' Star', 173, 174
Ward, Skip, 109–12
Warner, Jack, 100
Wasserman, Paul, 187, 188, 222
Wayne, John, 50, 51, 78, 91–4, 138, 218, 223, 241
Webb, Jack, 51, 80, 241
Weiss, Don, 12, 85–7, 102
We're Not Married, 53, 240
Werner, Oskar, 102–4, 122, 241
Whatever Happened to Baby Jane?, 82
Whitman, Stuart, 241
Widmark, Richard, 15
Wild One, The, 63, 65–7, 123, 126, 240
Wimmington, Richard, 100
Winters, Shelley, 241
Woodstock Little Theatre, 45–8
Woodward, Joanne, 195
Woolcott, Alexander, 46

Wyler, William, 53

Wynn, Keenan, 9, 65, 98, 110, 221, 241, 242

Young, Terence, 12, 14, 203–15, 243

You're in the Navy Now, 50-2, 240

Zaitz, Anthony W., PhD, 177

Zannuck, Darryl, 53